A CENTURY OF BANK RATE

OTHER BOOKS BY R. G. HAWTREY

Published by Longmans, Green & Co. Ltd.

———

CAPITAL AND EMPLOYMENT, SECOND EDITION
CURRENCY AND CREDIT, FOURTH EDITION
ECONOMIC ASPECTS OF SOVEREIGNTY, SECOND EDITION
ECONOMIC DESTINY
THE GOLD STANDARD IN THEORY AND PRACTICE, FIFTH EDITION
TOWARDS THE RESCUE OF STERLING
BRETTON WOODS FOR BETTER OR WORSE
CROSS PURPOSES IN WAGE POLICY
THE POUND AT HOME AND ABROAD

A
CENTURY OF BANK RATE

by

R. G. HAWTREY

Routledge
Taylor & Francis Group

LONDON AND NEW YORK

First published 1938 by Longmans, Green & Co.
Second edition published 1962 by Frank Cass Publishers

Published 2013 by Routledge
2 Park Square, Milton Park, Abingdon, Oxon OX14 4RN
711 Third Avenue, New York, NY, 10017, USA

Routledge is an imprint of the Taylor & Francis Group, an informa business

ISBN 13: 978-0-714-61228-7 (hbk)

PREFACE

HAVING undertaken to give a series of three *Alfred Marshall* Lectures at Cambridge in November, 1937, on *A Century of Bank Rate*, I was confronted with the fact that, though there is a profusion of statistical material available, this material had never been systematically analysed in the manner which appeared to me requisite for the elucidation of the subject. It seemed essential to do something towards filling the gap, and in pursuing that object I found that I had gone a long way beyond my primary purpose of supplying a statistical background for the lectures. In the lectures no more than a brief summary of the results that emerged from my statistical investigations was possible. In the present volume the statistical material, which is set out in detail in the Appendices, provides the basis for a historical survey of the period from 1858 to 1914, the Antonine age of Bank rate. For both the earlier and the later history of the subject the interpretation of the statistical evidence is assisted by the pronouncements of the Bank of England made in the course of official inquiries, the Parliamentary Committees of 1832, 1840–1, 1848 and 1857–8, and the Macmillan Committee of 1929–31. But for the all-important middle period very few such pronouncements are to be found.

I have to thank Sir Cecil Kisch for very valuable help in preparing a portion of the statistical material, and the Bank of England for kindly confirming some of the data employed. But the sole responsibility for the facts as well as for the opinions remains mine.

I have written this book in a private and personal capacity, and nothing in it is to be associated with my official position at the Treasury.

R. G. HAWTREY.

September, 1938.

CONTENTS

FOREWORD TO NEW EDITION

CHAPTER I

THE ORIGINS OF THE TRADITION

CHAPTER II

BANK RATE AND GOLD, 1858–1914

CHAPTER III

BANK RATE AND GOLD, 1859–1914 (*continued*)

CHAPTER IV

BANK RATE AND DEFLATION, 1914–32

CHAPTER V

BANK RATE AND CONSOLS

CONTENTS

CHAPTER VI

LONG-TERM AND SHORT-TERM RATES OF INTEREST

CHAPTER VII

THE RATE OF INTEREST AND THE PRICE LEVEL

CHAPTER VIII

LATER REFERENCES TO THE TRADITION

CHAPTER IX

PAST AND FUTURE

FOREWORD TO NEW EDITION

PROJECTS OF STABILISATION

In 1937, when I delivered the lectures which were afterwards expanded into this book, I had long been advocating a monetary policy of stabilisation of the purchasing power or wealth-value of the money unit. The resolutions adopted at the Genoa Conference of 1922, recommending international co-operation in the regulation of credit "with a view to preventing undue fluctuations in the purchasing power of gold", held out great hopes, but bore no fruit. The restoration of the gold standard by Great Britain and other countries in 1925 seemed in the eyes of most people a sufficient stabilisation of their money units. Their hopes were falsified by the crises of 1931 and 1933, which started the great depression of the nineteen-thirties, and led to the renewed suspension of the gold standard in Great Britain and America.

The Monetary and Economic Conference, which was inaugurated by the League of Nations in 1933, produced a resolution recommending that central banks should introduce into their credit policy a bias tending to correct any excess or deficiency of business activity in the world. "The central banks", it said, "will have done what is in their power to reduce fluctuations in business activity, and thereby also undue fluctuations in the purchasing power of gold."

This phrasing evidently betrayed doubts as to the power of a central bank to exercise any considerable control over the flow of money. It was little use urging a stabilisation policy on the monetary authorities of the world so long as they were completely sceptical of their power to carry it out.

It was the prevalence of this scepticism that led me to choose A Century of Bank Rate as the subject of my lectures in 1937. My purpose was to show that the reliance on Bank

rate as the instrument of monetary policy had been evolved through a century of experience, and that despite changes this experience was applicable to the problems of monetary policy in 1937.

CHANGES 1832—1937

The changes had undoubtedly been great. In 1937 the gold standard was in abeyance, whereas the experience of the years 1833-1914 had been obtained under the gold standard, and Bank rate policy had been governed by gold movements. The detailed statistical material (in the Appendices) revealed what had not been fully appreciated before, the importance under nineteenth century conditions of fluctuations in the interior demand for gold (pp. 49-54). When the market rate of discount in London was very low, the country banks did not hasten to send superfluous gold coin received from their customers to London to be invested in bills. A rise in the rate would make it worthwhile to do so, and the gold which they sent to London found its way forthwith into the Bank of England's reserve.

The power of attracting gold from the country banks, like the attraction of gold from abroad, though of immediate help in making good a shortage of reserves, was not a help but a hindrance in the more fundamental purpose of tight credit in restricting demand. A spell of high Bank rate would restore the reserve in a few weeks, only to be followed by a loss of gold as soon as the rate was lowered. Hence the violent zigzags which appear in Appendix I up to about 1880. Only after repeated alternations of high and low rates, would the expansive tendency of credit be effectually checked (pp. 64-5).

It was the growth of branch banking through amalgamations and mergers which eventually ended these fluctuations of interior demand (pp. 55-6). The disuse of gold coin and the abandonment for practical purposes of the fixed fiduciary issue system have made the reserve position independent of movements in the circulation of currency. But the attraction of money from abroad remains as a complication in estimating the effect of a high Bank rate.

The gradual disuse of bills of exchange in the financing of internal trade (pp. 56-61) tended to make traders more sensitive to the terms of borrowing.

Since 1914 far wider fluctuations of price levels and wage levels had become possible than before. The fluctuations of prices were not only in terms of inconvertible paper units, but in terms of gold and of money units fixed in gold. The world had a foretaste of what this change meant in the violent inflation and deflation of 1919-22 (pp. 130-4). The return to gold in 1925 brought hopes of relative stability, which were shattered by the crises of 1931 and 1933 (pp. 143-5), and the ensuing appreciation of gold, which reduced the world price level by more than half (p. 251).

THE GREAT DEPRESSION

The great depression of the nineteen-thirties has passed into history as a unique period of misery and distress. The helplessness of successive Governments in Germany, faced with six million unemployed, led directly to the accession of Hitler to power, and so to the second World War.

People concerned in public affairs are apt to treat monetary policy as a technical matter which the normal practical man need not trouble to understand. The great depression is often regarded as a visitation comparable to Attila "the Scourge of God", to the Tartar invasions, or to the Black Death, instead of being the inevitable consequence of more than doubling the wealth-value of the world's money unit.

Even those who recognise that the depression was a monetary phenomenon are not always alive to the train of causation which brought it about.

In my *Good and Bad Trade* (1913) I showed how the effect of the rate of interest on short-term borrowers is modified by the prospect of rising or falling prices, and how a low rate might fail to revive demand in a depression. I pointed out (p.186) that, "in order to counteract the effect of falling prices, bankers fix a rate of interest lower than the natural rate by the rate at which prices are believed to be falling", but "if the rate of depreciation of prices is actually *greater*

than the natural rate of interest, . . . nothing that the bankers can do will make borrowing sufficiently attractive. Business will be revolving in a vicious circle: the dealers unwilling to buy in a falling market, the manufacturers unwilling to maintain their output in face of ever-diminishing orders."

The present volume (pp.250-3) gives a slightly different account of this "stagnation" of business. Since it is the *expectation* of falling prices that influences the borrowing traders, account must be taken of the circumstances which cause such an expectation. A fall of prices in the recent past is in itself just as likely to cause an expectation of a recovery as of a further fall. The sign that prices of goods are too high relatively to demand is the accumulation of unsold stocks. Traders who are encumbered with such an accumulation cannot be tempted to order more, however liberal the facilities for borrowing. In such circumstances the vicious circle is more correctly described in terms of redundant stocks than of falling prices. A fall in demand leads to an accumulation of stocks, the accumulation of stocks leads to a decline in orders, the decline in orders leads to a decline in output, thus to a decline in incomes, a decline in sales and a renewed accumulation of unsold goods (p.62).

BANK RATE AFTER ITS FIRST CENTURY

My century of bank rate may be said to have begun with the recommendation of the representatives of the Bank of England in 1832 for the repeal of the laws against usury (p.16), and to have ended with the reduction of Bank rate to 2 per cent on the 30th June 1932. For two-thirds of the thirty years that have passed since that reduction Bank rate may be said to have had no history. Apart from the ephemeral rise to 4 per cent on the outbreak of war in 1939, it remained at the traditional minimum of 2 per cent till it was raised to 2½ on the 8th November 1951. Up to the outbreak of war it was beyond dispute that industry needed an expansion of demand, and the question of raising Bank rate to bring about a contraction did not arise. When the

war came, reliance was placed on controls, and without free markets there was no scope for monetary management through the rate of interest. After the end of hostilities, controls were not immediately relaxed, but it was soon clear that they were failing to prevent inflation. The removal of price controls in America in 1946 let loose a flood of redundant money, and the rise of American prices led inevitably to corresponding rises in other countries which were maintaining fixed rates of exchange on the dollar. In Great Britain wartime controls had had the same result of accumulating a mass of redundant money. So long as price controls were effective, the outlet for spending was limited by the available supplies valued at controlled prices, and there was no more than a trickle of spending to drain away the redundant money. The rise of prices in 1946-8 started the idle money circulating and initiated an orgy of inflation.

When there were two thousand millions of superfluous money for spending, dear money could do little to check expansion. Bank rate remained quietly at 2 per cent, and overdraft rates low.* But the rise of prices was itself steadily eliminating the redundant money. The rise was accelerated when in 1949 the dollar value of the pound was reduced from $4·03 to $2·80. Thereafter the pound had not merely to keep pace with the declining wealth-value of the dollar, but had in addition to make up for the abrupt increase in the sterling equivalent of dollar prices by 44 per cent. In 1952 the gross national product reckoned at current prices was 59 per cent greater than in 1946, while bank deposits had increased only 19 per cent. The redundant money had practically been absorbed.

From that juncture there starts a new chapter in the history of Bank rate. The rise from 2 per cent to 2½ immediately on the change of Government was no more than a signal that the long sleep was over. But devaluation had failed to ensure a favourable balance of payments, and in March 1952 Bank rate was raised to 4 per cent. That was

---

*The traditional minimum of 5 per cent on overdrafts had long been in abeyance (see my *The Pound at Home and Abroad*, p.6).

not a high rate, but it is the extent of a rise rather than the level the rate rises to that influences borrowing (see pp.240-3), and a rise by more than one point on one day has always been unusual. A slackening of the inflationary tendency had already been felt before the end of 1951, and how much the Bank rate contributed to the process it would be difficult to estimate. Anyhow the balance of payments was satisfactorily restored, and the reserve of gold and dollars rose from £602 million in June 1952 to £1,078 million in June 1954.

Before the end of 1954 the position had begun to deteriorate; an adverse balance resulted in a loss of reserves. Bank rate was put up to 3½ per cent (27 Jan. 1955) and 4½ (24 Feb.), and in July, when the effect appeared insufficient, a "credit squeeze " was imposed: the banks were to effect a "positive and significant reduction" in their advances. This was done. The total of the Clearing Banks' advances was brought down from £2,186 million in June 1955 to £1,851 million in December. Yet the reserves fell in the same half-year from £957 million to £757 million. At last Bank rate was put up to 5½ per cent (16 Feb. 1956). A slight improvement became visible but in the latter part of the year was interrupted by the Suez crisis. A loss of reserves amounting to £254 million was partly made good by a drawing of £201 million from the International Monetary Fund. The Suez crisis was a transitory disturbance, and in Feb. 1957 Bank rate was reduced to 5 per cent. The reserve was then £744 million, or, if the £201 million received from the I.M.F. be excluded, £543 million. An increase of £106 million brought it at the end of June 1957 to £850 (649) million. But thereupon another crisis boiled up, and something like a panic led to Bank rate being put up from 5 per cent to 7 in September.

All this time inflation was raging. At a time of rapid technological improvement and rising productivity the rise of prices gives an inadequate measure of an inflationary tendency. The rise of wages is a better indicator, and in the five years 1946-51 the wage level (men's hourly earnings) rose 36 per cent.

The situation was comparable to that of 1919-20 (pp.212-14). If the short-term rate of interest was to deter borrowers, it would have to be high enough to outweigh the speculative gains traders were expecting to make from rising prices, and so to stop their anticipatory purchases of goods. The successive rises of Bank rate to 4½ and 5½ per cent were not high enough.

The devaluation of 1949 resulted in the pound being undervalued. British costs expressed in dollars, and in those money units which had not been devalued, had become too low, and British exports were underpriced.* British manufacturers encountered a state of intensified demand which was reflected in the demand for labour. The rise in wages and prices since 1949 had been far from sufficient to restore equilibrium, and there was a clear prospect of a further rise.

At last the rise of Bank rate to 7 per cent (involving an overdraft rate of 8) broke the spell. For the moment the anticipatory purchases were checked. But the expectation of rising wages and prices continued. For, so long as the pound was undervalued, there was an excessive demand for British products in export and import markets.

The high Bank rate damped down demand at home, and mitigated the strain on the labour market. But it did not completely relieve the strain. Overtime was diminished, but unemployment, though slightly increased, remained abnormally low. For the productive resources released by the decline of demand at home became available to increase exports.

In 1920 the expectation of rising prices was based on the visible fact that the Government was paying its way by inflationary methods. A high bank rate was required so long as the expectation so founded continued. The Government had in December 1919 imposed a limitation on the issue of currency notes, and in April 1920 brought out a budget promising a substantial surplus. The 7 per cent Bank rate of April not only checked anticipatory purchases, but led people to believe that the deflationary measures

*See *The Pound at Home and Abroad*, pp.7-8 and 123-33.

of the Government would be effective. There was no longer any ground for expecting demand to expand or prices to rise.

In 1957 the position was different. The contractive effect of a high Bank rate is transitory. Once traders have adjusted their stocks to the state of credit, the contractive effect ceases. A trader who wants to reduce his stocks restricts the orders he gives for replenishment to something less than the amount he disposes of by sale. When he has achieved the desired reduction of stocks, his orders are once again equal to his sales. That stage may be long delayed by the vicious circle of deflation (pp.61-2) but so long as there was an insistent demand from abroad for the under-priced British exports, the vicious circle could not be joined. The contractive effect of the 7 per cent Bank rate was felt up to the summer of 1958. By that time the returns of overtime worked showed a reduction from 12·23 million hours in August 1957 to 9·26 million in August 1958. Bank rate had been reduced by steps to 4½ per cent, and was further reduced to 4 on the 20th November 1958.

The year 1959 saw a marked revival of activity. A growing demand was evidenced first by a big increase in overtime, and then, in the first half of 1960, by a resumption of the rise of wages. Bank rate was put up to 5 per cent (21 January 1960) and 6 (23 June), but there was little if any effect on productive activity. The clear inference should have been that the state of demand and the prospect of rising prices had again induced anticipatory purchases. And there was in fact a sharp increase in imports. Yet Bank rate was reduced to 5½ per cent (27 October 1960) and 5 (8 December). The reserve position looked highly favourable; after repayments amounting to £97 million to the International Monetary Fund, the reserves were increased in the second half of 1960 by £121 million. But the gain was delusive. It was due to a big influx of money from abroad, which raised the overseas sterling holdings outside the Sterling Area from £803 million in December 1959 to £940 million in June 1960, and £1,407 million in December 1960. If a high short-

term rate of interest is to attract foreign money, there must be confidence in the money unit. The favourable conditions of 1958 and 1959 had re-established confidence in sterling, and the attraction of a yield of 6 per cent on securities repayable in a few years exerted a powerful pull, even after Bank rate had been reduced. The huge inflow, depending on foreign confidence in sterling, concealed from the public a heavy adverse current balance.

After the turn of the year, the reserves began to suffer losses, and in March 1961 the statistical return of the Balance of Payments disclosed an adverse current balance, in the second half of 1960, of £265 million (later corrected to £215 million). There resulted acute anxiety, which soon developed into panic. There was a flight from sterling, which would have reduced the reserves from £1,037 million at the beginning of June to £553 million at the end of July, if they had not been supplemented by £323 million from foreign central Banks under the Basle Agreement in March. Once again Bank rate was raised to 7 per cent (26 July 1961) and for the moment confidence was restored.

THE DEVALUATION PANICS

The crisis of 1961, like that of 1957, was one of confidence in sterling. There was a fear that the pound would be again devalued. A strangely misplaced fear!

People feared devaluation because successive British Governments showed by their pronouncements that they themselves feared devaluation. From time to time they had been warning the public that exporters could not stand any further increase in wages, and protesting that every effort must be made to maintain the dollar value of the pound at $2·80. A recognition that the pound was greatly under-valued at that rate would have made nonsense of the warning and the protest, but the authorities never thought it necessary to examine the situation from that point of view.

It is astonishing that so misguided a belief was generally accepted, even with the authority of the Government and their advisers behind it. The explanation, I think, has been

that whatever the cause of an adverse balance may be its immediate impact is felt in an excess demand for foreign exchange, and a tendency for the country's money to be offered at a discount. People suppose that a depreciation of the money unit in terms of foreign units is the natural corrective of the adverse balance; and so it is when the adverse balance is due to an over-valuation of the money unit, as in 1931. But the root cause of an adverse balance of payments is excess spending, spending, that is, in excess of current receipts. Over-valuation causes an excess by reducing the current receipts from foreign demand. Declining orders cause unemployment in export industries. But excess spending arising in any other way has the same effect.

An under-valuation of the money unit might be expected to have a favourable effect on the balance of payments. And so long as industry is under-employed it does. But when full employment is reached, output encounters a limit, and exporters fail to meet the foreign demand. They do not seek export orders, or when they get them, they are late in delivery. Low-cost manufacturers do not put up their prices to what the demand can stand, and much of the favourable effect of the under-valuation is lost in the under-pricing of exports.

And under-valuation may actually have an unfavourable effect on the balance of payments through its reaction on the credit system. For it induces a state of markets in which traders expect costs and prices to rise, so that a higher short-term rate of interest is needed to have a given deterrent effect. When the banking authorities fail to appreciate this, they miscalculate the rate of interest appropriate to a given situation. In 1957 and 1961 a 7 per cent Bank rate was supposed to be desperately high, and only to be resorted to in a great crisis. The 6 per cent of 1960 or the 5½ of 1956 seemed severely high rates, and the 4 per cent of 1959 a moderate and prudent rate. In the circumstances of the times 4 per cent was "cheap money", 6 per cent was very mildly deterrent, 7 per cent could just be regarded as high. The deterrent effect even of 7 per cent was largely psychological,

and it may be that without the expectations aroused by it a still higher rate would have been needed. The excess spending which causes the adverse balance takes shape in the anticipatory purchases which lax credit encourages. The authorities believe that they have been keeping a tight hand on credit. When they find the country troubled by an apparently inexorable inflation and by repeated crises in the balance of payments, they are blind to the effect of what is really cheap borrowing and they look elsewhere for the explanation. When the Radcliffe Committee was asked on its appointment "to exclude exchange rates " from its inquiries, (Evidence, Question 982) Ministers must have felt very confident that $2·80 was just the right rate, and need not be inquired into.

RETROSPECT

When we look back on the monetary experience we have had since 1932, surely the moral to be drawn from it is above all the vital importance of maintaining stability of the value of the money unit. The depression of the nineteen-thirties was due to the doubling of the wealth-value of gold. And since 1934, when the present gold value of the American dollar was fixed, the value of gold as measured by the American wage level (hourly earnings in manufacturing) has fallen by three quarters.

The International Monetary Fund revived the gold standard, and based it on the American dollar. As the gold standard was practised in the nineteenth century, every country was free to depart from it or to alter the parity of its money unit. Now a change of parity requires the consent of the Fund. That consent was obtained and acted upon by Great Britain in 1949 with deplorable results. The pound already tied to the dwindling dollar, had to dwindle all the more.

Both the public and the politicians who take the responsibility of leading them are constantly exercised in their minds about rising prices, rising wages, crises in the balance of payments, and measures for the control of credit which

seem to restrict economic progress. They never seem to be aware that these are all aspects of one single question, the wealth-value of the pound, and that the wealth-value of the pound is dictated by the rate of exchange on the United States.

To unstable money are to be traced nearly all our economic troubles since 1918: the unemployment of the inter-war years; the over-employment and scarcity of labour since the second World War; the labour unrest incidental to perpetual wage demands; the hardships and dislocation caused by the declining value of small savings, annuities and endowments; the vexation of continual price rises even for those whose incomes on the whole keep pace with them; the unmanage-ability of the credit system and the resulting crises; the collapse of the prices of Government securities through distrust of the unit in which they are valued.

The dollar-value of the pound at $2·80 being accepted as the fixed basis of British monetary policy, the reserve of gold and dollars has naturally become the basis of day-to-day monetary policy. As the availability of the reserve is un-affected by changes in the note issue, management has become a matter exclusively of the balance of payments.

I have referred at the outset (p. xi) to the scepticism of the monetary authorities as to their power so to regulate credit as to maintain monetary stability. This scepticism has, I think, increased. At any rate they seem always to be unwilling to trust to Bank rate alone as a regulator. For example the resort to the "credit squeeze" in 1955, and to "special deposits" in 1961 to reduce the liquid resources of the banks. Yet the decisive effect of 7 per cent in 1957 and 1961 is hardly to be denied.

The book has been reprinted without alteration except corrections of misprints and one or two verbal errors.

July 1962   Ralph Hawtrey

CHAPTER I

THE ORIGINS OF THE TRADITION

INTRODUCTION

IN the years preceding the outbreak of war in 1914 the
reliance of the Bank of England on its discount rate or
" Bank Rate " as the means of regulating its reserve had
come to be universally accepted. The Bank was responsible
for the currency of the country, and its responsibility was
centred in the reserve of the Banking Department. Under
the Bank Charter Act of 1844 the fiduciary issue of Bank of
England notes was a fixed quantity, and the reserve represented the margin of surplus currency which the Bank was
free to pay out without transgressing the limit so imposed
upon it. If the reserve showed signs of falling to a dangerously low level, the Bank would raise the Bank rate till
the reserve was restored. If the reserve rose unnecessarily high, the Bank rate was reduced.

This procedure had become a firmly established tradition—
so firmly established that the reasoning on which it had been
founded had been clean forgotten. When it was dug up in
the course of the inquiries of the Cunliffe Committee in
1918 and the Macmillan Committee in 1930-1, it was regarded
rather as an academic exercise than as a serious practical
doctrine.

In recent years the traditional Bank rate policy has been
frequently challenged. It has been challenged on the
ground that it is injurious to trade and industry and sacrifices
their interests to a pedantic monetary correctitude. It has
been challenged on the contradictory ground that its supposed efficacy is a fiction based on fallacious reasoning.

The object of the present work is to show how the Bank
rate tradition grew up, what was in the minds of those who
originated it, to what extent their intentions were realized

in the experience which followed, and what is its virtue in the circumstances of the present day and the future.

The opening chapter deals with the period in which the policy was enunciated and took form. The century covering the history of Bank rate begins with the amendment of the usury laws in 1833, but a preliminary account of the proposals and of the experience that gradually led up to that measure is necessary to make the story complete.

This first period covers the Parliamentary inquiries of 1832, 1840–1, 1848 and 1857–8. Here we have the authoritative representatives of the Bank of England first explaining why they desired power to raise their discount rate without the restraints imposed by the usury laws, and then at subsequent inquiries subjected to examination and criticism in regard to the manner in which this power, when it had been granted, was used.

It becomes clear that the policy was throughout regarded as a device for regulating the *currency* ; it was a monetary application of a form of credit control. It is also revealed that the authorities of the Bank of England embarked on the policy with their eyes open to its dangers and drawbacks. They were aware of the injurious consequences of deflation, but they believed them to be unavoidable if the paramount object of a currency unit fixed beyond all doubt in terms of gold was to be gained.

In Chapters II and III we pass to the history of Bank rate in the period from 1858 to 1914. We no longer have the assistance of Parliamentary Committees as a guide to the interpretation of policy. That of 1875 on Banks of Issue hardly touched the subject. The Royal Commission on the Depression of Trade in 1885–6 and that on Gold and Silver in 1886–8 elicited no significant pronouncements from the Bank of England, though the evidence received by the latter is noteworthy for the formulation of the theory of credit regulation by Marshall.

Consequently in these chapters we have to go straight to the facts, and to interpret them in the light of the pronouncements of policy recorded up to 1858. Chapter III

sets out the statistical material in chronological sequence. Chapter II serves as an introduction to Chapter III, indicating the principles illustrated by the statistical data, so as to supply a theoretical basis for the interpretations suggested in the latter chapter. These chapters are mainly concerned with the movements of gold, exports and imports and interior demand, which are set out in detail in Appendices I and II.

Chapter IV carries on the story from 1914 to 1932.

Chapter V passes to the statistical investigation of another aspect of the subject, the relation of the long-term rate of interest to Bank rate. Appendix I records the price of Consols (or, from 1879 to 1888, the price of $2\frac{1}{2}$ per cent. annuities) on the day preceding every change in Bank rate from 1844 to 1932. Chapter V analyses the data thus presented, and Chapter VI supplies a theoretical discussion of this part of the subject and generally of the relations between the long-term and short-term rates of interest. Chapter VII is concerned with the relations of the rate of interest to movements of the price level and to monetary conditions, with special reference to events since the War.

Chapter VIII is devoted to a number of pronouncements throwing light on the Bank rate tradition from Bagehot in 1873 to the Macmillan Committee in 1931.

Finally, Chapter IX contains a general survey of the subject with reference to the future as well as to the past.

HENRY THORNTON

The practice of using the Bank of England's discount rate as an instrument of monetary regulation may be said to start from the Bank Charter Act of 1833. The exemption of the discount on bills up to three months from the operation of the usury laws by Section 7 of that Act permitted the Bank for the first time to raise its discount rate above 5 per cent.

The idea was thirty years older. It was originated, I believe, by Henry Thornton, who, when giving evidence

before the House of Lords Committee on the Bank Restriction in 1797, remarked on " the unnaturally low rate of interest resulting from the usury laws, which confine the rate of discounting at the Bank to 5 per cent." " There might be," he said, " a much greater disposition to borrow of the Bank at 5 per cent. than it might become the Bank to comply with." He recurred to the subject in his *Enquiry into the Nature and Effects of the Paper Credit of Great Britain*, which appeared in 1802. " The Bank," he wrote, " is prohibited by the state of the law from demanding, even in time of war, an interest of more than 5 per cent., which is the same rate at which it discounts in a period of profound peace." The demand for loans from the Bank depends, he said, " on a comparison of the rate of interest taken at the Bank with the current rate of mercantile profit." " At some seasons an interest of 6 per cent. per annum, at others of 5 or even of 4 per cent., may afford that degree of advantage to borrowers which shall be about sufficient to limit, in the due measure, the demand upon the Bank for discounts."

Only by limiting discounts was it possible to limit the Bank's note issue, and so to prevent inflation.

THE CREDIT SYSTEM OF THE EARLY NINETEENTH CENTURY

To make clear the commercial and financial organisation which elicited Thornton's comments, it will be necessary first to enter into a brief description of the credit system of the early nineteenth century, and especially to show the part played in it by bills of exchange.

A bill of exchange is an instrument for assigning the rights in a debt from one creditor to another. It is an order to the debtor to pay to the new creditor. It is written or " drawn " by the old creditor, and, to become binding, must be acknowledged or in technical language " accepted " by the debtor.

Under medieval conditions, as soon as the trade between any two distant places (even within the boundaries of one country) developed beyond casual and occasional adventures, and assumed some degree of regularity, the merchants

in one such place would have agents to transact their business in the other. The agent would sell his principal's goods and hold the money received at the latter's disposal. The merchant would direct his agent whether to use the money to buy more goods or to apply it to any other purpose. The earliest commercial bills of exchange were drawn by merchants on their agents, and were simply directions for the disposal of money in the agents' hands. But by the eighteenth century the agent was beginning to drop out. The merchant sending goods to a distant place would draw a bill on the purchaser himself, instead of on an agent. That necessitated a prior agreement by the latter both to purchase the goods and to accept the bill, but, as communications improved, such agreements became more practicable. Nevertheless the functions of the agent could not be wholly dispensed with. The bill, when accepted by the purchaser on whom it was drawn, became the vital evidence of his debt to the seller, and someone had to take charge of it on behalf of the latter. It was to render these services in respect of the bills drawn for the internal trade of the country that the English banking system of the eighteenth century had grown up. The country banks of that time were primarily an organisation for dealing with bills, not only for discounting them, but for presenting them for acceptance, holding them in safe keeping, and collecting payment on maturity. Their note issues and deposits were originally incidental to these functions; traders made their bills payable to the banks, and were willing to leave the proceeds of discount or collection on deposit, or to draw them out in the convenient form of bank notes.

The merchant in any part of England would usually pay for his purchases by accepting bills drawn upon him by the sellers, and would receive payment by drawing bills on his customers. Payment might also be made by means of bills already in the possession of the purchaser and endorsed by him to the seller, or it might of course be made in cash. When a bill was drawn, the foundation of the bargain was that the purchaser should make payment at an agreed

future date.   The bill was merely an instrument for assigning the debt so created to another creditor.

If a merchant's purchases and sales were paid for exclusively by the drawing of three months bills, his payments and receipts would be a perfect trace of his purchases and sales three months in arrear.   He would at any time be paying for what he bought three months before, and receiving payment for what he sold three months before.   There would be an excess of payments over receipts equal to the value of the goods bought and not yet sold up to three months before.   This excess (along with the expenses incurred in his business) might be met out of his own capital.   But it would be a widely fluctuating amount, and if his capital was sufficient to cover the maximum excess of payments over receipts, then at times when the excess was below the maximum he would hold a balance of idle cash. Idle cash is a loss.   And this loss could be avoided if the merchant so limited the capital employed in his business that it was just enough when the excess of his payments over his receipts was at a minimum, and relied on getting some of his bills discounted whenever the excess rose above the minimum.   In effect he might be increasing his business and supplementing his capital to the requisite extent by the discounting of bills ; or, if his business did not expand to this extent, he might build up a private fortune in securities or property outside the business.   The private fortune being withdrawn, the capital remaining in the business would be no more than the essential minimum ; so equally in this case the usual practice would be to provide for the fluctuating excess of payments over receipts beyond the minimum by getting bills discounted before maturity.

A wholesale dealer selling to retail dealers would probably draw bills on them, but many of the bills would be small and local, and he would not rely on getting them discounted.   He would assume the burden of financing the retailers from his own capital.   The retailers would need the credit accorded to them by the bills in some instances to enable them to give credit to customers and in others to

allow for the time taken to sell off each consignment of goods bought.

Manufacturers, like merchants, would be financed by bills. A manufacturer who drew bills for the goods he sold, and accepted bills drawn on him for the materials he bought, would have to pay wages and other expenses of production in cash. But that did not necessarily mean that he would depend to a greater extent than the merchant on getting bills discounted, for he might meet this cash outlay from his own capital. Like the merchant he would cover the variable margin in excess of his minimum working capital by getting bills discounted. For the manufacturer the variable margin would include the goods he has produced but not yet delivered and those he has delivered but has not been paid for.

Bills on London

Bills might be drawn on traders in any part of the country, but from the early days of the credit system there was a marked tendency for bills drawn on London to predominate. The more substantial merchants, those whose transactions were not merely local in character, would nearly always have either a head office or an important agency in London, and to all such the centralisation of receipts and payments was a great convenience. Even traders who had no London establishment tended in course of time to arrange with their bankers to have the bills drawn on them made payable in London.[1]

In consequence of the monopoly of joint-stock banking enjoyed by the Bank of England till 1826, the banking system was in the hands of numerous banks most of which were small and none could have a capital exceeding the fortunes of six partners. Few banks had any branches, and none had an extensive branch system. One of the principal functions of the banks in any locality was to act

---

[1] That arrangement, relating merely to the place at which the trader undertakes to make payment, must be distinguished from the case where the banker himself accepts the bill on behalf of the trader.

as correspondents of banks in other places for the purpose of presenting bills drawn on that locality for acceptance and payment. A bank would need to have correspondents in all the places with which its customers ordinarily did business, and above all it would need a London correspondent. Every country bank would hold a reserve of London funds composed partly of a balance with its correspondent bank and partly of accepted bills payable in London.

The accepted bills might be left in London with the correspondent bank to be presented for payment on maturity, or sold in the discount market should funds be needed earlier, or they might be returned to the country bank to be available in local dealings. The country bank would employ these London funds to meet the needs of customers arising from liabilities for the purchase of goods or investments or for maturing bills in London. The reserve would be fed by the London receipts of country customers, by maturities of bills, and by the sale of bills in the London discount market. One country bank would acquire London funds from another in exchange for local bills or in settlement of balances. Any country bank would possess a considerable amount of local assets, not only local bills, but also advances to customers. Even in those days advances were a substantial item.

London was also the principal centre for foreign trade. The system of merchants' agencies persisted longer in international trade than in domestic trade. In the early nineteenth century the great merchants had not yet been transformed into merchant bankers, but most of the foreign exchange business was already concentrated in their hands. Any merchant who had an agency in a foreign centre was in a position to arrange for the acceptance and payment of other merchants' bills on that centre, or to buy such bills outright.

In proportion as the export and import trade of the country came into the hands of British merchants, the financing of the trade was centralised in London. Not

only did the merchants accept bills payable in London
when they bought imports, but British manufacturers for
export sold their goods to the British merchants and drew
bills on them likewise payable in London. The smaller
merchants would draw bills on the country to which the
exports were sent for sale and would sell the bills to the
greater merchants. The greater merchants might get the
bills discounted in the country of destination, but alternatively they might hold the bills to maturity and depend
on their own capital to cover the cost of the goods in the
interval. There were also foreign merchants dealing in
British imports and exports and financing them in the
corresponding manner, but by the end of the eighteenth
century the predominance of the British merchant and
therefore of the bill on London was becoming established.

Thus it was usual for any trader, whether merchant,
wholesale dealer or manufacturer, at all times to be both
debtor and creditor on bills, debtor on those he had
accepted, and creditor on those in his own hands. And
he would probably from time to time sell a portion of the
bills coming into his hands to meet current liabilities.

The London Discount Market

A country bank discounted bills for its customers, but
the extent of its lending was limited by the amount of its
note issue and deposits and the need of a cash reserve. By
lending it created deposits which its customers could draw
upon, and, if it lent too much, their payments to customers
of other banks would exhaust its cash reserves. Even if
the payments were made in the Bank's own notes, these
would be presented for payment as soon as they had been
deposited in another bank.

If some banks received more bills from their customers
than they could safely discount, others received less. The
bills drawn on local traders, which a country bank received
in the course of its business, would not be readily marketable, and would probably be held till maturity. But bills
on London were a suitable asset for any bank, whether in

London or in the country. Any bank with an excess of bills on its hands became a seller of bills on London, and it was to provide facilities for the sale of such bills that the London discount market came into existence. Bills were offered for sale direct by the traders themselves as well as by banks. The buyers of bills were those banks which did not receive enough bills from their customers to employ their funds.

The banks in the manufacturing districts were sellers of bills. The greater part of the output of such a district was for sale elsewhere, either in another part of the country or abroad, and bills would be drawn on the purchasers. An agricultural district would be more nearly self-contained and would draw relatively few bills ; its banks would be regular buyers of bills in the London market. The banks in the City of London received the bills drawn in the course of foreign trade, while those in the West End received no bills from their customers, and were buyers of bills in the market.

That there were considerable areas of England in which the country banks seem to have been almost indifferent to conditions in the London discount market and went on year after year paying interest on deposits, charging interest on advances, and even discounting trade bills at unchanging conventional rates, is to be explained I think by the fact that in such districts the local demand for bills happened to be approximately equalled by local deposits.

At first the bill market was composed of mere brokers, who found buyers of bills to suit the sellers, and were paid by commission. About 1827 the practice began of lending money at call or short notice to bill brokers on the security of bills, and it soon grew.[1] It was impossible for a bank to select bills with maturities to suit its future uncertain needs for cash, and it was inconvenient either to be perpetually buying and selling bills or to hold a large enough cash reserve to cover all contingencies. A loan at call to the bill-broker, earning a rate of interest a fraction less

[1] See W. T. C. King, *History of the London Discount Market*, p. 67.

than the market rate of discount on bills, was a simple solution of the problem.   And it suited the bill-brokers too, for the needs of the banks for cash were mostly for payments to one another, so that loans called up would be balanced by new money lent.   But that was not always so.   There might be an excess of bills created in the country as a whole.   If for any reason there was increased activity of business, more bills would be drawn for the sale of more goods.   Manufacturers, receiving increased orders, had to discount bills to provide cash to pay wages and other expenses of production.   Additional currency would thus be created to pay additional incomes, and the additional incomes would generate increased demand.   A vicious circle of expansion would be joined. Eventually the additional purchasing power would attract additional imports from abroad.   There would be a twofold drain of gold, an internal drain to meet increased demands for currency and an external drain to pay for the excess imports.

The Bank of England and the Gold Reserve

The demand for gold was concentrated upon the reserve of the Bank of England.   The country banks drew what they needed from the London banks, and the London banks proceeded to sell bills in the discount market.   But if there was a general shortage of cash, so that the sellers of bills in the market predominated over the buyers, there was no way of providing for the unsold residue of bills unless the Bank of England would take them.   The practice had grown up of the Bank of England acting as the lender of last resort[1]; it was expected to discount all eligible bills offered, whether by merchants or by bankers, and any bill on London maturing within ninety-five days and bearing two good English names (one being the acceptor) was eligible.

It was found, however, occasionally, under conditions of extreme pressure on the reserve, that the Bank could not afford to assume this responsibility.   Thornton referred

---

[1] See my *Art of Central Banking*, pp. 116–26.

to " a determination, adopted some time since by the bank
directors, to limit the total weekly amount of loans furnished
by them to the merchants. The adoption of a regulation
for this purpose seems to have been rendered necessary by
that impossibility of otherwise limiting at all times the
Bank of England paper. The regulation in question I
consider as intended to confine within a specific, though in
some degree fluctuating, sum the loans of the bank, for the
sake of restricting the paper."

When the Bank of England placed a limit on its discounts and absolutely refused bills, the whole credit
system was endangered. Merchants who had relied on
the bills they held as the means of raising cash would find
themselves compelled to default on their own acceptances
unless they could realise some other marketable assets.
The prices of goods and of securities would be depressed by
forced sales, and doubts of the solvency of the merchants
whose names appeared on bills would lead to discredit of
the bills.

No doubt Thornton, when he wrote, had in mind the
attempt made by the Bank of England in December, 1795,
to ration discounts. The attempt to limit its note issues
by this method failed, for it did not avert the suspension of
gold payments fourteen months later. Under the Bank
Restriction that began in 1797 the Bank was no longer
restrained by any consideration of its gold reserve; it
became free to discount eligible bills without limit. And
as notes down to one pound had been put into circulation
concurrently with the suspension of gold payments, gold
was no longer needed for internal circulation at all.

THE BULLION COMMITTEE

It was this state of things that led to the appointment of
the Committee on the High Price of Bullion in 1810, in
the proceedings of which Henry Thornton took a prominent
part. In its Report the Committee found fault with the
reliance of the Bank of England on the soundness of the
bills it discounted as the sole safeguard against inflation,

without regard to their quantity, and recurred to the question of the usury laws (p. 51). "The law, which in this country limits the rate of interest and of course the rate at which the Bank can legally discount, exposes the Bank to still more extensive demands for commercial discounts. While the rate of commercial profit is very considerably higher than 5 per cent., as it has lately been in many branches of our foreign trade, there is in fact no limit to the demands which merchants of perfectly good capital and of the most prudent spirit of enterprise may be tempted to make upon the Bank for accommodation and facilities by discount."

The implication here is the same as in Henry Thornton's work ; the increase in the bills held by the Bank of England tends to bring about a corresponding increase in its note issue, and the latter increase can best be prevented by a rate of interest which is a deterrent on the former increase. To be a deterrent, the rate must offset the prospect of profit from the transactions intended by the borrowers, and, if the anticipated profit rises, the rate of discount ought to be free to rise without regard to any statutory limit.

BANK RATE IN 1822 AND 1825

As it turned out, the first occasion on which a change in the discount rate became a practical issue involved not a rise but a fall.   In the early part of the eighteenth century the Bank of England's discount rate had for twenty years been no more than 4 per cent.   From 1742 to 1773 the rate of 4 per cent. had continued for foreign bills (except for an interval at 5 per cent. from 12th December, 1745, to 1st May, 1746) though inland bills had been charged 5 per cent. Thereafter the rate had been 5 per cent. for both classes of bills, and still was when the pound was restored to gold parity in 1819, and when convertibility into gold coin was resumed in 1821.

But whereas 5 per cent. had been an unduly low rate during the Napoleonic Wars, now under conditions of

deflation that had since supervened it had become an unduly high rate. The Government was faithfully carrying out the recommendation of the Resumption Committee of 1819 to repay the Bank's advances, and the resulting gap in the Bank's assets could only be filled by discounts or by gold. But the Bank's discount rate of 5 per cent. was so far above the market rate that no bills were offered for discount, and the note issue could only be maintained in so far as gold could be attracted. The scarcity of currency thus occasioned by the Bank's policy led to open disagreement between the Bank and Government.

The Prime Minister, Lord Liverpool, speaking in the House of Lords in 1822, described as extraordinary and injurious the refusal of the Bank of England to discount at a lower rate than 5 per cent., when the market rate of interest was not more than four. " Finding it impossible," he said, " to induce the Bank to lower the rate of interest on their discounts, conformably with the expectations held out in 1819, His Majesty's Government resolved on borrowing four million pounds on Exchequer Bills from the Bank with a view to applying that sum in some manner to the relief of the country." (Quoted in W. M. Acworth's *Financial Reconstruction in England, 1815–22*, p. 106.)

The Bank yielded, and on the 20th June, 1822, reduced its discount rate to 4 per cent. How far this step contributed to the state of expansion and activity which started in 1824 and culminated in the crisis of 1825 it would be difficult to say with confidence. It is remarkable that when the crisis broke out, with its accompaniment of failures and panic, in the autumn of 1825, the rate was not at first altered. It was only on the 13th December, when the Bank adopted the policy of lending freely, that the rate was put up to the permissible maximum of 5 per cent.

The deterrent effect of that rate under crisis conditions was *nil*. There were other devices than the discounting of bills for raising short loans, and these show the intensity of the pressure ; for example in the proceedings of the

Committee of 1832 on the Bank of England Charter it was stated that early in December, 1825, " Consols were 75½ for money and about 80⅛ for the account, which account day was within twenty-five days of the day mentioned." That works out at 6 per cent. for twenty-five days, and the calculation made by a member of the Committee that it was 72 per cent. per annum was an under-statement.

It can hardly be said that at this time Bank rate was being used as an instrument of credit regulation. The foreign exchanges had already been made favourable and the external drain of gold stopped in October, as a result of the deflationary power of the crisis itself, and the last spasms of the internal drain were met by the re-issue of £1,000,000 of one-pound notes, which had been put aside when notes below five pounds had been withdrawn, and had not been destroyed or cancelled.

After the crisis of 1825 an Act was passed prohibiting the issue of notes below five pounds from April, 1829. This applied to the Bank of England and to the private banks in England and Wales (but not in Scotland or Ireland, where one-pound notes had been in vogue even before 1797). The change was an important one, for it made gold coin indispensable for use as a hand-to-hand currency. So long as there was no gap between the smallest bank note and the largest sum that could conveniently be paid in silver coin, it was possible to meet a demand for currency in any district where the banks of issue were trusted without any absorption of gold at all. Even the reserves of the banks might take the form mainly of London funds. In practice, no doubt, there was some demand for sovereigns everywhere as soon as the resumption of gold payments (1821) made them available. But the suppression of all notes below five pounds meant that thenceforward a demand for currency would be expressed more immediately and insistently in a demand for gold coin. And the Bank of England could not again meet an internal drain by opening a forgotten chest of one-pound notes. It must depend exclusively on its metallic reserve.

A CENTURY OF BANK RATE

The Committee of 1832

In 1832, when a Parliamentary Committee was constituted to consider the conditions on which the Bank of England's Charter should be renewed, the Directorate of the Bank of England came forward with a positive recommendation for the repeal of the laws against usury, or at any rate for such amendment as would give them a free hand to charge a deterrent rate of discount.

As George Warde Norman, one of the most influential directors, put the case, " if the rate of interest should rise much above 5 per cent., the Bank must either over-issue or be obliged to resort to measures to contract its discounts, which might lead to very serious effects, such as rejecting private paper capriciously for no other reason than because enough had been discounted already." (Qn. 2430.) Horsley Palmer, the Governor of the Bank, put forward the same argument, and expressly linked up the over-issue of currency with the price level and the foreign exchanges. " Over-issue," he said, " means excess of prices having relation to the prices of other countries." (Qn. 371.) Asked, " by what test would you generally measure an over-issue," he replied, " by the foreign exchange."

The argument put forward by Norman and Horsley Palmer differed in one respect from Thornton's. Thornton's argument was based on " a comparison of the rate of interest taken at the Bank with the current rate of mercantile profit " ; his supposition was that the merchant who thought he could make a profit in excess of the rate of interest would be tempted to extend his borrowing. Norman compared the Bank's discount rate not with the current rate of mercantile profit but with the current rate of interest.

Neither statement of the case is satisfactory. Thornton's comparison of the rate of interest with the rate of profit is vitiated by the fact that while interest is calculated per unit of time, profit is a margin between the buying and the selling price and is independent of time ; the relation

between the two depends on the time for which interest has to be paid.

Norman's comparison of the Bank's rate of discount with the market rate presupposes that the market rate could rise above the statutory maximum. Possibly it could ; there might be an illicit market, and there were various legal or at any rate colourable evasions open to the ingenious lender. But so long as the Bank of England was willing to lend an indefinite amount at 5 per cent., the market rate for bills classed by it as eligible could not rise higher. What Norman really meant was that the rate of interest might rise virtually or potentially above 5 per cent., in the sense that if the market were allowed to work freely at that rate a disequilibrium would be caused in the form of over-issue.

And this virtual rise of the rate of interest might be attributable to just such an expansion of profits as Thornton had in mind. It would not arise from a direct comparison of the rate of interest with the rate of profit, but the expansion of profits would be a sign of increased demand for commodities, and demands for credit from traders who wished to increase their working capital would result.

If the rate of interest were free, this pressure to borrow would cause the rate to rise. But if the rate of interest were limited then as soon as the limit was reached and the private banks found themselves unable to deter borrowers, further demands for credit would all be concentrated on the Bank of England. Thus the power to raise the rate of discount was required to deter borrowers. That did not mean that the trader would abandon an enterprise altogether on the ground that the charge for interest on his temporary borrowing would eat up the whole of his profit ; he could usually reduce the charge for interest by shortening the interval between purchase and sale, that is to say, by postponing purchases of goods. (Hastening sales is not so easy ; it involves a sacrifice of price.)

The recommendation of the Bank was adopted, and the usury laws were so amended by the Act of 1833 as not to

apply to the rate of discount on bills of exchange maturing within three months.

BANK RATE FROM 1825 TO 1844

The market rate of discount had fallen from 5 per cent. at the end of 1825 to 4½ and 4 per cent. in the summer of 1826 and 3 per cent. in June, 1827. Bank rate had been reduced from 5 to 4 per cent. on the 5th July, 1827, and remained at that level (though the market rate occasionally fell as low as 2½) till July, 1836. By that time the severe depression which had followed the crisis of 1825, and had lasted with little relief till 1832, had made way not merely for revival but for a state of activity which caused some anxiety. There was a drain of gold to the United States, where the reduction of the gold contents of the dollar in 1834 had raised the coinage ratio of gold to silver from 15 to 1 to 16 to 1, and practically involved a transition from a silver to a gold standard. At the same time unsound credit conditions had been developing in the United States, and early in 1837 failures occurred among English merchants with American interests.

Bank rate had been raised to 4½ per cent. on the 21st July, 1836, and to 5 on the 1st September. From November, 1836, to April, 1837, a market rate of discount prevailed of 5½ per cent., a rate which would have been illegal before the amendment of the usury laws. The Bank of England's rate, however, remained at 5 per cent. Credit expansion was checked in England by the failures, but it continued on the Continent, and there resulted an inflow of gold from the Continent to England. Bank rate was reduced to 4 per cent. on the 15th February, 1838, and the market rate even fell in May to 2½ per cent.

At the end of 1838, however, crisis conditions developed in France and Belgium, and there soon followed an outflow of gold from England, which was intensified by payment for imports of corn to supplement deficient crops. On the 16th May, 1839, Bank rate was raised to 5 per cent., on the

20th June to 5½, and on the 1st of August to 6. The market rate rose to 6½.

This was the first occasion on which the Bank rate policy was seriously relied on. The Directors of the Bank, however, were unwilling to go beyond 6 per cent., and they had to call other measures in aid. They obtained credits of £2,000,000 in Paris and £900,000 in Hamburg, which relieved the strain on the bullion reserve. And they also reduced the limit of maturities discounted by the Bank from the customary ninety-five days to sixty. That meant applying an absolute refusal to those who brought longer bills to be discounted, but it caused far less embarrassment than a more general refusal, because most people who had any bills probably had some shorter ones, and even those who had none but long bills might get accommodation from those who had short ones, so long as these latter could get money from the Bank. In fact the discount market as a whole held enough short bills to raise the money it required from the Bank.

Bank rate was reduced to 5 per cent. on the 23rd January, 1840, but the Bank's gold reserve continued at an inconveniently low level for some time. The market rate of discount rose to 6 per cent. in November, 1840, and again to 5½ in November, 1841. It was only in April, 1842, that Bank rate was reduced to 4 per cent., and there then followed a period of very cheap money, the market rate actually falling below 2 per cent. in May, 1844.

THE BANK CHARTER ACT, 1844

The next stage is marked by the passage of the Bank Charter Act in 1844. The separation of the Issue Department and the Banking Department of the Bank by that Act was intended to make the business of note issue purely mechanical. There was a fixed issue against securities, initially £14,000,000, but to be increased as the note issues of the country banks were surrendered or ceased from any cause, and any additional issue could be made only against an equal addition to the metallic reserve. It was intended

by this device to relieve the Banking Department, which held the deposits, from the exceptional responsibilities devolving on a bank of issue, and to enable it to carry on business on the same footing as any other bank.[1]

Pushed to its logical conclusion that meant that the Bank would no longer undertake to be the lender of last resort. It would be free, on the one hand, to refuse to discount bills beyond such limit as seemed convenient, and, on the other, to get its share of the discounting business of the market, and for that purpose to offer to discount bills at a competitive rate. When the Act came into operation at the beginning of September, 1844, the market rate of discount was 2 per cent., and the Bank rate was reduced forthwith from 4 to 2½.

The Bank found itself in the midst of one of those long spells of cheap money which have become the familiar sequel of a financial crisis or a period of great credit pressure. The bullion reserve was at the very high level of £15,209,000. The Bank in regulating credit was intended to have regard to the reserve in the Banking Department. The notes in the Banking Department were simply the excess of the Bank's legally permissible note issue over the actual circulation. In other words the reserve was the amount of currency which the Bank could pay out without infringing the limit imposed by the Act of 1844 on its fiduciary issue. At the start in September, 1844, when the bullion was £15,209,000 the reserve was £9,033,000. In the autumn of 1845 there was some loss of gold, and the reserve fell to £5,937,000. The rate was put up to 3½ per cent., and by the end of August, 1846, the bullion had reached £16,366,000 and the reserve £9,940,000, and the rate was lowered to 3 per cent.

THE CRISIS OF 1847

Trade revival had been in progress for several years, and the credit situation was not free from special complications.

---

[1] See Parliamentary Committee of 1848 on Commercial Distress, answers of the Governor of the Bank to Questions 2652–3.

The speculation in railway development, which had been interrupted by financial stringency ten years before, had been resumed and was in full swing. And a deficient harvest in 1846 involved exceptionally heavy importations of foreign corn. To counteract the adverse effect on the balance of payments would have required a substantial credit contraction. No steps were taken in the direction of contraction till January, 1847. On the 14th January Bank rate was put up to 3½ per cent., and on the 21st to 4.[1] By that time £3,000,000 of bullion had been lost since August, 1846, and even 4 per cent. was a low rate. It was only on the 8th April, when a further £3,500,000 of bullion had gone and the reserve was reduced to £4,391,000 that Bank rate was raised to 5 per cent. And the Bank, counting itself free to behave " like any other bank," at the same time resorted to a partial refusal to lend.

For the moment this procedure was successful ; the reserve had fallen on the 17th April, 1847, to £3,087,000 but by the 19th June had recovered to £6,544,000. But the new Act had been placed in a sinister light. It had been interpreted to mean that if the reserve fell to zero, the Bank would refuse to lend at all. There would be no lender of last resort, and the discount market would dry up altogether. The prospect held out to those accustomed to finance all transactions in commodities with bills of exchange was nothing less than a complete breakdown. Any solvent trader might find himself committing an act of bankruptcy simply because the usual channel for raising the means of payment was closed to him. Each failure would destroy the guarantees for the bills on which the defaulting trader's name appeared, and would plunge the holders of those bills deeper into embarrassment.

Gold began to ebb away again. Early in August, 1847, the reserve had shrunk to £4½ millions. Bank rate was

---

[1] It was on the 15th January, 1847, that the Bank of France departed from a long-established practice of maintaining an unvarying discount rate, and raised its rate from 4 per cent. (at which level it had been since February, 1820) to 5.

put up to 5½ per cent., the first time since 1839 that it had been above 5.

In September the elements of unsoundness in the credit situation began to become manifest. The bad harvest of 1846 had led to very high prices of cereals, and a sudden collapse of prices in the summer of 1847 precipitated a number of failures among traders who had been speculating in wheat. Tension passed into panic. That of itself stopped the external drain of gold, but a general reinforcement of cash resources in coin and notes all over the country gave rise to an internal drain. Nothing less than legal tender would serve the purposes of country banks which had no current accounts at the Bank of England, and even the London banks felt the need of an ample supply of currency on the premises. In virtue of the Act of 1844, the withdrawal of notes from the Bank of England depleted the banking reserve just as much as the withdrawal of coin. The reserve fell to £3,071,000 on the 16th October and to £1,994,000 on the 23rd October.

The Bank did not refuse to lend or even restrict its lending. It displayed a livelier recognition of the responsibilities of the lender of last resort than under the pressure of the preceding April. Nevertheless it seemed to be rapidly approaching the abyss. The withdrawal of £2,000,000 more of currency would leave the Bank unable legally to meet its liabilities to its depositors in any form of currency, including its own notes.

It was in these circumstances that the Government of the day wrote a letter to the Bank recommending the Directors " to enlarge the amount of their discounts and advances on approved security," and promising an act of indemnity should this course involve an infringement of the law limiting the fiduciary issue. And the letter stipulated that " in order to retain this operation within reasonable limits," a rate of interest not less than 8 per cent. should be charged. Bank rate was raised accordingly to 8 per cent. on the 25th October, 1847.

Thus Bank rate was assigned a leading part in the drama.

The primary purpose of the Act of 1844 had been to secure the convertibility of the Bank of England note by a limitation of the issue. If the system relied on for that purpose was to be suspended, some other safeguard was essential. The desired alternative was found in a high Bank rate, the deterrent effect of which, as we have seen, had been gaining recognition for a number of years. But 6 per cent. had been found insufficiently deterrent in 1839, and the Bank was already charging rates far above its nominal 5½ per cent. Bank rate for the longer or less eligible bills. The Government therefore required the rather sensational rate of 8 per cent. to be charged as a condition of the breaking of the law.

BANK RATE FROM 1847 TO 1857

The fear of a rigid refusal of discounts once dispelled, the drain of currency ceased. The reserve touched a minimum of £1,606,000 at the end of October, and then began to recover. The law was not broken. On the 20th November, 1847, the reserve was £4,719,000 and steadily rising, and on the 22nd (a Monday) the Bank rate was reduced to 7 per cent.[1] By the 27th of January, 1848, or within ten weeks, it had fallen to 4 per cent. There was some hesitation in reducing it lower. But the cheap money policy of 1844 to 1846 had not been condemned. So long as the Bank did not set the pace towards lower discount rates, there was no reason why it should not continue the practice of following the market downwards. With bullion at £14 millions and the reserve at £10¾ millions, the rate was reduced in June, 1848, to 3½ per cent. In November, 1848, it fell to 3 and a year later, in November, 1849, the reserve having topped £12,000,000, it was reduced to 2½. For three and a half years more the rate remained low, varying only between 2 and 3. Two per cent., which has ever since been the accepted minimum, was in operation

[1] It was then, as it still is, the practice of the Bank Directors to meet on Thursdays to decide whether any change should be made in Bank rate. A change on any other day of the week was made on the individual responsibility of the Governor, and was exceptional.

for nine months of 1852. It was only in June, 1853, that the rate was raised to 3½, the reserve having dropped below £9,000,000. From then till the beginning of October, 1853, the reserve gradually fell to £6,800,000 and Bank rate was raised by stages to 5 per cent. In 1847 a reserve of £6,800,000 had only brought the rate to 4 per cent., and 5 per cent. had been imposed when the reserve had fallen to £3,500,000. The Bank remembered, no doubt, that it had been blamed for its tardiness on that occasion.

At the end of March, 1854, England was involved in the Crimean War. Bank rate was still at 5 per cent., but at the beginning of May the reserve fell to £4,600,000 and the rate was raised to 5½. War did not bring inflation, and if there was any inflationary tendency it did not prevail. Presently the reserve began to recover, and Bank rate was reduced step by step till in June, 1855, it was 3½ per cent., and the reserve exceeded £12,000,000.

That however was only a transitory phase. The reserve melted away and in October, 1855, fell below £5,000,000. Bank rate was raised to 6 per cent. for bills with not more than sixty days to run and 7 per cent. for longer bills, and there followed two years of pressure during which (except for one interval of three months at 4½ per cent. in the summer of 1856) the rate oscillated between 5 per cent. and 7.

It was at this time that the Bank of France began to rely on relatively frequent alterations of its discount rate in imitation of the practice of the Bank of England. The rate of 5 per cent. put in force at the beginning of 1847 had remained unchanged through all the varying fortunes of that year till the 17th December, when the rate reverted once more to 4 per cent. It was then left undisturbed (even by the Revolution of 1848 and the suspension of specie payments) till it was reduced to 3 per cent. on the 3rd March, 1852.

In 1853 the approach of the conflict with Russia brought advances of the discount rate to 4 per cent. in October and to 5 in January, 1854.

A usury law still existed in France and limited the rate of discount to 6 per cent. Under the influence of growing activity it was raised to that level on the 25th September, 1856. The Bank of France was relieved from the operation of the usury law by the law of 9th June, 1857, and from that time had the same freedom as the Bank of England to vary its discount rate.

Revival had reached a high level of activity in England in 1853 before the outbreak of war. On the restoration of peace at the beginning of 1856, business resumed where it had left off, perhaps with some added impetus. By then the flow of gold from the newly discovered mines in California and Australia into Europe was beginning to give a further stimulus. Sauerbeck's price index, having dropped from 95 in 1847 to 74 in 1849, rose to 102 in 1854 and 105 in 1857. An excessive credit expansion was developing, and the increased monetary circulation of the world was straining the gold supply.

THE CRISIS OF 1857

It was in the United States that an unsound credit position broke out into a crisis at the end of August, 1857. News in those days took a fortnight to cross the Atlantic. The first stages of the American crisis became known in England early in September. As news of its successive phases arrived, the crisis was revealed to be one of extreme severity, and its repercussions on the British financial system were profound. The exchange on the United States became violently unfavourable, and gold was withdrawn for export thither in considerable quantities. The credit of merchants and banks with American connections was shaken, and big failures occurred. Distrust grew into panic, and the Bank of England had once again to meet a formidable demand for currency. Bank rate had been at 5½ per cent. since July, and was raised by successive stages between the 8th October and the 9th November to 10 per cent. The Bank had placed no restriction on the granting of discounts, and had relied only on the high Bank rate

as a deterrent. But it had become manifest that the deterrent was insufficient. On the 12th November the bullion had fallen to £6,524,000 and the reserve was no more than £581,000. On that day came a letter from the Government, following the precedent of 1847, and promising indemnifying legislation if the Bank should find it necessary to break the law limiting the fiduciary issue. A high rate of discount was again made a condition, but this time Bank rate had already reached 10 per cent., and the letter merely stipulated that it should remain at that rate.

On this occasion the law was actually broken. The fiduciary issue was temporarily increased by £2,000,000, notes to that amount being handed over by the Issue Department to the Banking Department in exchange for securities. The actual excess issue at its greatest was below a million. As in 1847, the external drain of gold had already ceased before the letter was written. But the internal drain of gold continued. The London banks were quite content to hold their reserves in the form of deposits at the Bank of England, and, so long as that was so, the accommodation granted to them did not diminish the reserve. The difficulty arose from the needs of the country banks and the Scotch and Irish banks, which required actual currency on the spot to meet the demands of distrustful depositors. In the particular case of Scotland the notes of the issuing banks retained the confidence of the public (even those of the Western Bank and City of Glasgow Bank, which suspended payment, were guaranteed by the other banks). But under an Act of 1845 any additional note issue had to be backed by an equal amount of coin, and there resulted a large demand on the Bank of England for gold to be hastily transmitted to Scotland.

It was perhaps hardly sufficiently realised at the time that these demands for currency for the banks at a distance from London could not be stopped or even greatly reduced even if the Bank of England absolutely refused to discount bills or to lend. These banks already held deposits with the London banks, and the London banks held deposits

with the Bank of England. If notes and gold were drawn out against existing deposits, an excess over the fiduciary limit might be unavoidable except by an actual suspension of payment by the Banking Department.

HORSLEY PALMER ON DEFLATION

The crises of 1847 and 1857 both formed the subject of Parliamentary inquiries, which tell us much of the considerations of policy involved. Horsley Palmer, who as Governor of the Bank had advocated the amendment of the usury laws in 1832, was examined by the Committee of 1848. In 1832 he had explained how a rise in Bank rate would make the foreign exchanges favourable by causing a fall of prices ; it would " tend to limit transactions and to the reduction of prices." In 1848 he had not abandoned his view that the discount rate was the right instrument with which to regulate the foreign exchanges, but he was most emphatic in limiting the use of it to cases in which the foreign exchanges were unfavourable. Asked if he thought it was a protection to the Bank of England in a time of pressure and panic to be able to raise the rate of interest to a great extent, say, to 8 or 9 per cent., he replied, " I think that it is extremely prejudicial to commerce, and that it is totally uncalled for when the exchanges are in favour of this country, which they must be at those times of commercial pressure." (Commons Committee, 1848, Qn. 2005.) In reply to Thomas Baring, who asked in what way he thought it prejudicial to raise the rate of interest, Palmer explained : " it presses upon all branches of commerce in a way that is most prejudicial to them ; the raising of the rate of interest, I am given to understand, stopped very largely the mercantile transactions of the country—exports as well as imports." (Qn. 2007.)

Presently Baring recurred to the subject and the following series of questions and answers ensued :

" It is by producing a fall in the value of all commodities in this country that you would correct the exchange ? "—
" Yes ; not merely in that way, but you would bring

capital to this country ; by the high rate of interest you
stop credit ; many persons trading with America or with
India and China have found money so extremely scarce
in this country that they have been forced to stop their
operations."

" It is by interference with trade that it acts," he asked,
" and not merely by the inconvenience that it occasions to
holders of bills ? "—" It causes the stoppage of trade,"
was the answer. (Question 2113.)

At that point James Spooner, a banker of Birmingham
and a champion of the inflationists, intervened and asked :
" What would be the effect on the manufacturers and
labourers in the country during such an operation ? "
Palmer replied : " It destroys the labour of the country ;
at the present moment in the neighbourhood of London
and in the manufacturing districts you can hardly move in
any direction without hearing universal complaints of the
want of employment of the labourers of the country."
Spooner went on : " That you ascribe to the measures
which it was necessary to adopt in order to preserve the
convertibility of the note ? " " I think," was the reply,
" that the present depressed state of labour is entirely
owing to that circumstance."

From one of the most influential representatives of the
Bank of England so outspoken a recognition of the price
paid in the form of trade depression and unemployment
for the maintenance of the gold standard is noteworthy.

JAMES MORRIS'S VIEWS

And at the same inquiry the Governor of the Bank,
James Morris, took a similar position, though not quite so
willingly. He explained that, when gold has been exported,
the means of getting back the gold is by making money
dear[1] and causing a fall generally in the prices of commodities. (Question 3278-9.) Cayley, a member of the
Committee, who, like Spooner, was an inflationist, put to

---

[1] By a long-established convention the rate of discount or the short-term
rate of interest is called the " price " of money, so that " dear money "
means a high rate, " cheap money " a low rate.

him that " the price of the convertibility of the note under that state of things is the disemployment of labour and the ruin of the merchants of this country." " The pressure which the export of the precious metals causes," replied Morris, " naturally will cause failures of parties who may have been overtrading, and will also cause a fall in the price of goods." Morris had been maintaining that, in raising its rate of discount, the Bank of England was not exercising its own volition, but was only doing what all banks were compelled to do in face of a shortage of currency. (Questions 3275–6—see below, p. 66.) Cayley was not satisfied, and he returned to the charge : " and it will lead," he urged, " to a disemployment of labour ? " " Probably for a time," admitted the Governor, " it may lead to a disemployment of labour." (Questions 3321–2.)

Neither Morris nor Palmer was prepared to say explicitly that if the rate of discount was not raised, and the convertibility of the note was sacrificed, the " disemployment of labour " could be avoided, but it is the inevitable inference.

A little later Cayley turned to the effects of cheap money. (Questions 3412–8) :

" Did not the cheapening of money in 1844 and 1845 lead to a rise of prices ? "—" Yes."

" Did not that lead to an increased consumption of commodities ? "—" No ; the cheapening of money will create a higher price of commodities and will naturally check consumption."

" Does not the cheapening of money lead to an increase of production ? "—" Yes."

" Does not that increase of production lead to an increased employment of labour ? " " Yes," replied Morris, but he went on to protest that he was not prepared to enter upon a theoretical discussion. He wound up, however, with, " If I am asked whether cheap money has a tendency to encourage imports into this country, I answer, yes ; an abundance of money creates a rise of price and encourages importations into the country."

" You say that the cheapening of money, by which I mean a lower rate of discount, would tend to increase importation ? "—" A cheapness of money, by which I mean a large circulation, tends to raise the prices of goods, and the high prices of goods naturally cause an importation into the country."

" Does not that under the present system tend to create an adverse balance of trade and to diminish exports ? "— " Undoubtedly it does."

.   .   .   .   .

" Under the present state of things, the system is safest under a comparatively small amount of imports ? "— " No, I do not mean to say that ; we are speaking of a year [1847] in which there has been a sudden and an enormous import of food."

" But when there is a great increase of consumption, which has been produced by an increase of employment of labour, that endangers the condition of the circulation ? "— " If there has been a very greatly increased consumption, necessitating a very large importation of foreign commodities, unless we have manufactures or securities to export in payment, the balance must be paid for in the precious metals. The importation of 1847 has been very much larger than the exportation of goods, and therefore the balance has been paid in bullion."

" A diminished power of consumption on the part of the public would have been rather advantageous than otherwise to the system of circulation ? "—" A diminished consumption would have checked importation."

" Then the more privation the public was subjected to, the safer the system of circulation ? "

James Morris was silent ; but the Deputy Governor, H. J. Prescott, intervened to answer : " It is necessary sometimes for the public to deny themselves, or for the country to deny itself, the consumption of certain foreign conmmodities, in order to restore the circulation to a proper state."

Inflationists such as Cayley and Spooner did not carry much weight in the political or economic world of 1848.

But their questions and the answers they elicited threw light on the assumptions of the Governor of the Bank and his colleagues. The kind of productive activity which prevailed in 1845 and 1846 was associated with an inflationary tendency ; the resulting expansion of the consumers' income attracted an excess of imports ; to maintain the gold standard, the " convertibility of the note," it was essential to correct that excess ; and the Bank of England relied on a high Bank rate to accomplish that result by compressing the consumers' income. Therefrom resulted the " privation " and the " disemployment of labour " which Cayley's questions led up to.

The Attraction of Foreign Money

But since 1832 another theory of the operation of a high Bank rate had come into vogue. Tooke explained it as causing an " influx of foreign capital into this country for investment." As Bagehot put it at a later date, " Loanable capital, like every other commodity, comes where there is most to be made of it. Continental bankers and others instantly send great sums here as soon as the rate of interest shows that it can be done profitably." (*Lombard Street*, p. 46.) But in the eyes of the Bank of England this was a tendency of secondary importance. Weguelin, the Governor of the Bank in 1857, stated to the Committee of that year : (Qn. 1212) " the raising of the rate of interest by the Bank of England so as to affect the profit of the exchange transaction has not, in my view, any very material effect as regards the righting of the exchange." Goschen pointed out a few years later, in his *Foreign Exchanges* (1861) how small was the gain from even a substantial difference of interest on a three-months' bill in comparison with an exchange risk.

If however Bank rate were put up to stop an outflow of gold, the exchange on the places to which the gold was going would already be at the export gold point, and could not become more adverse so long as the gold standard was effectively maintained. Subject to that condition there

was no exchange risk, and a high Bank rate would attract foreign balances and diminish or even stop the outflow of gold. And in any country which was a large and regular producer of gold, since the exchange on London might be expected to remain at the gold export point, the exporters of gold would never count on an exchange gain and might be induced to hasten the despatch of the gold to take advantage of a high rate of discount even for a few weeks.[1]

It may undoubtedly be assumed that the Bank of England was glad to take advantage of this effect of Bank rate for what it was worth. But the recurrent insistence of Governors and Directors on the effect of Bank rate on the price level shows that their main reliance was on that and not on the attraction of foreign money. And it is significant that at the times of crisis when the Government intervened and made a high Bank rate a condition of the suspension of the fiduciary limit, the foreign exchanges had on both occasions already become favourable, and the attraction of foreign money was hardly thought of.

EFFECT OF BANK RATE ON THE TRADER

Bank rate was regarded as essentially a monetary instrument. It was raised to prevent an over-issue of notes. Formerly the Bank had been accustomed to contract its note-issue by selling securities. But, if there was any pressure in the money market, the sales of securities were immediately offset by increased discounts, and the assets and therefore the liabilities of the Bank remained undiminished. After the experience of April, 1847, the Bank definitely abandoned the expedient of refusing to lend. The use of Bank rate as a deterrent on borrowers was then the only policy available.

In the years 1853–7 the Bank endeavoured to apply this deterrent to keep the expansive tendency during the active phase of a trade cycle within bounds. In the two years from October, 1855, to October, 1857, Bank rate averaged no

---

[1] For an analytical examination of the international migration of funds seeking temporary investment see my *Art of Central Banking*, pp. 181–5 and 406–25.

less than 5·7 per cent., but the reserve remained persistently low. Only once did it touch £8,000,000 and on numerous occasions it fell below £5,000,000. When the crisis came, and Bank rate was advanced on the 19th October, 1857, to 8 per cent., the Governor, Neave, explained that this had less effect than in 1847 because people had become accustomed to 6 or 7 per cent.

Every one took for granted that a high Bank rate was an effective deterrent on borrowing, but it is remarkable how little consideration was given to the precise manner in which the deterrent worked. Horsley Palmer said in 1832 that it tended to diminish transactions, and in 1848 that it caused a stoppage of trade. G. W. Norman went to the root of the matter when he told the Committee of 1840 that a rise in the rate of discount " makes merchants less disposed to buy or more disposed to sell." (Question 1918.)

When Charles Turner, a Liverpool merchant, was examined by the Committee of 1848, Spooner tried to induce him to admit that a high rate of discount was directly injurious to the small manufacturers.

" I think," replied Turner, " if they can get money the rate of interest is not a consideration."

" Not a consideration to meet their existing engagements ; but do you believe that they would enter into new engagements and employ their men to work for them, if they were aware that they could not get their bills discounted without paying the rate of 8 per cent. ? "—" There is great difficulty in a man stopping his works and throwing his men out of employment ; if they supposed that the rate of interest would continue for any length of time, I do not think they would go on ; but we naturally supposed that that rate of interest would not continue for any period."

" Have you any idea what the average rate of profit of small manufacturers is ? "—" No."

" Suppose it should turn out that the average rate of profit which the small manufacturer gets is from 8 to 10 per cent., should you not think that raising the discount

of those bills to 8 per cent. would stop him entering into new engagements ? "—" It would depend upon how long he thought it would continue ; if he thought it was only to continue for a short time, he would go on, because if he discharged his workmen he would have fresh workmen to hire, and the interest of his machinery, whatever it might be, would be going on and depreciating in value."

" If it turns out to be the fact that a great many manufacturers did stop in consequence of their knowing the high rate of interest fixed, should you then say there was no mischief done by fixing the rate of interest at 8 per cent. ? "
—" I never meant to say that it occasioned no inconvenience, but I consider that the benefit was greater than the inconvenience."

Neither Turner nor anyone else would deny the fact of a great decline in manufacturing activity and consequent unemployment. But Turner's answer to Spooner's argument was nevertheless sound. The direct increase in a manufacturer's costs on account of a rise in the rate of discount was trifling. If he had to calculate the price he would ask when offered an order, the difference between 8 per cent. and 4 per cent. on a portion of his working capital during the currency of a three months' bill would be only 1 per cent. on that portion and much less than 1 per cent. either on his turn-over or on his total capital. The item is negligible in comparison with the loss involved in leaving his works idle.

On the other hand the merchant can regard each purchase of goods as a separate venture ; practically the whole capital involved is working capital, the cost of the goods themselves. And by *postponing* his purchases he can reduce the amount of capital employed without curtailing the scale of his operations at all. The additional charge imposed upon him by a rise in the rate of discount affects him like a tax on the holding of goods. The tax may be a light one, but the subject of the tax, the amount of goods held in stock, can be varied so easily that it will be responsive even to a light tax. And when the merchants post-

pone purchases, the effect is felt by the manufacturers in reduced orders. The action so lightly taken by the former involves the latter in tribulation.

We must not forget that trade in those days was financed by bills. It was the seller of goods who drew the bill, and, if the bill was discounted before maturity, it was to supply *him* with cash. When a trader decided to curtail or postpone his purchases of goods his immediate cash position was not affected ; he merely avoided giving an acceptance, and eased his cash position only three months later. When the rate of discount rose, the loss fell on those traders who found it necessary at the time to replenish their cash by selling bills, either the new bills representing new transactions or old bills representing sales of goods some time before. A trader in that position could not escape the loss. He might seek to do so by selling goods for cash. But then the purchaser would be equally unwilling to raise cash by himself selling bills, and the cash price of goods would fall.

The trader selling goods in the ordinary course of business would find the effective price of the goods diminished by the increased discount on the bills drawn. Even if the difference were something less than 1 per cent., it would make a transaction with a narrow margin of anticipated profit perceptibly less attractive. But to postpone a sale on that ground would be to speculate on the pressure being relieved by the time the goods came to be sold. It is in the motives of the purchasers of goods rather than of the sellers that we must look for the effect. For the purchaser who becomes the acceptor of a three-months bill commits himself to finding the cash at maturity, and the cautious trader will postpone the purchase and so avoid burdening his position three months hence. Even if his commitments are relatively light, and he can look forward to a surplus of cash, the realisation of that expectation will depend on the bills he holds for his sales of goods being met at maturity. Under the bill system traders were terribly dependent on one another's solvency. A " shock to credit "

would result in a general reluctance to purchase goods by the acceptance of bills.   A decline of orders to manufacturers would follow, and so general depression and unemployment and a fall of prices.

THE BANK OF ENGLAND AND THE DISCOUNT MARKET

The Parliamentary Committee of 1858 described the Bank of England as " the bank of last resort in a panic." (Sec. 17 of Report.)   One of the documents placed before them was a letter from the Governor, Weguelin, written to the Chancellor of the Exchequer in November, 1856, in which he said : " the Bank is expected to open its doors to all comers, and make advances to any amount, provided only good banking security, such as unexceptionable bills of exchange, are tendered to it."   When the Bank was called on to render this service, as it commonly was at times of pressure, without any suggestion of panic, it was not usually to other banks.   In fact the London bankers from 1825 onwards made a point of never offering bills for rediscount.

While the banks both in London and the country received the bills on the more obscure acceptors from their customers, the first class bills, those for example drawn on the great merchants (and later the merchant bankers) to finance foreign trade, were to a great extent disposed of in the discount market and either sold to banks by the discount houses or held by the discount houses themselves. The banks were thus ordinarily buyers of bills and could strengthen their cash by ceasing to buy ; if that was too tardy an expedient, they called up the money they lent to the discount houses.

Thus the discount market supplied the banks with the essential rediscounting facilities.   When the banks were strengthening their cash, the discount houses found themselves with more bills and less money.   In those circumstances the market rate of discount rose and, as soon as it was higher than Bank rate, either the traders would themselves bring new bills direct to the Bank of England or the

discount houses would get some of the bills they already held rediscounted.

In 1858 the Bank of England preferred the former system, and it announced that for the future it would not discount bills for the discount houses, and would only grant them advances (outside the quarterly periods of pressure) by special arrangement. This course was not ultimately compatible with the call money system, which for the banks was a substitute for rediscounting. Instead of sending bills to the Bank of England the banks would call up money from the discount houses. But if the money called exceeded the amount of bills falling due, the discount houses could not find the total except by selling or pledging some of their bills. And there was no source from which they could raise money except the Bank of England. But it was not till 1890 that the Bank definitely accepted the discount houses as the principal channel through which bills came for rediscount.

Bank Rate and the Quantity Theory

The monetary policy underlying the proposals put forward in 1832 by the Bank of England for the use of Bank rate was based on the quantity theory of money. The intention was, by varying the discount rate, to regulate the amount of bills brought to the Bank of England, and so to control the volume of currency against which those bills were held. But the policy was by no means dependent on the quantity theory. In fact the discount rate modified the quantity of currency by modifying activity ; the latter was cause and the former was effect. The link between the quantity of currency and the price level existed (though not in so rigid a form as was then supposed). But the variations in the quantity of money and the price level were effects of a common cause, the variations in the consumers' income, and it was these latter that were influenced by the discount rate.

A rise in the discount rate diminished productive activity and with it the consumers' income because it

made traders less disposed to buy and the orders given to producers fell off. And when a reduction in the discount rate relieved the pressure on buyers, the resulting increase of orders stimulated productive activity and enlarged the consumers' income. Those reactions were not dependent on the associated changes in the quantity of currency.

By the consumers' income I mean simply the total of incomes expressed in monetary units.[1] It is much more fundamental in monetary theory than the quantity of money. The consumers' income is the source of general demand, composed of consumption demand and of the demand for capital goods.[2] For though it is traders, not consumers, who buy capital goods for use in production, the funds used by the traders are ultimately derived, through the investment market, from the consumers' income.

And while the consumers' income is the source of demand, demand in turn is the source of the consumers' income. That is to say, the money spent on the purchase of goods is the source of the incomes of those who produce and deal in the goods. So long as an unchanging stream of money continues to flow through the consumers' income to demand and back through demand to the consumers' income, activity will be maintained. If at any stage a part of the stream of money is intercepted and absorbed, the stream is diminished and activity falls off ; if at any stage money is released and the stream is enlarged, activity is increased. In the former case the receipts of some group of people exceed their disbursements and they absorb cash ; in the latter the disbursements of some group exceed their receipts and they release cash. The absorption or release of cash may occur among consumers, in the investment market, in industry. Wherever it occurs, an absorption of cash causes a shortage of demand and compresses the consumers' income ; a release of cash causes an expansion of demand and enlarges the consumers' income.[3]

A rise or fall of Bank rate may be regarded as a device

---

[1] See my *Art of Central Banking*, Chapter III.
[2] See my *Capital and Employment*, pp. 66–9.
[3] See my *Capital and Employment*, pp. 64–6, 145–6 and 154–161.

for causing an absorption or release of cash on the part of dealers in commodities. In the case of a rise of the rate, they buy less than they sell. The diminution in the consumers' income is caused directly as the orders to producers are reduced. In the case of a fall of Bank rate, dealers buy more than they sell and the consumers' income is enlarged in consequence of increased orders to producers.

There will also be some effect on the investment market, a matter which we shall consider in Chapters V and VI. And there may be some effect on consumers, but consumers as such buy little with borrowed money except investments. Hire purchase agreements are more analogous to borrowing for investment than to borrowing for working capital. The stocks of goods held by consumers not for enjoyment but as " working capital " are small.

CHAPTER II

BANK RATE AND GOLD, 1858-1914

GOLD RESERVES AND INTERIOR DEMAND

THE Parliamentary Committee of 1858 marks the end of the period in which we have the motives and policies of credit regulation discussed in all their aspects and laid bare for all to see. Thereafter it becomes necessary to infer motives and policies from the action taken, though a certain amount of guidance is to be derived from unofficial comment, some of which was no doubt more or less in touch with the Bank of England Directorate and reflected something of their views.

The broad conclusion to which an examination of the facts leads us is that the policy followed in the use of Bank rate from 1858 to 1914 continued on the whole to be guided by the principles enunciated in the earlier period. Since the aim of the Bank of England was to keep its banking operations within the limits appropriate to its reserve, the reserve is always the governing factor. Any change in Bank rate is usually associated in an obvious manner with the state of the reserve, and, even where this is not so, that is because causes were believed to be at work to affect the reserve in the near future, such as the existence of gold in transit.

The changes in the reserve were due to two sets of causes, exterior and interior. The exterior causes took effect through the net exports or imports of gold ; the interior included both the increase or decrease of currency in circulation, and the industrial demand for gold as a material. An increase or decrease of currency in circulation affected the reserve in the same manner whether it was gold coin or Bank of England notes, since under the Act of 1844 every note in excess of the fixed fiduciary issue had to be covered by its value in gold.

If for any interval of time we calculate the difference
between the net import or export of gold and the net
increase or decrease of the reserve in the Banking Department of the Bank of England, we arrive at the interior
movement. We have weekly statistics of imports and
exports of gold made up, like the Bank of England return,
to every Wednesday. But we have no direct statistical
information to enable us to separate this interior movement
of gold into the industrial demand on the one side and the
increase or decrease in the currency in circulation on the
other. Nor are the statistics of exports and imports complete, for when gold coin was in active circulation considerable quantities were carried in and out of the country by
travellers. On balance there was probably a net outflow
from this cause, and an abatement has to be made from the
apparent interior demand on that account, as well as on
account of the industrial demand, to arrive at the true
increase (or decrease) in the monetary circulation. Another
unknown quantity is the amount of gold in the hands of
bullion dealers. Imported gold would sometimes be withheld for a time from sale to the Bank of England in the
hope of an export demand or an industrial demand at a
price above the Bank's buying price. It would only be a
matter of a few days, but that might on occasion be enough
to introduce a material error into the estimate of interior
demand.

Gold reserves in the nineteenth century were small
relatively to the amount of gold coin in circulation, at any
rate up to about 1890. Jevons estimated the monetary
gold in the United Kingdom in March, 1868, at £95,000,000,
composed of £80,000,000 in sovereigns and half-sovereigns
and £15,000,000 in the form of bullion or foreign coin in the
Bank of England. Therefore the coin and bullion in the
Bank of England, varying as it did in the 'sixties between
£12,000,000 and £24,000,000, never exceeded a third of the
gold in circulation and was sometimes less than a sixth.

In the case of France we find that at the end of 1861,
after net imports of gold amounting since 1848 to more than

three milliards and a quarter, the gold in the Bank of France was no more than 229 millions of francs or £9,000,000. That does not mean that the gold coin in circulation had increased by three milliards or £120,000,000, but after all deductions for the industrial demand and undisclosed exports, the addition to the circulation must still have been very large in comparison with the reserve.

In the years 1874–8, when France was in process of returning to gold payments after the suspension of 1870, French net imports of gold exceeded two milliards. The gold in the Bank of France rose from 611 millions of francs at the end of 1873 to 1530 millions at the end of 1876, but by the end of 1878 had fallen to 983 millions. Only 372 millions of the two milliards remained there, the rest having gone for the most part into circulation.

It was only with the big growth in the output of gold that occurred after 1890 that the gold reserves of the great central banks began to absorb a substantial proportion of the world's monetary gold.

So long as the reserves of the Banks of England and France were the only considerable concentrated gold holdings in the world, and were small fractions of the gold in active circulation in the two countries, the dominant influence in monetary regulation was bound to be the issue of currency into circulation and its withdrawal.

It was these movements that had to be influenced if the work of Bank rate as a monetary instrument was to be done. When gold was attracted from abroad or let go, it was ultimately the monetary circulation in foreign countries that had to be modified, for otherwise the gold movement would soon be reversed.

INTERNATIONAL INFLUENCE OF LONDON

Even by the middle of the nineteenth century the international influence of the Bank of England over credit had become great. The predominance of the British merchant in international trade had been growing. Soon after 1830 we find traces, at first in the American trade, of the

London acceptance business. But long before that business, as ultimately practised by the accepting houses, came into vogue, the bill on London was making its way. When a British merchant acted as intermediary between an importer of goods in a foreign country and an exporter either in Great Britain or in another foreign country, the exporter would draw bills not on the ultimate importer but on the British merchant. The British merchant might draw bills on the foreign importer, but these bills would probably not be readily negotiable ; he would treat them as a mere record of debts and hold them till maturity. The original bills drawn by the exporter on the merchant would very likely extend over the time required to sell the goods in the importing country and to remit the proceeds to England. Any further credit to be given to the importer the merchant could readily provide for out of his own resources, supplemented if need be by the sale of bills drawn by him on British purchasers of goods in connection with other transactions. Thus the imports into a foreign country with inadequate credit facilities might be financed in large part by bills on London.

And it was found that the system could be extended. It was not at all essential for the British merchant to be an intermediary in the actual purchase and sale of the goods ; his intervention might be limited to accepting the bills. The foreign importer would buy the goods direct from the exporter, and the exporter would be told to draw bills upon the British merchant, who would charge a commission for the service so rendered. The British merchant, who thus transformed his business into that of a merchant banker or accepting house, relied on the foreign importer remitting the amount of the bill to London in time for its maturity. The system depended on the merchant banker's knowledge of the probity and solvency of the foreign merchants he accommodated. In its early days the system was not free from abuses. The American crisis of 1837 led to three important failures of British mercantile houses which had been accepting bills for a commission. In

1857 there were some failures of houses which had embarked upon the accepting business imprudently with inadequate capital. But by that time the system was firmly established in the hands of the great merchant bankers, who knew how to guard against its dangers and abuses, and thenceforward it contributed greatly to the international influence of the London money market.

When Bank rate rose, the cost of carrying stocks of goods was increased not only in Great Britain but all over the world, wherever the buyers of goods were accustomed to tell the sellers to draw on London. The tendency to slow down purchases of goods was thus spread abroad, and that limitation of transactions involving the " disemployment of labour," which Horsley Palmer explained to be the purpose of raising Bank rate, took on an international character.

When British merchants, and foreign merchants financed by bills on London, alike became reluctant to buy, the sales of goods not replaced by equivalent purchases yielded a balance of money which came to London to pay off the corresponding indebtedness. This tendency, like that of surplus funds available for temporary investment to be attracted from abroad by the high rates obtainable in the London money market, was an immediate and transitory effect of dear money.

EFFECTS OF BANK RATE ON MONETARY CIRCULATION

But at the same time there were the more permanent effects in limiting transactions or compressing the consumers' income, not only at home but abroad. If this deflationary process went faster at home than abroad, it made the foreign exchanges favourable and occasioned an inflow of gold. But it sometimes went faster in some foreign country (particularly in case of a financial crisis there) and caused an outflow. But in any case the progress of deflation gradually released currency from circulation both at home and abroad, and there appeared an accumula-

tion of redundant gold coin in the Bank of England and the Bank of France, or, in later years, in central banks generally. It was this release of gold from circulation that was the real purpose of a high Bank rate. So long as the Bank of England and the Bank of France were both short of gold, any measure adopted by either to attract gold would be sure to evoke a counteracting measure from the other. Only when a surplus of gold began to appear in the gold-using world as a whole could either relax the pressure. And, as soon as one did so, the other could do the same.

Thus the working of a high Bank rate to restore the foreign exchange position under nineteenth-century conditions can be put in three stages. There was the first impact when foreign funds were attracted to London, for temporary investment, to gain a higher short-term rate of interest, and when merchants were liquidating capital employed in international trade. There followed a second stage in which activity in British industry was abated, and the resulting decline of purchasing power resulted in a reduction of imports visible and invisible. Finally the deflationary process was felt abroad, partly from the direct effect of dear money in London on international trade, partly from the measures taken by the Bank of France and other foreign credit systems in view of their loss of gold to Great Britain.

It was only the last stage that really accomplished the object of the rise of Bank rate. So long as it had only attracted gold through a *differential* effect as between Great Britain and other countries, the position was precarious ; the pull of London would inevitably provoke a contrary pull from other centres. But when deflation spread to foreign countries, and the expansion in their monetary circulation was successfully checked (or if need were reversed), the supply of gold in the gold-using world became adequate, and, as matters were actually managed, probably redundant.

Similarly the working of a low Bank rate has the same

three stages, first, the immediate transfer of money abroad, then a monetary expansion at home relative to monetary conditions abroad, and finally a monetary expansion abroad, and only the last stage completes the operation. The history of Bank rate is made up of alternating periods of stringency and ease, each usually extending over some years. In a period of stringency recurrent applications of dear money are needed to correct a persistent tendency of the reserve to fall below the prudent limit. There are intervals when in response to dear money the reserve has filled up and the pressure is relieved, but the reserve soon ebbs away and dear money has to be re-imposed.

At last the corner is turned, possibly at the cost of a financial crisis. There follows a period of ease, when the reserve grows bigger and bigger in spite of cheap money. Presently currency begins to pass into circulation again, but cheap money continues with little interruption so long as the reserve, though falling, remains above the prudent level. Eventually, however, the demand for currency becomes so insistent that the pressure of dear money has to be administered to maintain the reserve, and ease once again gives place to stringency.

THE GOLD POSITION, 1858–1914

We may regard the manipulation of Bank rate in the period from 1858 to 1914 as a method of regulating the flow of new gold into circulation not only in the United Kingdom but in the rest of the world. At the outset the annual output of gold had been enormously increased by the discovery of the Californian goldfield in 1849 and of the Australian in 1851. At a time when the world's monetary stock of gold (apart from hoards in the East) was estimated at little more than £200,000,000, the annual output suddenly rose in 1853 to £31,000,000, and from 1860 to 1890 settled down at something well over £20,000,000 with a slight tendency to fall off in the latter part of the period. Then began the South African production which, along

with the application of improved methods to other gold-fields, gradually raised the annual output to £90,000,000 in 1908 and £97,000,000 in 1913.

Up to 1871 there was little monetary demand for gold outside Great Britain and France, especially after the suspension of the gold standard in the United States in 1862, and the output, being far in excess of the requirements of natural growth, caused a monetary expansion in both countries. The expansion was restrained in some degree by the existence of bimetallism in France. Part of the gold displaced silver, which found its way to the silver-using countries in Europe and the East. But still the monetary expansion was considerable. From the beginning of 1858 to the end of July 1871 the net imports of gold into the United Kingdom were about £74,500,000, and as the Bank of England's reserve rose from £6,614,000 to £17,410,000 and the fiduciary issue was increased by £525,000 (in 1861 and 1866), the interior demand was £64,000,000.

From August, 1871, to the end of 1888, the net imports of gold were only £4,700,000. The reserve fell on balance by some £6 millions, and the fiduciary issue had been increased by £1,450,000 so that the interior demand in seventeen years had been only £12 millions, or under £700,000 a year, contrasting with £4,700,000 a year in the preceding 13½ years. The reason for the difference was not the slight falling off that occurred in the world's output of gold, but a great extension of demand. In July, 1871, Germany adopted the gold standard, and in two years imported £50,000,000. The immediate effect on the gold position was mitigated by the release of gold from France, where the gold standard had been suspended in 1870. But in 1874 began an accumulation of gold by France preparatory to resumption, an accumulation destined to exceed £80,000,000 by 1878 ; and before this was over there began an equal absorption by the United States, which in the course of seven years retained the whole of its own gold output and imported £38,000,000. Thereafter up to 1890,

though such spectacular movements were not repeated, there was a steady extension of the gold-using world and of the demand for monetary gold.

After 1890 the spread of the gold standard continued and was indeed accelerated, but owing to the enormous increase in output there was, as before 1871, a superfluity of gold. British imports of gold in the 25½ years from the beginning of 1889 to June, 1914, amounted to no less than £154 millions. The reserve increased by £17¾ millions and the fiduciary issue was increased by £2,000,000. The interior demand was therefore £138 millions or an annual average of nearly £5½ millions.

For the whole 56½ years from January, 1858, to June, 1914, the interior demand was £214 millions. The increase in the monetary circulation (gold coin and Bank of England notes) probably did not exceed £80,000,000. The balance was mainly the industrial demand, but a part was accounted for by wastage and undisclosed exports.

It is the monetary demand that Bank rate aims at regulating. We need therefore some independent statistical measure of the monetary demand. For this purpose probably a wage index corrected for unemployment will be a tolerable approximation. For the years 1850 to 1910 we have Mr. G. H. Wood's index of wages, and from the year 1880 this overlaps with Professor Bowley's index which goes down to 1914. For unemployment we have the percentage unemployed in trade unions.

The long-period movements of the interior demand for gold correspond satisfactorily with these indices. The big absorption of gold from 1858 to 1871 was accompanied by a rise of the wage index (starting at 100 in 1850) from 110 in 1858 to 155 in 1873. Unemployment fluctuated, and fell to an exceptionally low level at the end of the period, being below 1 per cent. in 1872.

In the following period the wage index fell from 156 in 1874 to 146 in 1879 and did not reach the former figure again till 1889. And unemployment (though it was only 4·9 per cent. in 1888) had been severe in the interval.

From 1889 to 1914 the rise in the wage index was resumed, and it reached 187 in 1910, and 198 (calculated from Professor Bowley's index) in 1914, while the spells of unemployment were shorter and less severe.

But when we turn to the fluctuations in shorter periods, we find that the effects of movements in wages and employment were interfered with by other tendencies, and in the earlier years the correlation is almost obliterated.

DEMAND FOR CURRENCY IN PANICS

One interfering cause, which was only operative on rare occasions, was the sudden accumulation of currency by the country banks under the influence of panic. Kirkman Hodgson of the Bank of England gave the Committee of 1875 on Banks of Issue a lively account of " all the issuing banks coming in 1866 almost in a run and pouring in their bills and their Consols to the Bank of England and saying, ' we must have this and we must take the Bank of England notes down with us to-night, because we shall have a run on us to-morrow '." (Question 7947.) In 1857 and 1866 this occurred at the culmination of periods of activity, and had the appearance of merely intensifying the interior demand and the ensuing reflux of currency into the reserve. But in 1878, on the occasion of the failure of the City of Glasgow Bank, there was an interior demand of nearly £6,500,000 in three months at a time of severe depression.

In 1857 and 1878 the panic-stricken absorption of currency by the country banks was followed by a rapid reflux. In the ten weeks from 18th November, 1857, to 27th January, 1858, £3½ millions returned to the Bank from interior circulation. In the eight weeks from 15th January to 12th March, 1879, there was a reflux of £6½ millions.

In 1866 on the other hand the reflux was very much less. In the nine weeks up to and including that in which Overend, Gurney and Company failed the interior demand exceeded £8½ millions, and before the reduction of Bank rate from 10 to 8 per cent. three months later a further £800,000

had been absorbed. Yet in the ensuing four months the reflux was only £2,645,000.

Accumulation of Currency at Times of Cheap Money

Panics are exceptional. But a scrutiny of the statistics of gold movements, especially in the period up to 1873, reveals a more persistent interference with the correlation that theoretically ought to hold between the interior demand for currency and the state of wages and employment. And this interference is intimately related to the working of Bank rate.

We find repeatedly that at times of depression there is a big interior demand, and at times of rising wages and active employment interior demand falls off and even becomes a negative quantity.

The interior demand was not exclusively monetary, for it included the demand for gold as a material of industry. But this latter demand would itself tend to be greater at a time of activity and less at a time of depression. Whatever weight we give to the non-monetary demand for gold increases the discrepancy to be explained. It is in the monetary sphere that we must look for the explanation.

The clue is to be found in the fluctuations of the discount rate. Cheap money prevailed at those times of depression at which interior demand was at a high level ; dear money prevailed at those times of activity at which interior demand was at a low level, or gave place to a reflux of currency. Dear money hastened the transmission of surplus gold coin from the country districts to London.

At this period branch banking had hardly begun to develop. And modern communications were still in a very imperfect condition. In 1867 little more than half the ultimate mileage of the British railway system had been constructed. The telegraph was a novelty. Even when the telegraph system was taken over by the Post Office in 1870, people feared it would be impossible to enforce secrecy. My relative, the late Sir Charles Hawtrey,

remarked in his reminiscences that in consequence of this misgiving many people were very chary of submitting any private matter to the perusal of the post-office clerks.[1] He proceeded to give examples of reputed " milking of the wires " or leakages of the contents of telegrams about race-horses. Whether such leakages were in fact at all common I do not know, but, if the fear of them prevailed, a country banker might be very chary of relying on the telegraph to send for gold in an emergency.

Under these conditions every country bank had to have an independent reserve of notes and coin, its funds on deposit or at call in London being too remote to be relied on for unexpected demands.

Some country banks would habitually pay out more currency than they received ; others received more than they paid out. The former would keep up their reserves by procuring notes and coin from London in exchange for bills, while the latter would from time to time send their superfluous currency thither. The currency sent to London by the country banks would be credited to their balances with their London agent banks, and then placed by them in bills or lent at call in the discount market.

At a time of slack business traders liquidate their stocks of goods. Under the bill of exchange system anyone whose purchases fall short of his sales finds after the appropriate interval that what he receives on maturing bills exceeds what he pays on his own acceptances falling due. The bills he has to get discounted to maintain his cash are a diminishing quantity. They may fall to zero, and he may accumulate an idle cash balance.

The country banks would thus find themselves receiving more in currency from their customers and less in bills. If they continued to send all their superfluous currency to London, the discount market would find itself short of bills. The rate of discount would fall, and, as the market would be experiencing a plethora of cash, Bank rate would

<hr />

[1] *The Truth at Last*, p. 63.

become ineffective. So would begin a period of cheap money, in which ultimately Bank rate would fall to its minimum of 2 per cent., and the market rate of discount lower still, sometimes below 1 per cent.

If discount rates fell very low, it might be hardly worth while to send gold coin to London. Sooner or later the demand for currency in the provinces might be expected to revive, and it would then become necessary to bring the gold back ; to cover the freight and insurance of the double journey out of a discount rate of, say, 2 per cent. per annum, perhaps even 1 per cent. or less, the gold would have to stay in London a long time.

What has to be explained is, it is true, not the mere retention of idle money in the country districts but the actual continued flow of currency thither. But the accumulation of idle money would not go on to an equal extent in all districts at the same time. Even in the depths of depression there would be some places that would be obtaining currency from London, and with the beginning of revival these demands would increase. At the same time there would be other districts accumulating gold coin and retaining it.

Not less paradoxical than a swollen interior demand at a time of depression, is the reduced interior demand, or even reflux of currency from interior circulation, at a time of activity. And, just as the former phenomenon was due to cheap money, so the latter was due to the dear money that accompanied activity. At times of dear money the banks would cut their cash reserves as fine as prudence would allow. Those accumulating currency in the provinces would hasten to send whatever could be spared to London in order to buy bills yielding 6 or 8 per cent. or more, while those needing currency would keep their requirements down to a minimum when raising funds meant discounting bills at such onerous rates. If a phase of dear money supervened immediately upon one of cheap money marked by a great accumulation of redundant currency in the country districts, a very large reflux of

currency might ensue before the redundant currency was dispersed.

This tendency of currency to accumulate in the provinces at times of cheap money, and to be attracted to London by dear money, was referred to in the evidence taken by the Gold and Silver Commission in 1886. Robert Giffen indicated it very tentatively : " I think I have observed that the raising of the rate attracts money out of the provinces and seems to bring money into the banks in some way." (Question 625.)

J. W. Birch, who had been Governor of the Bank of England in 1880, was in a position to be more definite : " With regard to what Mr. Giffen said about attracting the hoards, what I suppose he has not seen quite clearly is this, that at times money is absolutely unlendable by the brokers in London. You cannot get even $\frac{1}{2}$ per cent. per annum for your money. Then the bankers, I imagine, would leave their money in the country, not to have the expense of sending to London. A considerable sum might thus accumulate. Another $\frac{1}{2}$ per cent. or 1 per cent. makes money lendable to the brokers, and then the bankers of the country send it up to employ it." (Question 1366.)

" Naturally," he added, " an exceedingly high rate [8, 9 or 10 per cent.] might induce country bankers to send up all they could lay hands on. The flow, when it gets to anything like that, is not so much from the country as from abroad."

That was said in 1886, when the effect of Bank rate on interior demand was already much less marked. From 1873 onwards it is often difficult to disentangle from seasonal fluctuations.

Seasonal Movements of Interior Demand

In view of the magnitude of disturbing causes we cannot arrive at an exact statistical measure of the allowance to be made for seasonal fluctuations, but we can readily obtain a broad general idea of them. It is convenient to take quarterly periods, but those ending with the calendar year

and its quarterly divisions are to be avoided, because the big displacements of currency round about the 31st December may involve in a few days sums comparable to an entire year's net interior demand, and fortuitous circumstances such as the proximity of that day to the Wednesday of the Bank return may vitiate all comparisons. I therefore take the year beginning on the first Wednesday in December and its quarterly divisions at the first Wednesdays in March, June and September.

The first quarter, comprising the months of December, January and February, tends to be one of reflux. Even in the years of big gold imports up to 1871 this was so on balance, though there were many occasions when there was a moderate interior demand.

But in every year from 1872 to 1913 there was a reflux, with the single exception of 1875. The average reflux in the quarter during those forty-two years was £2,669,000.

The months of March, April and May which make up the second quarter, always include Easter. In that quarter there was invariably a positive interior demand, and it was usually large. For the forty-two years 1872 to 1913 it averaged £3,770,000. The other two quarters both showed a positive average, £1,626,000 for June, July and August, and £576,000 for September, October and November, but on occasions there was a reflux in these quarters.

CHANGES DUE TO BRANCH BANKING

There were profound changes after 1873. By about 1880 the nineteenth-century system of communications had been practically completed. And branch-banking was being steadily extended.

It was the growth of joint-stock banking that made branch-banking possible on a large scale, for the capital of a private partnership was never sufficient for anything more than a local organisation. But in 1870, though the displacement of private banks by joint-stock banks had made great progress (partly by amalgamation and absorption), branches had not been extended far beyond purely local

systems. If a bank in a provincial town had half-a-dozen or a dozen branches in its immediate neighbourhood, the head office and branches were likely either all to need currency or to accumulate currency at the same time. It was only when the branches extended into places of different economic type that the currency movements would be more or less complementary. A banker would not fetch gold from London if he had a superfluous accumulation of currency at a branch of his own bank fifty or a hundred miles away.

As the railway system and the branch banking system grew, the farmers and country traders who had to keep hoards of currency because there were no banking facilities within convenient reach became less and less numerous. Redundant currency throughout the country passed more quickly into the hands of the banks, and was more readily redistributed by them in response to local needs. The continued interior demand for gold at a time of depression and cheap money was no longer called for.

The substitution of a relatively small number of large banks with extensive systems of branches for the numerous independent country banks, each with no more than local connections, brought another change. The inequalities in the amount of accommodation required by the customers of different banks were diminished. When some banks found a difficulty in lending locally the resources they received from their depositors, and others found their deposits insufficient to meet the needs of borrowers, it was almost necessary for traders to obtain credit in marketable form. Banks could get bills rediscounted or the traders themselves, when their bankers could not afford to lend more, could leave the banks out and sell bills in the discount market.[1] When branch banking developed so far as to link together districts where there was an excess of deposits and districts where there was a deficiency, it was no longer necessary to embody credit in a negotiable instrument.

[1] The majority of the so-called " country banks " were in great provincial centres and their customers included important industrialists and traders known to Lombard Street.

The banker could allow his customer a simple loan or overdraft, possibly with collateral security, but without any idea of ever assigning the debt to another creditor. Traders learnt to prefer the simplicity and privacy of this system. The acceptor of a bill is the debtor of an unknown creditor against whom default is an act of bankruptcy. For a trader who obtains an advance from his banker, and pays cash instead of accepting a bill, the only outstanding liability is a purely private matter between him and the banker.

In international trade the convenience of bills of exchange was great enough for them to survive. But the internal bill began to die out after 1880 and by 1900 was of greatly diminished importance. Statistical evidence of the process is to be found in the yield of the stamp duty on bills of exchange, which has remained unchanged since 1862. In 1869 when bank clearings were £3,626 millions the duty yielded £731,000. We may estimate (after allowing for bills payable abroad) that nearly one-third of the clearings represented the payment of maturing bills. In 1904, when clearings were £10,564 millions, the duty yielded £700,000. A threefold increase in clearings was accompanied by an actual decrease in the yield of the duty on bills.

It was estimated that £285,000, or more than 40 per cent. of the duty in 1904 came from " inland bills." But inland bills are defined for this purpose as those both drawn and payable in the United Kingdom, and include all those drawn by British exporters on British banks and accepting houses. The proportion of bills that were drawn to finance external trade was therefore much more than three-fifths. These bills were quite enough to provide the discount market with more business than ever. A considerable proportion of the home trade bills that had dropped out had never been regularly marketable.

The Rate of Interest on Loans and Overdrafts

What was the effect of this change upon Bank rate?

Bank rate was a discount rate ; it had no direct relation to bank loans and overdrafts.   Nevertheless the practice grew up of linking the rate for loans and overdrafts directly to Bank rate ; a bank would stipulate for a rate ½ per cent. or 1 per cent. above Bank rate.

As the late Walter Leaf wrote in 1926 (*Banking*, p. 177), " the rate, for bank loans is, with very few exceptions, based upon bank rate.   The most usual rate for loans which may be regarded as fair banking risks, the average rate, in fact, for advances on what may be called average security, is generally ' one per cent. over bank rate varying.'   In addition to the rate for the loan, the banks almost always protect themselves by charging a minimum below which bank rate will not be followed."   And Leaf indicated a minimum of 5 per cent. as normal.

By the time that was written the progress of bank amalgamation had tended to standardise practice to some extent.   But the variations that survived even among the branches of a single big bank were many.   Further back in the past the variety of practice was such that it would be difficult to formulate general rules at all.   In the nineteenth century there were parts of England which were quite detached from the influence of the London discount market and Bank rate.   The banks sought to attract depositors by offering to pay, say, 2½ per cent. on deposits. When money was dear in London, the depositors never thought of asking for more ; but when money was cheap, they did not expect to receive less.   The banker had to keep an adequate margin between the interest he paid and the interest he received, and consequently would not reduce the former below 5 per cent.   In a district which was, for banking purposes, approximately self-contained, so that the banks did not often have either to buy or to sell bills in the London discount market, these fixed rates might go on year after year and decade after decade, till at last the local banks were amalgamated or absorbed by big joint-stock banks with head offices in London.   Even mergers of this kind did not necessarily and immediately

alter the practice, but the tendency was for relations with the London discount market to become closer and closer, and for the fluctuations in the rates there prevailing to be reflected in the deposit and overdraft rates in the country.

On the other hand, before the days of amalgamations, any banker who found himself a regular or frequent seller of bills in the London market was bound to charge his own customers a commensurate rate. He could not afford to accommodate them at a lower rate than he would have to pay for raising cash in London. Districts in which more bills were regularly drawn than the banks could hold would thus be closely associated with the London market and the rates prevailing there.

The association was perhaps a little looser in the case of districts with an insufficiency of bills drawn locally, which would be regular buyers of bills in London.

Even if in some districts the minimum rate mentioned by Walter Leaf was a survival of a former fixed rate, a minimum had no doubt also prevailed in the other districts where the London rate had always been more or less closely followed. It must be remembered that before the amendment of the usury laws in 1833 the London rate itself had for long periods been practically fixed at 5 per cent., and Bank rate had never fallen below 4.

But the minimum has never applied to all advances without exception. Bankers have always been willing to make a special bargain with any customer who pressed for it, provided his account was sufficiently valuable to justify it.

To many customers the interest charged on an overdraft is a trifling matter. One who derives his income from a salary or from professional fees would probably not overdraw more than a few hundreds at a time, and would not waste a bank manager's time by bargaining about a matter of 1 per cent. on such a sum for a few months. It is to the trader, whose requirements in the matter of advances arise not out of the disbursement of his income, but out of his turnover, on which his income is a small

percentage, that the rate charged is a material consideration. And the trader would usually be an important enough
customer to be able to stipulate for an advantageous
rate.

Moreover the minimum rate did not necessarily apply to
the customer who could put up gilt-edged or even readily
marketable securities as collateral. One who could do so
was not dependent for his credit on the banker's knowledge of his affairs, and, if dissatisfied, could go forthwith
to another bank. He could therefore insist on a competitive
rate on advances if he cared to ask for it.

The rule, as enunciated by Leaf, applied to advances
" on what may be called average security," and that may
be interpreted to mean on security arising out of the business for which the advances were granted, such as a lien on
the commodities bought by a merchant, or a deposit of
debentures on a producer's own concern.

Thus the late Sir Felix Schuster, when interviewed by
the American Monetary Commission in 1908 (Bank rate
being then 2½ per cent.) said, " at the present moment I
would say a three months bill is worth 1⅞ and a three months
loan would be worth perhaps 3½." (*Interviews*, page 45.)
He was referring to loans with collateral in the form of
marketable securities (not necessarily gilt-edged). He
had previously mentioned that such collateral was almost
invariably required in London, so it is clear that his answer
had no special reference to Stock Exchange loans.

The Macmillan Committee stated in paragraph 70
of their Report that " the rate of interest charged on loans
and overdrafts is ½ per cent. to 1 per cent. above bank rate,
with an agreed minimum of commonly 4 to 5 per cent."
That statement was much too unqualified. When Mr.
John Rae of the Westminster Bank was giving evidence,
Professor Gregory asked him, " do you make your loans at
½ per cent. over Bank rate, with a minimum of 5 per cent ? "
His reply was, " we have a great many of them."

" So," said Professor Gregory, " if Bank rate goes down
from 4½ to 4, no difference is made in those loans ? "

" Well," answered Mr. Rae, " you would get your customer coming in.   He does not last very long on a 1 per cent. difference."   (Questions 2438–9.)

When I myself appeared before the Committee, Mr. McKenna asked me (Question 4331), " are you aware that below a certain point cheap money, as you know it, has little or no effect upon trade, because banks do not lend below that point ? " But he tells me that his question was not intended to apply to advances made on gilt-edged collateral.

Sir Ernest Harvey, the Deputy Governor of the Bank of England, did, it is true, remark : " We have always understood that there are minimum rates at which money is lent to trade, and that the minimum in most cases would not be below, if indeed as low as, $4\frac{1}{2}$ per cent." (Question 7597.) But this statement does not purport to be of universal application, and it was only introduced incidentally in order to explain the view which he attributed to the Bank of England, that a reduction of Bank rate below $4\frac{1}{2}$ per cent. in 1928 would not have made any difference.   In any case it was not an adequate explanation, for, when Bank rate was $4\frac{1}{2}$ per cent., loans and overdrafts would be granted at 5 or $5\frac{1}{2}$; they would not reach a minimum of $4\frac{1}{2}$ till Bank rate was reduced to 4, and in some instances to $3\frac{1}{2}$.

It is, I think, quite evident that the exceptions to the practice of making a minimum charge are numerous and important.   Almost any customer of good credit who thinks the matter worth pressing can get the minimum waived.   And it must be remembered that very many joint-stock companies maintain a reserve of Government securities that can be pledged, while in the nineteenth century, before joint-stock companies became common, the assets of a firm were legally indistinguishable from the private fortunes of the partners, who would often possess considerable holdings of marketable securities.

Undoubtedly the application of the minimum in a proportion of cases does in some degree impair the effect of a reduction of Bank rate below, say, 4 per cent.   But even in

these cases the effect of such reductions is not altogether excluded. For the banker who is receiving no more than 2 or 3 per cent. on most of his short-term investments is naturally particularly glad to lend to a customer whom he can legitimately charge 5 per cent., and such a customer will find the obstacles to an overdraft surprisingly easy to surmount.

Loans and overdrafts may be expected to be more sensitive than bills to the rate of interest. The drawer of a bill is the *seller* of goods, to whom the discount appears in the shape simply of an abatement from the price. In the case of a loan or overdraft the borrower is the buyer, and the interest is to him a charge for holding goods in stock. Under the loan and overdraft system a trader can immediately diminish the amount to be paid for interest by postponing his purchases, or, with given purchases, by arranging for deliveries to be deferred. Under the bill of exchange system such postponement only relieves his position after, say, three months, when the bills fall due, and does nothing for him in the interval.

There is statistical evidence that business became more sensitive to Bank rate after 1873. In the thirty years from 1844 to 1873 there were eleven occasions on which Bank rate was raised to or above 6 per cent., their total duration being 200 weeks. In the forty years 1874 to 1913 there were only eight such occasions with an aggregate duration of fifty-five weeks. Probably this growing sensitiveness was partly due to traders having learnt what to expect. If, when Bank rate rose to 6 per cent., they all expected one another to become reluctant buyers, they would become reluctant buyers, and business would decline without the rate being raised any higher.

THE VICIOUS CIRCLE OF EXPANSION OR CONTRACTION

But why, it may be asked, was there ever any want of sensitiveness? Why did not a rise or fall of Bank rate have its due effect promptly and certainly ? The explanation is to be found in the principle of the vicious circle, the

inherent instability of credit. Economic activity generates
incomes, incomes generate demand and demand generates
activity. When activity falls off, incomes fall off, demand
falls off, and there results a further falling off of activity ;
and when activity is stimulated, incomes expand, demand
is increased and activity is further stimulated. In virtue
of this cumulative effect, any tendency towards either
increased or decreased activity is amplified and gets a
firmer and firmer hold till something happens to break the
vicious circle. For whatever cause may have originated
the increase or decrease of activity, the resulting increase
or decrease of demand is a new fact accentuating the
tendency.

Now a rise of Bank rate is expressly intended to restrain
activity. It does so by making traders less willing to hold
stocks of goods with borrowed money. When, as G. W.
Norman put it, traders become less disposed to buy and
more disposed to sell, manufacturers receive less orders,
pay less wages and make less profits. There is a shrinkage
of incomes which is reflected in a shrinkage of demand.
Sales fall off, and the retail and wholesale dealers find that
after all their stocks resist reduction. The decrease of
their purchases has failed to attain its full effect in that
direction because it has been followed by a decrease of
sales. But just because their sales have fallen off they will
aim at a greater reduction of stocks than before. They will
cut down their orders to manufacturers still more.

Similarly a reduction of Bank rate makes traders more
willing to hold stocks of goods with borrowed money, and
more disposed to buy. Manufacturers receive more orders,
pay more wages and make more profits. The consequent
expansion of incomes and of demand results in increased
sales, and dealers find that their increased orders have
failed to produce the desired increase in stocks. And
because of the increased sales they aim at a greater increase
in stocks than before.

When activity has taken hold, an apparently high Bank
rate may fail to check it. To be successful, the rate must

be high enough to counteract this intensified desire to increase stocks.

And when demand outstrips productive capacity, there will be an accumulation of forward orders, which will keep producers busy even after the demand has begun to fall off. When the demand for the product of a particular industry increases to such an extent that the industry's productive capacity is strained, the first symptom of strain is delay in the delivery of the goods ordered. When producers find that they cannot keep pace with orders, they raise their prices, and, if they are satisfied that the increase in demand is not merely temporary, they take steps to extend the capacity of the industry.

At a time of expansion of general demand all industries, or nearly all, find themselves in this position. They cannot all extend capacity at the same time except to the very limited extent that the productive resources of the producers of capital goods will allow. Therefore they have to rely on raising their prices to keep demand within limits, but the rise of prices always lags some time behind demand. When the expansion of demand is progressive, so that a succession of price rises is called for, the majority of industries are likely at any given time to be working through an accumulation of past orders. If pressure is then applied through a rise in Bank rate, and traders wish to hold smaller stocks of commodities, the effect will be felt first only in a reduced volume of forward orders, and the activity of producers will be little if at all diminished. The consumers' income will be sustained and with it general demand. There may therefore be a considerable interval before the corner is really turned and the vicious circle of inflation broken.

INTERMITTENT ACTION OF BANK RATE

There were reasons also why the application of dear money was apt to be intermittent. The purpose of a high Bank rate was to limit transactions or to compress the consumers' income, but the action taken by the Bank

was guided not primarily by evidence of the state of business but by the state of the reserve. As we have seen, a high Bank rate had certain superficial short-period effects in the direction of increasing the reserve. It would attract foreign balances, it would induce merchants to postpone their purchases of goods abroad, and it would lead the country banks to send their superfluous currency to London. The reserve might thus be very rapidly raised from a dangerously low level to an apparently ample amount, and the Bank would reduce the rate before the underlying tendency to increased activity was reversed. Soon the reserve would fall away again, and the same treatment would be repeated. It is like a mechanical lighter that over and over again fails to ignite. In the period 1871–4 we find this well exemplified.[1] There are half-a-dozen successive spells of dear money, each occasioned by a big drop in the reserve, and in the intervals the Bank rate drops to 3½ or 3 per cent. After 1874 this is less noticeable, and later on the alternations of interior demand for gold and its reversal became very much less. Nevertheless the oscillations between dear and cheap money were still noticeable in the years 1888–91. In 1899–1901 there was one drop to 3 per cent. between rises to 6 and 5 per cent. In the period of dear money in 1906–7, however, the rate did not fall below 4 per cent., and the reaction in business had already been started before the American crisis caused a renewed rise in October, 1907.

In the course of revival from the depression of 1908, there were oscillations between 5 and 3 per cent. in 1909 and 1910, but, once activity was established, the rate was kept at 4½ to 5 per cent. from October, 1912, to January, 1914, a period of fifteen months.

This last time of activity immediately before the war differs from all previous applications of dear money both in the narrow range of rates and in the limitation of the maximum rate to 5 per cent. On no other occasion had an expansive movement been checked without a resort at

[1] See below, pp. 90–6.

least to 6 per cent. The reserve, apart from seasonal fluctuations, was remarkably steady during these years. The seasonal fluctuations had become much more marked than twenty or thirty years before, but their character was so well understood that they did not involve any big changes in Bank rate. Perhaps this steadiness of the reserve was due to the final elimination of the accumulations of currency in the country districts which had been so perplexing an influence in 1872 and 1873.

It was at times of dear money that the dispersal of these accumulations produced its disturbing effect. But there were times when the policy of cheap money was also interrupted, for example when there was a scarcity of gold between 1875 and 1888. During those years the Bank was repeatedly led by a decline in its reserve to raise its rate to 5 per cent. or more, at times when, far from there being any danger of excessive expansion, the vicious circle of contraction was already at work. That happened at the beginning of 1876, in the autumn of 1877 and in the summer of 1878. And when a renewed depression set in after 1882, there were spells of 5 per cent. in 1884 and 1886.[1]   In the periods of depression either before or after the years 1875 to 1888, when there were long spells of cheap money with no serious interruption, revival would begin at an earlier stage.

It was the aggravated depression of these years that led to the appointment of the Royal Commission on the Depression of Trade in 1885. According to their final report, dated 1886, the Commission found general agreement that depression, in the form of " a diminution and in some cases an absence of profit, with a corresponding diminution of employment for the labouring classes," had existed, with the exception of a short period of prosperity enjoyed by certain branches of trade in the years 1880–3, ever since 1875.

For this state of things the Commission adduced a variety of causes ; but among them was one, the appreciation of the standard of value, gold, which appeared to them so

[1] See below, pp. 96–9 and 103–4.

important as to call for a separate inquiry.   It was on their
recommendation that the Gold and Silver Commission was
appointed in 1886.

THE BANK'S POWER OVER THE MARKET

In both 1848 and 1857–8 the representatives of the Bank
of England maintained in their evidence before the Parliamentary Committee that the Bank had no independent
power over the rate of discount.   It had to conform to
market conditions like any other bank.   Asked why, when
there is an export of gold, the Bank raises the rate of
interest, the Governor, James Morris, replied : " if the
amount of circulation in the country is diminished by an
export of bullion, the value of money rises ; and if the Bank,
in common with all other bankers, did not take steps for
the purpose of protecting their reserves, it would be acted
upon in consequence of the additional demand arising from
the greater value of money."   And in answer to a further
question : " as far as the export of gold goes, we consider
it merely as an indication that money will be dearer ; I
can only repeat what I stated previously, that the effect of
an export of bullion is to contract the general state of the
circulation, and the value of money rises ; and unless the
Bank and all other bankers took steps to raise the rate at
which they employed their money, there would be an
increased demand upon their reserves."   (Committee of
1848, Questions 3275–6.)

In 1857 the then Governor, T. M. Weguelin, took a
similar position but with some qualification.   Asked, " do
you believe that the rate of discount is fixed by the competition in the market, and that in fixing a certain amount
for their own discounts the Bank follow and do not lead ? "
he replied : " they invariably follow in a decline of the rate
of discount ; and I should say also they practically follow
in a rise ; but there is no doubt that the Bank, when there
is a rise in the rate of discount, has a greater power over the
money market of fixing the rate of interest for a short

period, than it has in the case of a decline in the rate."
(Committee of 1857, Question 476.)

Bagehot held that " a bank with a monopoly of note
issue has great sudden power in the money market, but no
permanent power ; it can affect the rate of discount at any
particular moment, but it cannot affect the average rate."
(*Lombard Street*, p. 111.) His argument was that if such a
bank lends at a low rate, the resulting increase of trade and
increase of prices lead to a further increase of borrowing.
" Any artificial reduction in the value of money causes a
new augmentation of the demand for money and thus
restores that value to its natural level."

To him it was an axiom that there must not be an
indefinite expansion of the currency. If, however, the
central bank has not merely a monopoly of note issue, but
power to expand or contract the currency indefinitely
without regard to convertibility or reserve proportions,
it can dictate the short-term rate of interest to the market.

It can keep the rate low by issuing whatever amount of
currency may be necessary to enable the market to satisfy
the demand for advances at that low rate, or it can keep the
rate high by keeping down the currency issued. The
consequences of so using its power may in either case be
disastrous, but that does not mean that the power itself
is limited.

Bagehot of course left these possibilities out of account.
He was assuming the supply of currency to be limited by a
metallic standard and a convertible note issue with a
rigid reserve law. With those assumptions the power of
the central bank would be restricted in both directions.
If it fixed the rate of interest too low, the expansive process
that Bagehot describes would give rise to a demand for
more and more currency, which would ultimately exhaust
the reserve. If the central bank fixed the rate of interest
too high, credit would contract, the demand for currency
would fall off, and the reflux of currency would fill up the
bank to the entire exclusion of any earning assets.

Bagehot compared the position of the Bank of England

to that of a single large holder of a commodity who " may, for a time, vitally affect its value if he lay down the minimum price which he will take, and obstinately adhere to it." (*Lombard Street*, p. 110.) But this understates the Bank's power. It is not merely that the Bank " used to be a predominant and is still a most important dealer in money." The Bank of England is the bankers' bank, and in that capacity the lender of last resort. It is rather in the position of a single wholesale dealer supplying a number of retailers. Its notes and deposits form the cash reserves of the other banks, and it can, by regulating the amount of its own advances, discounts and investments, modify the amount of these cash reserves at its discretion. Under the operation of the nineteenth-century gold standard the Bank of England's power in this respect was limited by its obligation to buy and sell gold in unlimited quantities within a fraction of the mint price. But that only meant that the Bank was placed under statutory directions as to the manner in which its power should be used, not that its power was in itself any the less.

The practical effect, however, was that the Bank's freedom was limited by market conditions very much in the manner that Morris and Weguelin said. At any rate up to 1890 the adjustment of Bank rate was very nearly automatic. When the Bank lost gold or the active circulation of notes increased, there was an equivalent decline in its deposits. The money available for the commercial banks was diminished, and the gap was made good by the sale of bills to the Bank of England. Thus the loss of gold or the increase of active circulation itself made Bank rate effective. In raising Bank rate under such conditions the Bank appeared to be merely following the market.

Only exceptionally did the Bank take the initiative in making the rate effective, if, for example, the commercial banks were expanding credit on a basis of redundant cash reserves at a time when a loss of gold and consequent stringency were to be expected in the near future. To make Bank rate effective, it was necessary to reduce the

cash reserves of the commercial banks, so that they would become unwilling to buy bills, and the bills would be brought either by traders or by discount houses to the Bank of England. The Bank could effect this result by itself simply borrowing like the discount houses from the commercial banks or other lenders of call money, or it could sell bills or other securities. Up to about 1890 the Bank abstained from entering the market as a borrower, partly because that course would have brought it more obviously into competition with the discount houses, partly because the transaction would have been legally indistinguishable from a deposit and inconsistent with the Bank's avowed practice never to pay interest on deposits.

At this period therefore the Bank had to rely on selling securities. But here a difficulty arose. At a time when Bank rate was not effective it presumably had no bills to sell, and in any case it never sold bills. It therefore had to sell investment securities such as Consols, and buying and selling Consols involved a risk of a capital loss—a very real risk if they were sold when Bank rate rose and bought back when it fell. To avoid this risk, the Bank resorted to the ingenious plan of selling Consols for cash and buying them back for the next Stock Exchange account, just as if it were arranging a carry over from account to account. It received money for the Consols sold, and paid the money out again at the account when they were bought back, and in the interval it had withdrawn the money from the commercial banks just as if it had carried out a simple borrowing operation. It could of course carry the transaction over at successive accounts so long as the state of the market might require.

This device, commonly called " borrowing on Consols " was all that the Bank allowed itself from 1844 till about 1890 in the way of what is now called an open market policy.

When the Bank of England gained gold, or the active circulation of notes fell off, its deposits were increased, the cash reserves of the commercial banks were in excess of requirements, bills ceased to come to the Bank and the

market rate of discount fell appreciably below Bank rate. If there was no prospective danger of stringency, the Bank would acquiesce in this condition of things. That would occur not only when Bank rate was in course of being reduced step by step, but also during those prolonged phases of cheap money which I have already had occasion to notice. Bagehot wrote in 1873 (*Lombard Street*, pp. 110–1) : " at all ordinary moments there is not money enough in Lombard Street to discount all the bills in Lombard Street without taking some money from the Bank of England," and drew the inference that Bank rate must always be effective. But the " ordinary moments " to which he referred excluded all these periods of superfluous gold.

The effect of the system followed was eventually to disperse any redundant gold and to reduce the reserve till bills came to the Bank, but thereupon Bank rate would be raised by steps till it became sufficiently deterrent to restore the reserve. The oscillations of the reserve were about a normal level at which the market just did not have to bring bills to the Bank. That did not mean that the Bank did no discounting at all. For it had regular commercial and private customers for whom the Bank of England was their sole or principal banker and who relied on it for advances and discounts in the course of their business. In 1878 the Bank adopted the practice of accommodating these customers at market rates without reference to Bank rate. The state of quiescence was reached when the reserve just filled the gap between the deposit liabilities of the Bank and its normal assets composed of its holding of Government securities and the advances and discounts provided for customers.

After 1890 the Bank began to aim at a higher standard of reserve. To prevent a growing reserve from making Bank rate prematurely ineffective, it was led to adopt more energetic measures than the old device of borrowing on Consols. The former objections to borrowing were waived, and the Bank took to borrowing directly from discount houses or banks or from large-scale lenders who would

otherwise have placed their money in the discount market.[1] Apparently it was ruled that the liabilities incurred through these borrowing operations were not legally deposits, for instead of being included among the deposits in the Return they were deducted from the securities.

Much interesting light is thrown on the day-to-day operations of the Bank of England in performing its task of regulating credit by contemporary comments in the financial columns of the newspapers, and particularly of the weekly *Economist* and *Statist* and of the monthly *Bankers' Magazine*. Extensive use has been made of these sources in some recent works. Mr. W. T. C. King's *History of the London Discount Market* and Mr. R. S. Sayers' *Bank of England Operations*, 1890–1914, have produced most valuable and interesting results from such investigations.

I have not attempted anything of the kind. For my present purposes Bank rate is itself at any given moment a sufficient indication of credit policy ; I have been content to note the movements of the fleet without entering into those of the fleet auxiliaries.

THE STATISTICAL MATERIAL

The statistical material on which the next three chapters are based is set out in the Appendices. The statistics available for the study of the money market are voluminous. There are daily quotations of discount rates and of prices of securities, and there are weekly Bank of England returns. From November, 1857, there are weekly statements of imports and exports of gold. These statements are for the week ending on Wednesday, the day on which the Bank of England return is made up. In Appendices I and II the interior demand for any period is assumed to be equal to the difference between the net imports of gold and the increase in the Bank of England's reserve (negative signs being attributed to net exports, a decrease or a reflux). In making use of these calculations we must not forget

[1] See R. S. Sayers, *Bank of England Operations*, 1890–1914, pp. 34–43.

that the day on which the arrival or departure of gold is recorded in the returns of imports and exports may not be the same as the day on which it enters or leaves the Bank of England. In other words gold in the hands of bullion dealers is counted as if it were in circulation. The amount may be considerable. One of the difficulties in handling statistics of gold movements is that the imports or exports on one day or even in one ship may be far from negligible, relatively to the net movement of many months. On only half-a-dozen occasions in the period from 1858 to 1913 did the net imports or exports of gold in a calendar year exceed £10,000,000. But the exports or imports in one week would often exceed £500,000 in the earlier years or £1,000,000 in the later.

And the statistics are by no means free from error. It is possible to check the weekly statistics of gold movements against the monthly, which appear in the regular trade returns, by comparing them in any period at the beginning and end of which a month ended on a Wednesday. That comparison is made in Appendix VI. In many cases the totals coincide exactly. In many others there are trifling discrepancies, representing no doubt minor corrections made subsequently to the necessarily hasty entries from which the weekly returns were compiled. But here and there we find very large errors. Sometimes the discrepancy is evidently due to the date of an item having been revised. Thus according to the weekly returns the exports of gold from 1st July, 1880, to 31st August, 1881, were £17,507,900 and according to the monthly returns £18,203,700. But for the following period 1st September to the 30th November, 1881, the respective figures were £5,869,500 and £5,151,800. It may safely be inferred that an export of about £700,000 was found, when the returns were revised in preparing the monthly statements, to have been erroneously attributed to September instead of August.

In the period from 1st October, 1874, to 31st March, 1875, the exports of gold according to the weekly returns

were £6,563,500 and according to the monthly £7,606,600. What the explanation of this very large correction may have been I do not know. A detailed examination shows that at any rate the greater part of it belongs to February, 1875. In the year 1874 the weekly and monthly figures agree quite well, but there was a very large correction in the imports of gold for the calendar year, when the annual statement of trade came to be made up. The imports were given in the annual statement as £18,081,000, whereas the total of the monthly figures was only £16,743,000.

Seyd in his *Bullion and Foreign Exchanges*, which was written in 1868, questions the accuracy of the Customs statistics on the ground of " the well-known practice of some shippers of bullion to omit declaring the value of the gold shipped by them ; the gold is frequently packed with and declared as silver in order to save freight."

Gold was conventionally subject to higher freight charges. How prevalent this misrepresentation was we have no means of knowing. But presumably, if the amount of gold involved was anything more than trifling, it was certain to be insured, and the shipper would surely hesitate to endanger his reputation for honesty in the eyes of the underwriters for the sake of the small gain to be made on the charge for freight.

In the years 1885 and 1886 errors appear to have been discovered long after even the annual statements of trade had been issued, and the totals of imports of gold were altered in the *Statistical Abstract* for 1889 from £13,376,000 and £13,392,000 to £12,576,000 and £12,951,000 respectively. The alterations were in the imports from the United States, and for the year 1885 it is possible to identify the particular week in which a consignment of £800,000 from the United States was recorded as that ended the 20th May. I have therefore been able to correct the weekly statistics. But for the year 1886 that has not been possible.

The daily statements of gold received from abroad by the Bank of England and withdrawn from the Bank

for export give an alternative means of calculating the movements of interior demand. But the results so obtained are incomplete, in that they omit all gold passing into or out of interior demand by other channels than the Bank of England. The amount of sovereigns so passing might sometimes be considerable, and imported bullion might be sold direct by dealers to industrial users. Possibly these daily statements from the Bank of England would provide a check on the weekly returns of the Customs by affording evidence in certain cases that the week in which a gold movement appeared in the reserve was not the same as the week in which it appeared in the Customs returns. But the particulars supplied are not in general sufficiently detailed to link up the two series of returns and I have not attempted any investigation on these lines.

In calculating the interior demand allowance has to be made for certain changes affecting the reserve :

The inclusion of silver bullion in the reserve in 1860–1 ;

Additions to the fiduciary issue either at a time of crisis (1857) or in place of lapsed country bank issues ;

The issue of Currency Notes in 1914.

Allowance also has to be made for gold set aside or released on account of the Indian Government. Gold set aside was excluded both from the reserve and from circulation, and is the equivalent of an export. Gold released is the equivalent of an import.

I have disregarded the note issues of the country banks. The gain in accuracy and completeness from taking them into account would have been very slight.

The weekly statistics of gold imports and exports are not available before November, 1857. After 1914, though they continue to be available, they are of little statistical value owing to the growing practice of earmarking gold, and also to the cessation of the use of gold coin in active circulation. Accordingly for the years 1915–32 the Appendix omits the statistics of net imports.

Appendix I records all the changes of Bank rate from 1844 to 1932 and the number of weeks each rate lasted,

along with the price of Consols on the day before the change (from 1879 to 1888 the price of 2½ per cent. annuities), and the reserve in the Banking Department in the last return of the Bank of England before the change.   For the years 1858–1914 it includes also the increase (or decrease) in the reserve up to the next change of Bank rate, the net imports (or exports) of gold and the interior demand (or reflux) in the same interval.

In some places the reserve position is shown at an intermediate date, when there was no change in Bank rate.   That is usually to mark the beginning or the end of a period of net gold export, but sometimes it is to show the state of the reserve at a time of crisis or disturbance.   When Bank rate was changed on any day other than a Thursday the reserve position is shown on the following Wednesday as well as on the preceding Wednesday.   Up to November, 1857, the Bank Return showed the position on Saturday.   Since then it has shown the position on Wednesday.

For the years up to 1914 I have included coin in the Banking Department in the reserve.   So long as gold coin was used in active circulation this was an effective part of the reserve.   For subsequent years the reserve has little significance.   It is omitted, and in its place we have the gold in the Issue Department and the active note circulation, including currency notes and excluding Bank of England notes in the Currency Notes reserve.   The variations in the former show the gain or loss of gold for monetary purposes, while the latter shows the amount of currency of unlimited legal tender in the hands of the public.

In using the price of Consols in any comparison allowance should be made for the accrued dividend.   Till 1888 dividends on 3 per cent. Consols were paid half-yearly on the 5th January and the 5th July.   Thereafter on the 2¾ and 2½ per cent. Consols they were paid quarterly.   On the 2½ per cent. annuities, they were paid half-yearly till 1884 and then quarterly.   Prices were quoted *ex dividend* about a month before the dividend date.

Appendix II shows the change in the reserve, the net

imports of gold and the interior demand quarter by quarter. The quarters are those beginning on the first Wednesday in March, June, September and December. The Appendix also shows the interior demand for each period of twelve months beginning with successive quarterly dates.

Appendix III contains the percentage of unemployed in Trade Unions and Mr. G. H. Wood's wage index for the years 1858 to 1913. The wage index for the last three years, 1911–13, not being available in Mr. Wood's series, has been calculated from Professor Bowley's index.

Appendix IV gives every change in the discount rate of the Bank of France from 1820 to 1931.

Appendix V supplies particulars of the principal periods of gold exports from 1858 to 1914. In most instances it merely summarises the details already given in Appendix I.

Appendix VI compares the weekly and monthly returns of gold imports and exports, wherever they can be totalled for coterminous periods between Wednesdays which happen to end months. The comparison is to be regarded merely as a check on the accuracy of the statistics. The discrepancies revealed are those which have survived after a careful scrutiny directed to discovering errors either of copying or of arithmetic. Numerous discrepancies of a unit or two are attributable merely to the vagaries of rounding up or down. More substantial differences are presumably due to corrections introduced when the monthly returns were compiled. The more remarkable of these are referred to above.

CHAPTER III

BANK RATE AND GOLD, 1858-1914 (*continued*)

Cheap Money and Interior Demand, 1858-60

AFTER the crisis of 1857, as after that of 1847, the relief of tension came quickly. On the 18th November, 1857, the first Bank return after the rise of Bank rate to 10 per cent. and the suspension of the fiduciary limit showed a reserve of £1,553,000. Since the securities in the Issue Department had been increased by £2,000,000, the limit had in reality been exceeded by £447,000. By the 23rd December, the reserve had risen to £7,971,000 and the fiduciary issue was reduced within its statutory limits. Bank rate was reduced from 10 per cent. to 8, and thereby, under the terms laid down by the Government, the right to exceed the limit was surrendered.

Net imports of gold in the five weeks had been £3,747,000, and £2,671,000 had therefore returned to the Bank from interior circulation.

Panic had resulted in the hasty withdrawal of enormous amounts of currency from London by the country banks, and much of this was now coming back.

Imports of gold continued, and, as the reserve rose, Bank rate was reduced by rapid steps, till on the 10th February, 1858, the reserve reached £11,446,000 and the rate was reduced to 3 per cent. In December, 1858, with a reserve of £13,357,000 the rate was reduced to 2½.

The spell of cheap money that ensued was not so long as that which followed the crisis of 1847. It lasted nearly two years, with one short break in May, 1859, when the rate was at 4½ per cent. for four weeks. That was due to a Stock Exchange crisis, provoked by the imminence of war between France and Austria over the Italian question. There was a long list of Stock Exchange failures, but the pressure passed away, and the liquidation was effected

without any serious disturbance of the credit situation.
By July, 1859, Bank rate was back at 2½ per cent.
Meanwhile recovery was making good progress. The
depression in 1858 had been severe. Unemployment had
risen to 11·9 per cent., and the wage index had fallen from
116 in 1856 to 110 in 1858. In 1860 the wage-index was
114 and unemployment was only 1·9 per cent.

The period of cheap money was brought to an end by the
advance of Bank rate from 3 to 4 per cent. on the 31st
January, 1860 (a Tuesday). Since the 10th February,
1858, there had been an interior demand of no less than
£13½ millions. Much of this must have been due to the
accumulation of idle currency by the country banks
(see above, pp. 50–5). In 1860, notwithstanding the
increased activity, the interior demand slackened off ;
from the 1st February to the 7th November, Bank rate
remaining at 4 per cent. with a short period at 5 in April,
the net interior demand was only £1,117,000.

AMERICAN ABSORPTION OF GOLD 1860–1

A new phase then began. The imminence of civil war
started an absorption of gold in the United States. The
election of Lincoln as President at the beginning of November, 1860, quickly precipitated the movement towards
secession in the slave-owning States of the South.

New York had long been the financial centre of the
country, through which the exports of the South were in
great part financed. It had become a creditor centre, in a
position to claim payment as the exports it had financed
came to be sold off in Europe. The South on the other
hand was a debtor country, discounting its exports and
importing on credit. The sudden approach of secession
and war caused a serious banking crisis in the South, and
the North began to absorb gold.

The United States and Australia were the two great gold-
producing countries of the world, and a great part of the
stream of gold that flowed through London normally came
from the former. When the United States suddenly

became an importer of gold, the monetary situation in Great Britain and Europe was violently disturbed.

This occurred at a time when London had already been losing gold. The bimetallic system in France had not been working quite smoothly. Owing to the big world output of gold which had been in progress for the preceding ten years, silver was at a premium. The Bank of France was therefore unwilling to pay its depositors and note-holders in silver coin, for which it could only ask the face value, and its gold holding was for the time being its only working reserve. Monetary expansion and business revival were giving rise to demands for currency. When silver had been the predominant medium, people had preferred notes to the bulky five-franc pieces, but the handy gold coin that was now being paid out suited them better still. The Bank of France, with an adequate metallic reserve on the whole, found itself faced with an inconvenient shortage of gold, and proceeded to procure gold from London through the medium of sterling bills in the hands of the Comptoir d'Escompte. At the beginning of November, 1860, Great Britain had, in this way, just suffered a net loss of gold by export amounting to £1,548,000 in seven weeks, and the reserve had been reduced to £7,166,000.

It was then that the exports of gold to America began. Three advances of Bank rate in a week (8th–15th November, 1860) brought it up from 4 to 6 per cent. A substantial reflux from interior circulation for the moment restored the reserve. And an arrangement was made to meet the French need for gold. The Bank of England had the power under the Act of 1844 of including silver bullion in the metallic backing of the note issue (up to one-fifth of the whole), and it took over 50,000,000 francs of silver from the Bank of France in exchange for gold.[1] As the exchange was effected at the market price, the Bank of France did not have to sacrifice the premium on silver.

---

[1] See Gabriel Ramon, *Histoire de la Banque de France*, pp. 284–5. The exchange of gold for silver was carried out gradually, and the maximum silver holding of the Bank of England at any one time was £1,644,000 on the 2nd January, 1861.

On the 29th November, 1860, the reserve being then £8,435,000, Bank rate was reduced to 5 per cent. But at the turn of the year seasonal demands for currency brought the reserve down almost to £6,000,000, and Bank rate was raised to 7 per cent. (7th January, 1861). Exports of gold continued, and a further advance to 8 per cent. followed on the 14th February. Once again there was a reflux of currency from interior circulation, which by the 20th March had restored the reserve to £8,325,000. From the 7th November, 1860, to the 20th March, 1861, there had been a reflux of £4,595,000 in all. But the absorption of gold by the United States persisted. In the first nine months of 1861 the net imports of that country were £7,000,000. The Bank of England's rate remained at 5 or 6 per cent. till the 15th August. By that time the Civil War in America was in full swing. Though the actual suspension of specie payments did not come till December, 1861, and the first Greenbacks were authorised by a Legal Tender Act in February, 1862, the issue of Government demand notes in a form to serve as currency was already beginning in the preceding summer. Under the influence of inflation the absorption of gold stopped.

Dear money in England had produced a deflationary effect. From January, 1860, to August, 1861, money had usually been dearer in London than in Paris. Now the reserve of the Bank of France began to decline, and the French Bank rate rose on the 26th September, 1861, to 5½ per cent., and on the 1st October to 6, whereas the Bank of England's rate was only 3½. Even this difference failed to bring relief to the French reserves, and in October the Bank of France had recourse to the same device as the Bank of England in 1839 ; it arranged with Rothschilds and other leading financial houses of Paris for London credits to a total amount of £2,000,000 on which the Bank of France drew sterling bills. By November, 1861, the pressure had passed, and the French Bank rate was reduced to 5 per cent. But throughout 1862 the French Bank rate remained higher than the English.

The year 1862 was one of cheap money, Bank rate never rising above 3 per cent. from the 7th November, 1861, to the middle of January, 1863. In fact a renewed depression had set in. The unemployment percentage rose from 1·9 in 1860 to 5·2 in 1861 and 8·4 in 1862. A serious dislocation was caused by the blockade of the Southern States of America and the " cotton famine " in Lancashire, but this did not begin till 1862. In 1861 the blockade was not effective and the cotton industry was not interfered with. Before the end of the year the price of raw cotton began to rise, but manufacturers had large stocks in hand and were glad to realise a profit on the corresponding rise in the manufactured products. The cause of the depression must be sought elsewhere, and we may conclude that the monetary stringency which accompanied the American crisis had interrupted the normal progress of the trade cycle, and interposed a premature depression.

THE CRISIS OF 1866

The depression was short. The year 1863, in spite of the cotton famine, was one of recovery, and 1864 was one of great activity. At the beginning of 1863 the reserve fell to £8,161,000 (28th January, 1863) and Bank rate was raised to 5 per cent. for three weeks. The reserve recovered to £10,000,000 but soon fell away again, and in the autumn it dropped below £7,000,000 (November, 1863). The rate moved up by rapid steps from 4 per cent. at the beginning of November to 8 on the 3rd December, 1863. That was the beginning of more than twelve months of dear money. The rate varied between 6 and 9 per cent., and did not drop below 6 till the 12th January, 1865. The average from the 5th November, 1863, to that date had been 7¼.

Interior demand in the year 1863 (twelve months ending the first Wednesday in December) had amounted to the considerable total of £6,716,000 ; in 1864 under the pressure of dear money it was only £2,106,000.

In the autumn of 1864 the stringency culminated in a spell of nine weeks at 9 per cent. The trade activity came to an end on the Continent. In England, however, it suffered no interruption, though there was a long tale of failures. The unemployment percentage fell from 2·7 in 1864 to 2·1 in 1865. On the 10th November, 1864, Bank rate was reduced from 9 per cent. to 8, and it fell step by step till it reached 3 per cent. on the 15th June, 1865. In the seven months interior demand had been only £828,000, and imports of gold had sufficed to raise the reserve from £7,907,000 to £9,966,000. But there followed a sudden revival of interior demand, which by the 4th October, 1865, had carried the reserve down to £5,106,000 in spite of imports amounting to £1,504,000. In nine days (28th September to 7th October, 1865) Bank rate was raised from 4 to 7 per cent., and at the turn of the year to 8 per cent. The reserve recovered to £8,804,000 on the 14th March, 1866, and Bank rate was reduced to 6 per cent. But by that time the financial community had been worked into a state of extreme apprehension. Great Britain had shared with Europe the high state of industrial activity that had prevailed in 1863 and 1864, but had not shared in the set-back which the Continent had suffered from the end of the latter year. Recent British legislation had facilitated the flotation of joint stock companies, and had thereby given a spurt to capital enterprise. One-eighth of the entire ultimate mileage of the British railway system was opened in the years 1861–6. The commitments entered into for capital outlay in this and other forms prolonged the activity into 1865 after it had been suspended on the Continent, and the concentration on capital outlay at home for a time prevented the expanded purchasing power from attracting an excess of imports. Unfortunately the stimulation of enterprise had been associated with some financial operations of a very undesirable character. A dangerous situation had developed. Great pressure was necessary to bring monetary conditions in Great Britain into due relation with deflation on the Continent, and this

pressure was being applied to a credit system weakened by flagrant departures from sound practice. I have already referred to the lending of money at call to bill-brokers or discount houses. It was adopted by bankers as an advantageous substitute for the holding of bills, avoiding the need for so selecting the bills they acquired as to mature at convenient dates. The call money took the place of a stock of short bills suitable for immediate realisation. Instead of selling bills the banks would call money from the discount market. This process took the place of direct rediscounting with the Bank of England, and it was essential that the money should be really available on demand. Any good bill complying with the customary conditions could be turned into cash at a moment's notice at the Bank of England, and the call money, if it was to serve its purpose, must be not less liquid.

Most of the call money was directly secured on bills of exchange, which guaranteed liquidity as well as safety. But, in dealing with the greater discount houses, the practice had grown up of leaving some of the call money without specific security. That allowed a fatal freedom in the selection of so much of the discount houses' assets as corresponded to the unsecured liabilities. A discount house that deposited unsound bills as security for its call loans would immediately incur discredit. If all its liabilities were secured, it could not hold any unpresentable bills except with its own capital. But in so far as it had unsecured liabilities, it could conceal the character of the corresponding assets.

Unfortunately the undesirable flotations of the years preceding 1866 had involved not only various finance companies and investment companies, the collapse of which would concern chiefly their own shareholders, but certain discount houses which had been perverted to improper uses.

The lamentable story of the failure of Overend, Gurney and Company has been told with admirable force and

insight in Mr. W. T. C. King's *History of the London Discount Market*. The firm had achieved an undisputed primacy in the discount market ; in fact half the business of the market was in its hands. Of the two partners who had built up the firm, Samuel Gurney died in 1856 and D. B. Chapman retired in 1857, and the business passed into younger and less experienced hands. A rogue insinuated himself into the confidence of one of the partners, and proceeded to exploit the credit of the firm in favour of various speculative or worthless concerns. So long as a liability could be expressed in the form of a bill, it could be placed among the firm's assets. If the worthlessness of the other names on it were not too evident, the endorsement of Overend, Gurney and Company would make it marketable, or alternatively it could remain unseen in the firm's portfolio. When Overend, Gurney and Company became a limited company in July, 1865, their deposit or call loan liabilities amounted to £14,400,000. Included in this total was a sum of £5,400,000 unsecured, under cover of which bad assets to an amount of £4,200,000 had been accumulated. By a special arrangement segregating the bad assets in a separate account, for which the partners who were transferring the business to the Company gave the guarantee of their private fortunes, any real knowledge of the state of the firm was withheld from the shareholders.

By the beginning of 1866 some suspicion of the embarrassments of the concern began to arise. The former partners were selling securities. There were some important failures which were believed to involve Overend, Gurney and Company in losses. At the end of January, 1866, the failure of the Joint Stock Discount Company (which had been formed in 1863) gave a severe shock to credit, and offered an ominous parallel on a smaller scale to what was in fact destined to happen to Overend, Gurney and Company. Deposits were by that time being withdrawn from the company in great volume.

The statistics of gold movements give evidence of a growing state of panic. In the seven weeks from 14th

March to the 2nd May, notwithstanding net imports of gold amounting to £890,000, the reserve fell from £8,804,000 to £5,636,000 ; there had thus been an interior demand of £4,058,000. Matters came to a head early in May. Bank rate was raised to 7 per cent. on the 3rd of May and to 8 on the 8th (a Tuesday). Late on the 10th the suspension of Overend, Gurney and Co. was announced. On Friday, the 11th, panic was let loose. Bank rate was raised to 9 per cent., and that evening the Bank of England laid a statement of the situation before the Government, and received a letter, modelled on the precedents of 1847 and 1857, permitting the fiduciary limit to be exceeded, provided Bank rate was not less than 10 per cent. On Saturday, the 12th May, accordingly Bank rate was raised to that level.

The panic of 1866 has remained famous in the financial history of London. A discount house discharges some of the functions of a bankers' bank ; its call loans are part of the reserve system of the banks. The failure of Sanderson and Co. at the height of the crisis of 1857 had contributed materially to its intensity, but that firm had quite a secondary position as a discount house in comparison with Overend's. The failure of the latter threatened the entire credit structure.

The letter of the 11th May by no means assuaged the panic. The urgent demands for currency in provincial centres continued. On the 16th May the reserve fell to £1,203,000, the interior demand having amounted to £4,805,000 in one week.

TEN PER CENT.

The fiduciary limit was not exceeded, the lowest point touched by the reserve (in the published accounts) having been £860,000 on the 30th May. But the recovery of the reserve was slow. The 10 per cent. Bank rate remained in force for three months, and when it was reduced to 8 on the 16th August, 1866, the reserve was still low at £4,611,000. Since the 30th May net imports of gold had

amounted to £4,185,000, but no net reflux of currency from the country had occurred ; there had in fact been a further interior demand of £434,000.

A circumstance that aroused much comment at the time was that though the discount rate of the Bank of France was only 4 and then, from the 26th July, 3½ per cent., the 10 per cent. rate in London failed to attract gold from France. The gold that did come was largely from the producing countries, Australia and the United States, and some actually continued to go from England to France. The difference between the discount rates of London and Paris was sufficient to cover an exchange risk of ½ per cent. on any bill or loan with more than a month to run. And indeed as the exchange was at times as unfavourable to London as it could be consistently with the maintenance of the gold standard, there was no exchange risk except through the contingency of a suspension of gold payments. Yet money apparently was not attracted.

At the time it was contended that this was due to foreign financial centres not appreciating the difference between a suspension of the fiduciary limit and a suspension of gold payments, or at any rate to their thinking that the former was likely to be the prelude to the latter.

A distrust of the currency may well have been a contributory cause of the reluctance to place money in London. The sudden narrowing of the discount market may also have contributed. Some of the most important channels through which foreign money could seek temporary investment had been suddenly severed.

But in any case the funds available for such international operations are not unlimited, and they may have been nearly exhausted during the preceding seven months of dear money. Seyd refers to an estimate of £40,000,000 to £60,000,000 of foreign money placed in first-class bills at the time.[1]

In the last three months of 1865 the French Bank rate had been 2 per cent. lower than the English, and then

---

[1] *Bullion and Foreign Exchange*, p. 569.

till the crisis of May, 1866, 3 or 2½ per cent. lower. That difference may well have been enough to attract very nearly all the available funds that were likely to move at all.

CHEAP MONEY, 1867–70

From the middle of August, 1866, the restoration of the reserve and the reduction of Bank rate made rapid progress. In six weeks the reserve rose from £4,611,000 to £8,680,000 (26th September) and Bank rate fell from 10 per cent. to 4½. By the 19th December, the reserve was £11,715,000 and Bank rate (on the 20th) 3½ per cent. But imports of gold were flowing in, and in the four months amounted to £4,459,000, so that the reflux of currency even then was no more than £2,645,000. In the ensuing two years the importation of gold continued in large volume. From the 19th December, 1866, to the 2nd December, 1868, the net imports were no less than £13,061,000. Yet at the end of the period the reserve was only £9,577,000, or £2,138,000 less than that at the beginning. Interior demand had thus absorbed over £15,000,000. Occurring at a time of severe depression, when the percentage of unemployed rose from 3·3 in 1866 to 7·4 in 1867 and 7·9 in 1868, while the wage index fell from 132 to 130, this was a repetition of the experience of 1858 and 1859.

The interior demand is to be explained as an absorption of currency by country banks at a time when discount rates were so low that it was not worth while to transmit it to London to be placed in bills.

That does not mean that there was no other contributory cause. After the activity of 1863–6, and the rise of the wage index from 117 to 132, there may well have been some continued absorption of currency by the wage-earning classes. Working-class earnings probably began to fall off soon after the crisis of May, 1866, but when earnings grow the adjustment of the wage-earners' cash balances takes time. The moment of maximum earnings is not the moment of maximum balances ; rather it is the moment of the maximum rate of growth of balances. If earnings reached

a maximum and then became stabilised, cash balances would be gradually adjusted to them ; after an interval they would be stabilised likewise. If earnings first reached a maximum and then began to decline, balances would for a time continue increasing after earnings had started to decrease. They would not begin to decrease till earnings so diminished that the reduction of balances by the losers more than offset the accumulation of balances by those who continued to gain.

The gain in rates of wages from 1863 to 1866 had been substantial, and nearly all of it was retained throughout the subsequent depression, so there may well have been a latent demand for currency among the working classes for some time after the crisis. But this could only account for a moderate part of the enormous interior demand in the years 1867 and 1868. And it must be remembered that the crisis itself had occasioned an interior demand of £9,000,000 in 2½ months, of which only £2,645,000 returned in the subsequent reflux.

Substantially the swollen interior demand of those two years must be attributed to the prevalence of cheap money. The yield of discounts and of call money was so low that the country banks did not send their redundant currency to London. Bank rate was actually lower than in 1858 and 1859. It was reduced to 2 per cent. in July, 1867, and so remained for sixteen months. It was this state of things that formed the subject of Goschen's essay, *Two per cent.* Bank rate did not rise above 3 per cent. till the 1st April, 1869.

Up to the end of October, 1868, the reserve was sustained, in spite of the big interior demand, by huge imports of gold. But there then came a reversal of the movement and on the 19th November, after a net export of £1,293,000 in three weeks, Bank rate was raised to 2½ per cent., and a fortnight later to 3.   From then till the end of March, 1869, exports and imports of gold practically balanced, but the interior demand continued. The actual amount, £560,000 in nearly four months, was small, but it was at a

season when there should normally be a reflux. The reserve fell below £9,000,000, and on the 1st April Bank rate was put up from 3 to 4 per cent. The response being insufficient, it was advanced to 4½ on the 6th May, and in the the next seven weeks there was a reflux of £2,760,000, most of which probably came from banks which were roused from slumber by the prospect of obtaining bills at 4½ per cent. With net imports of £1,579,000, that raised the reserve from £7,577,000 on the 5th May to £11,916,000 on the 23rd June, 1869, and cheap money once again became possible. The rate did not fall quite so low as in 1867 and 1868, but from 14th July, 1869, to 13th July, 1870, it remained at 3 or 2½ per cent. and there was an interior demand of £4,280,000. This was not quite on the previous scale, and by this time business was reviving. Unemployment fell from 7·9 per cent. in 1868 to 3·9 in 1870 and the wage index rose from 130 to 133. We may infer that the accumulation of idle money in the country banks had practically come to an end, and that renewed activity was making itself felt in a demand for currency.

THE FRANCO-GERMAN WAR

Imports of gold continued on a high level, and sufficed not only to meet the interior demand but to raise the reserve from £10,857,000 on the 14th July, 1869, to £12,100,000 on the 13th July, 1870. At that point a new phase began. Very suddenly there appeared the threat of war between France and Germany, quickly to be realised in actual hostilities. By the 3rd August the reserve had fallen to £9,331,000, practically the whole loss being due to interior demand. This sudden absorption of £2¾ millions of currency occurred in face of a rapid rise of Bank rate to 6 per cent., and is to be regarded as a sign of loss of confidence, a repetition on a small scale of the effects of the great panics. But this time it was very transitory. Big imports of gold, amounting in eight weeks to £6,100,000, raised the reserve to £14,083,000 (28th September, 1870), and in addition met a further interior demand of £1,348,000.

By that time Bank rate had been reduced to 2½ per cent. ; the reduction from 6 per cent. had taken only seven weeks. Bank rate in Paris remained at 6 per cent. (the level to which it had been raised on the 9th August, 1870) but with an inconvertible currency, involving an indefinitely increased exchange risk, the disparity of rates did not attract gold to Paris.

For the next five months the flood of imports of gold abated, but it set in again in March, 1871, and from the 1st March to the 26th July amounted to £7,438,000, raising the reserve from £13,310,000 to £17,410,000, or £2,000,000 above the highest figure ever reached before. Interior demand in five months was £3,338,000.

These imports of gold were due to the suspension of specie payments in France on account of the war. The actual amount of gold displaced from France by the inconvertible paper currency was not very great, but up to then France had regularly absorbed a great part of the world's output of gold. In the ten years 1860-9 the average net exports of gold from Great Britain to France had exceeded £5,000,000. This outlet was now closed. The resulting superfluity of gold permitted the continuance of cheap money, though the growing activity of business might well have been regarded as a ground for caution.

The Gold Standard in Germany

A new demand was now to descend upon the gold market. The war was over, and one of the first steps taken by the newly formed German Empire was to adopt a gold standard and a gold coinage. The free coinage of silver was suspended on the 3rd July, 1871, and almost immediately Germany began to acquire gold.

This demand for gold was at once felt by the London market. Net exports of gold from the United Kingdom from the 26th July to the 11th October amounted to £4,974,000 and combined with an interior demand of £4,371,000 to reduce the reserve from £17,410,000 to £8,065,000. Bank rate was hastily raised from 2 per cent.

to 5 in seventeen days (21st September to 7th October). The effect was surprising. By the 15th November despite a further net export of gold to the amount of £1,270,000 the reserve had risen to £14,126,000. There had been a reflux of currency from the interior of £7,331,000. And the reflux continued till on the 13th December the reserve was £15,649,000, and on the 14th Bank rate was reduced to 3 per cent.

Exports of gold had abated during November, but were quickly resumed, and from the 6th December, 1871, to the 15th May, 1872, amounted to £4,298,000. And at the same time interior demand revived. In April Bank rate began to go up, and on the 9th May, the reserve then being £9,929,000, reached 5 per cent. In six weeks a reflux of currency of £2,234,000, and net imports of £1,430,000 raised the reserve to £13,593,000 and Bank rate was back at 3 per cent. (20th June, 1872).

Once again there was an immediate revival of interior demand, and in July renewed exports of gold began to be felt, though only on a very modest scale. It was the interior demand of £4,896,000 that had reduced the reserve to £8,922,000 by the 2nd October, 1872. Bank rate had been gradually rising, and on the 3rd October was put up to 5 per cent. Further advances to 6 per cent. on the 10th October and 7 on the 9th November, proved effective ; the reserve rose to £13,063,000 on the 27th November, and successive reductions brought Bank rate down to 3½ per cent. on the 30th January, 1873, with the reserve at £15,125,000. Practically the whole gain was 'ue to a reflux of currency amounting to £6,051,000, net imports having been insignificant.

The very large reflux on this occasion and also that at the end of 1871 may possibly have been swollen by transactions incidental to the German purchases of gold. The German authorities certainly kept the monetary conditions in London under close observation, and might well think it prudent, when pressure developed, to release gold they were in course of acquiring, and to make it available to the

Bank of England. But that would not account for the appearance of a net reflux over any considerable period. The acquisition of gold in advance of actual export by the German purchasers or by bullion dealers acting as their agents would for the moment increase the apparent interior demand. But from the commencement of the German purchases of gold in July, 1871, to the reduction of Bank rate at the end of January, 1873, there was on balance a reflux of several millions, which can, I think, only be explained as the attraction of currency from the country banks by dear money.

THE CRISES OF 1873

In February, 1873, an outflow of gold by export began again, and Easter, which fell on the 13th April, brought a seasonal interior demand. On the 7th May, the reserve was £10,278,000 and Bank rate was raised from 4 to 4½ per cent. on that day (being a Wednesday). Two days later an acute financial crisis broke out in Germany, where the process of receiving payment of the war indemnity of five milliards from France had induced a state of inflated credit. Vienna, in virtue of its close commercial relations with Germany, was also involved.

On Saturday, the 10th May, 1873, Bank rate was raised to 5 per cent., on the 17th to 6 and on the 4th June to 7. The German absorption of gold was for the time being suspended, and it was net imports of gold that raised the reserve from £9,814,000 on the 4th June to £13,287,000 on the 20th August. Such reflux of currency as occurred was moderate and transitory, and on balance it was insignificant. Since her suspension of the free coinage of silver in July, 1871, Germany had imported £50,000,000 of gold, of which nearly half had come from England.

The year 1873, which is conspicuous on account of twenty-four changes of Bank rate, the greatest number ever recorded in one year, was to see yet another major disturbance On the 19th September there broke out a violent crisis in the United States. That country was still

under a regime of inconvertible paper, the United States notes or Greenbacks first issued during the Civil War, and the reaction of the crisis on Great Britain and other countries with metallic currencies was not so direct as under the conditions of 1857. But still there were some of the symptoms of panic. The Bank of England's reserve fell from £13,239,000 on the 24th September to £9,954,000 on the 1st October, mainly on account of an interior demand of £2,801,000. A fortnight later it was only £7,861,000. In the three weeks, the net loss of gold by export had been £1,109,000, and therefore the interior demand had been £4,269,000.

Bank rate, having gone up to 4 and 5 per cent., was advanced to 6 on the 14th October and 7 on the 18th. Still the reserve flagged. On the 5th November it was only £8,071,000. The rate was raised to 8 per cent. (1st November) and then to 9 (7th November). On the 20th November, a reflux of currency having raised the reserve to £9,702,000, the rate was reduced again to 8 per cent. The reflux was then reinforced by a moderate importation of gold, and further reductions brought the rate down to 4½ on the 11th December, the reserve then being at the comfortable level of £12,462,000. The total net reflux of currency from the 15th October to the 10th December had been £3,707,000. But though dear money had once again drawn currency from the country, it must be remembered that the amount was less than the panic demand which had occurred immediately before.

Interior Demand and Reflux 1871–5

It can, I think, be inferred that the first application of 5 per cent. in 1871 had swept up much of the loose currency from the country banks, that the advance to 7 per cent. in 1872 had brought in most of the rest, and that there was relatively little to be attracted even by 9 per cent. in 1873. The following table summarises the alternations of interior demand with reflux in the three years.

	Interior Demand	Reflux
11th October–13th December, 1871	—	£8,768,000
14th December, 1871–8th May, 1872	£2,145,000	—
9th May, 1872–19th June, 1872	—	£2,234,000
20th June–2nd October, 1872 ...	£4,896,000	—
3rd October, 1872–29th January, 1873	—	£6,051,000
30th January–7th May, 1873 ...	£2,347,000	—
8th May–9th July, 1873... ...	—	£1,454,000
10th July–24th September, 1873	£1,394,000	—
25th September–15th October, 1873	£4,269,000	—
16th October–10th December, 1873	—	£3,707,000

In the whole period of two years and two months there was a net reflux of £7,180,000. Yet it was a time of quite exceptional economic activity. Unemployment fell from 1·6 per cent. in 1871 to 0·9 in 1872 and was still only 1·2 per cent. in 1873. The wage index rose from 138 in 1871 to 155 in 1873 (and was still rising, for it was 156 in 1874).

We have here a much more striking example of the power of dear money to attract a reflux of currency than in 1860–1. On that occasion Bank rate rose to 8 per cent., and there was a reflux of £4,595,000 in 4½ months. But 1860 was a year of much more moderate activity and this spell of dear money was accompanied by a decisive reaction.

The reflux of the years 1871–3 had been preceded by a more persistent interior demand. The enormous absorption of currency at the time of the crisis of 1866 had only been very partially offset by the reflux in the latter part of that year. The country banks had apparently adopted a more ample standard of reserves and stocked themselves with currency accordingly.

From the 19th December, 1866, to the 11th October,

1871, interior demand had amounted to the enormous total of £32,808,000. Therefore, when Bank rate was rapidly advanced from 2 to 5 per cent. just before the latter date, there must have been a vast quantity of idle currency ready to come to London as soon as a remunerative yield could be obtained from the discount market.

Even in 1873, when the disposable currency had nearly all already been drawn to London, the net interior demand was surprisingly small. And we have evidence that even at that stage dear money had a great power of retaining currency in London, for as soon as the pressure was released there was a very large interior demand. From the 8th January, 1874, to the 11th November, 1874, Bank rate did not exceed 4 per cent., and there was a net interior demand, calculated from the weekly returns of imports and exports of gold, of £7,324,000. But this is an understatement. For the final trade returns for the year contained a correction, the total imports of gold being shown as £1,338,000 higher than in the monthly returns (with which the weekly returns corresponded). The true interior demand was something like £8¾ millions.

And the interior demand continued high till the autumn of 1875. From the 11th November, 1874, to the 13th January, 1875, Bank rate being 5 and 6 per cent., it slackened, amounting in the two months to only £603,000. But from then to the 6th October, 1875, according to the weekly returns, it was £7,785,000. Here again a correction has to be made. An export of approximately £1,000,000 in the monthly returns for February 1875, seems to have been omitted from the weekly returns,[1] so that the true interior demand was £6¾ millions.

The trade activity continued into 1874 and even into 1875 with little abatement. The wage index reached its maximum of 156 in 1874, and was still as high as 154 in 1875. Unemployment rose to 1·7 per cent. in 1874 and 2·4 in 1875, but even the latter figure was very low. Only

[1] In the six months from October, 1874, to March, 1875, the monthly returns show exports of £7,606,000, whereas the weekly returns which exactly coincide for that period, show £6,561,000 only.

the wholesale price level presaged a serious depression, falling from 111 in 1873 to 96 in 1875.

It was not a time of extremely cheap money. There were occasional descents of Bank rate to 3, 2½ and at one time even to 2 per cent., but the average was fairly high at 3½ per cent. The high interior demand evidently had nothing in common with that which had prevailed in 1858-9 or 1867-8. The net imports of gold were large, amounting between 7th January, 1874, and the 6th October, 1875, to £16,000,000, notwithstanding the commencement of a French absorption of gold with a view to a resumption of convertibility. The German demand for gold, however, was also reviving, and in the last three months of 1875 Great Britain sustained a net loss by export of £4,900,000.

The Demand for Gold 1876-8

On the 6th January, 1876, the reserve had fallen to £8,132,000, and Bank rate was raised to 5 per cent. There immediately followed a reflux of currency, which by the 23rd March, in conjunction with imports of £933,000, had raised the reserve to £13,487,000. On this occasion the response of the gold imports was more noteworthy than the reversal of the interior demand. For the latter was mainly seasonal. It was not exclusively so, for the reflux in the quarter ending the 1st March, 1876, was £3,180,000 and was somewhat above the average.

In April, 1876, the reserve remaining high, Bank rate was reduced to 3 and then to 2 per cent.

Gold imports continued to flow in, and the net gain in the six months to the 20th September amounted to no less than £11,800,000. On the other hand interior demand remained low, and the reserve rose to the unprecedented figure of £22,244,000.

From September, 1876, however, the gold position underwent a change. Several countries had in principle adopted the gold standard since 1871, but, except Germany, they had not been in a position to acquire much gold. They had a " limping " standard, the old standard silver coin re-

maining in circulation as tokens, and, under conditions of declining trade activity, they needed little or no addition to their supplies of currency. The result was that the French accumulation of gold which started in 1874 was met at first without drawing gold from Great Britain. The net imports into France were as follows :

1874	...	£17,325,000
1875	...	£18,835,000
1876	...	£20,119,000
1877	...	£17,431,000
1878	...	£9,449,000

The total was no less than £83,000,000, the net exports from the United Kingdom to France in the five years being £14,500,000. By no means the whole of the world's output of gold passed through the London market, and there were large movements from one European country to another.

The maximum French demand for gold occurred in 1876, and it was from the middle of 1876 that the United States began also to accumulate gold. In the first instance they absorbed little more than the output of their own mines. But even that was an important change, for the yearly output had been averaging some £7,000,000, and was rising. The monetary gold stock of the United States rose from $130,000,000 on the 1st July, 1876, to $256,000,000 on the 1st July, 1879, an increase of over £25,000,000. The German demand also, having recommenced in 1875, absorbed some £20,000,000 from that year up to 1879.

From September, 1876, the Bank of England's reserve began to be reduced by net exports of gold. Bank rate however remained at 2 per cent. till May, 1877. By that time the net exports of gold had amounted to £9,611,000 and the reserve had fallen to £10,927,000. Bank rate had been at 2 per cent. for fifty-four weeks, and interior demand over the whole period had been £3,054,000. The growing trade depression was still on a very moderate scale. The wage index in 1877 at 151 was still actually higher than in 1872 and unemployment was only 4·7 per cent. An

interior demand of £3,000,000 in a year would correspond
sufficiently closely with these conditions, without assuming
any considerable accumulation of idle currency retained in
the country in consequence of the unremunerative discount
rate.

Bank rate was put up on the 3rd May, 1877, but only to
3 per cent. Whether in consequence of that moderate rise
or by chance, there followed an importation of gold and a
reflux of currency, and on the 12th July, the reserve having
recovered to £13,911,000, Bank rate returned to 2 per cent.
But the recovery was delusive. Renewed exports of gold
and interior demand brought the reserve down to £9,431,000
on the 10th October. Bank rate went up to 3 per cent. on
the 28th August, 4 per cent. on the 4th October and 5 per
cent. on the 11th. At the end of January, 1878, it was back
at 2 per cent. The reserve was then £12,982,000. The
exports of gold had barely been checked, but there had been
a reflux of currency amounting to £3,713,000.

Of this reflux £1,630,000 occurred in January, and may
be regarded as seasonal. The rest was, no doubt, a true
manifestation of the power of dear money to attract idle
currency to London. This effect, however, had become
noticeably less marked than in 1871.

Continued gold exports diminished the reserve, and
presently there was a seasonal reappearance of an interior
demand. In July, 1878, the reserve fell to £9,000,000 and
Bank rate was raised to 3½ and then to 4 per cent. (1st
August).

When that failed to reverse the adverse tendency, it was
put up to 5 per cent. on the 12th August (a Monday).
The tide of exports was effectively turned. By the 4th
September, 1878, the reserve had risen to £10,301,000.
Nevertheless Bank rate remained at 5 per cent.

THE CITY OF GLASGOW BANK FAILURE, 1878

There was an underlying weakness in the situation. The
depression that began in 1875 had at first been very mild.
And the eighteen months of uninterrupted cheap money

which began in April, 1876, might have been expected to promote a return to activity without any serious trouble at all. But cheap money had come to an end with the imposition of the 5 per cent. Bank rate in October, 1877, and, after an uneasy interval, 5 per cent had returned. The business situation had deteriorated, and unsound positions which had been successfully concealed were threatened with exposure. On the 2nd October, 1878, the gathering storm burst. The City of Glasgow Bank suspended payment. An investigation of its affairs disclosed a lamentable tale of extravagant lending and falsified balance sheets. The direct losses ran to several millions and unlimited liability involved the shareholders in calls which ultimately amounted to £2,750 for every £100 of paid-up capital. The full extent of the losses was only made known gradually, but the immediate shock to credit was severe. There were several large consequential failures. As in previous crises there was a sudden interior demand for currency. In the week following the failure the interior demand amounted to £953,000, and in the following week, that ending on the 16th October, to £2,669,000, making £3,622,000 in a fortnight. On the 9th October, the reserve was still as high as £10,215,000 and Bank rate remained at 5 per cent. But on the 14th October, the following Monday, in view of the rapid loss of currency, it was raised to 6. Imports of gold had been pouring in ever since the rise of Bank rate to 5 per cent. in August, and they were accelerated by the further rise. On the 21st November, the reserve being £12,311,000, the rate was reduced to 5 per cent. During the continuance of the 6 per cent. rate there had been some reflux of currency, but when it was reduced there was a recrudescence of the interior demand. From the 20th November, 1878, to the 1st January, 1879, it amounted to £4,193,000, and from the 2nd October, 1878, to the 1st January, 1879, to £6,465,000. A part of this was due to seasonal requirements (a little exaggerated owing to the Bank return being made up to the 1st January), but far the greater part was due to panic.

The City of Glasgow Bank was a big and important institution, but the failure of a bank is by no means so far-reaching in its effects as the failure of a discount house. Early in the new year the currency withdrawn from the Bank of England began to flow back. From the 1st January to the 12th March, 1879, the reflux amounted to no less than £6,731,000. The excess over the normal seasonal reflux may be estimated at about £4,000,000.

GOLD AND THE DEPRESSION OF 1875–9

On the 12th March the reserve was £19,302,000. Bank rate had already come down to 3 per cent., and was reduced to 2½. On the 9th April, immediately before Easter, in spite of the seasonal demand for currency, the reserve was still as high as £18,662,000 and the rate fell to 2 per cent.

For a time the imports of gold continued, though since the reduction of the Bank rate in the new year they had come in reduced volume. The reserve reached a maximum of £21,372,000 on the 30th July. But then began a net export of gold on a great scale. That was due to an increase of the American demand. Up to the middle of 1879 the United States had absorbed little gold beyond the output of the American mines. But in the twelve months beginning 1st July, 1879, their net imports were no less than $77,000,000 and in the following twelve months $97,500,000. At this time France was exporting gold and German imports were on a moderate scale. Nevertheless the American demand was heavy enough to involve the Bank of England in large losses of gold by export. In 7 months (30th July, 1879, to 3rd March, 1880) net exports were £10,353,000. But there was a reflux of currency of no less than £5,542,000. The fall in the reserve was therefore £4,800,000 and left it at the relatively high level, according to the standards then accepted, of £16,561,000.

The depression had been greatly aggravated by the crisis and dear money of 1878. In 1879 the unemploy-

ment percentage rose to 11·4, the wage index fell to 146, and the wholesale price index to 83. The reflux may have been swollen by a belated return of some of the currency absorbed at the end of 1878. But even so it is remarkable that though Bank rate did not rise above 3 per cent. there was no evidence of an accumulation of idle currency in the country banks.

It was the reflux that permitted the continuance of cheap money. And now at last came the long deferred signs of revival of business, which had been deteriorating ever since 1874. Since the 9 per cent. Bank rate of November 1873 there had been four successive spells of 5 or 6 per cent., 6 per cent. in November, 1874, 5 per cent. in January, 1876, 5 per cent. in October, 1877, and 6 per cent. in October, 1878. This was a striking departure from the practice adopted in earlier depressions. The four weeks at 4½ per cent. in May, 1859, made a very slight interruption of cheap money at a time when recovery was already well under way. The same is true of the five weeks at 4½ per cent. in May, 1869.

In January, 1876, 5 per cent. was imposed for only three weeks, and there followed eighteen months of cheap money. Whether revival was really beginning before the reintroduction of dear money in October, 1877, the statistical material does not enable us to say. But in any case the longer spell of seven weeks at 5 per cent. spoilt the prospect, and the five months' spell at 5 and 6 per cent. that was soon to follow was the prelude to the worst year since 1858. In fact gold could only be set free to meet the demands of France, Germany and the United States by compressing the consumers' income. Of that process the fall in the wage index and the price level and the rise in unemployment were evidence. So long as it continued, and produced the requisite reflux of currency, the exports of gold could go on. Whenever the reflux of currency was insufficient, Bank rate had to be raised. The rise gave momentary relief by attracting foreign money, but, unless the depression was sufficiently intensified, a renewed loss of gold was

bound to follow. It was the stringency and crisis of 1878 that at last brought British industry to a sufficient state of prostration to free the Bank of England from anxiety in regard to the reserve. The Bank cheerfully watched its reserve fall from £21,372,000 in July, 1879, to £12,578,000 in January, 1881, before raising the rate to 3½ per cent.

TRADE REVIVAL AND RENEWED DEPRESSION, 1880–6

A recovery of the reserve to £16,580,000 on the 16th February, 1881, which permitted a return to 3 and then 2½ per cent., was mainly seasonal. In the summer the reserve fell away again. The exports of gold had abated in the earlier part of the year, but set in again in August, and Bank rate was raised to 4 per cent. On the 6th October it was put up to 5 per cent. and on the 30th January, 1882, to 6. The reserve on the 1st February, 1882, had sunk to £9,175,000. The reduction since the 16th February, 1881, was due to net exports of £7,856,000. There had on balance been a trifling interior demand.

The exports of gold had been accentuated in consequence of the crisis in Paris in January, 1882, resulting from the failure of the *Union Générale*. The loss of gold by export stopped almost immediately after the rise to 6 per cent. In fact the importation into the United States was ceasing, in consequence partly of the silver legislation which went far to satisfy the need for currency with silver certificates.

By this time revival had blossomed out into real activity. There was nothing like the inflation of 1872–3. In fact the wage index remained at 147 for the three years 1880–2. Unemployment having dropped from 11·4 per cent. in 1879 to 5·5 in 1880, fell further to 2·3 in 1882. This improvement soon made itself felt in a revived interior demand. At first there was a rapid increase in the reserve from £9,175,000 on the 1st February, 1882, to £15,113,000 on the 22nd March. Imports of gold accounted for £2,654,000, and a reflux of currency for the balance of £3,284,000. The reflux, however, like that of a year before, was mainly seasonal. And in the next five months

(to 16th August, 1882) there was an interior demand of £5,805,000. The reserve fell to £10,691,000 and Bank rate was advanced to 4 per cent. and on the 14th September to 5.

In 1883 business began to fall off, but at first only very slightly. There was a small net import of gold in the year, and a small net reflux of currency. Bank rate oscillated between 3 and 4 per cent.

In 1884 the set-back to trade became more marked. The wage index was, it is true, a little higher at 150, but the percentage of unemployed rose to 8·1. In the first half of the year the reserve was improved by the arrival of imports of gold from the United States, and by the 19th June Bank rate had come down to 2 per cent., the reserve being £15,867,000.

At this period the extension of the gold standard had made a large number of countries potential absorbers of gold, and the international market did not depend so much as formerly on the action of two or three principal countries. In the second half of 1884 the United States imported a small amount of gold, but it was chiefly due to miscellaneous demands that there was a net loss of gold. From the 18th June to the 5th November, 1884, there was a fall of £6,350,000 in the reserve (to £9,517,000) composed of net exports, £3,086,000 and interior demand, £3,264,000. The interior demand had not been purely seasonal, and the greater part of it had occurred during sixteen weeks of 2 per cent. Bank rate. In view of the state of growing depression, we can infer that the tendency of currency to accumulate in the country banks when discount rates were very low, though undoubtedly much diminished, had by no means entirely ceased to operate. The experience that followed goes to confirm this view. For, when Bank rate rose to 5 per cent. on the 6th November, 1884, there began at once a reflux of currency that eventually amounted to £7,754,000. From the 5th November, 1884, to the 18th March, 1885, the reserve rose from £9,517,000 to £18,270,000, net imports being only £1,000,000.

A reflux on such a scale was far in excess of any seasonal movement. Moreover, it was followed by an almost equally striking revival of interior demand as soon as cheap money was restored. From the 18th March to the 11th November, 1885, the reserve fell by £6,497,000, and, as net exports were only £237,000, interior demand was no less than £6,260,000.

These two big movements did, it is true, correspond fairly closely in time with normal seasonal fluctuations, but they were far greater in amount.

Dear money had again been applied at a time of growing depression. And it was a fairly stiff dose ; for the 5 per cent. rate remained in force for twelve weeks. Unemployment rose to 9·3 per cent. in 1885 and 10·2 in 1886. The wage index fell to 148, the price index to 69.

Activity of Business and Zigzags of Bank Rate

Once more Bank rate went up to 5 per cent. in December, 1886, and remained there for seven weeks. But in the course of the following year a real improvement began to be felt. Unemployment in 1887 averaged 7·6 per cent. From that point recovery made steady progress till in 1889 unemployment had fallen to 2·1 per cent. and in 1890 the wage index had risen to 163. The interior demand also rose. If we average the interior demand over the whole period from 1876 to 1887 (taking the year ending on the first Wednesday in December to eliminate the cash disturbances at the turn of the year), we find that it is a minus quantity. There was in fact a net reflux in the twelve years of £4,211,000, or an annual average of £351,000. For 1888 there was an interior demand of £1,809,000, the highest since 1882. In 1891 it had rise to £7,980,000, the highest since 1874.

In this period of active trade Bank rate performed oscillations which are reminiscent of the years 1871–3, though the zigzags were much less violent. After being at 4 per cent. all through the autumn of 1887, the rate fell between January and March, 1888, to 2 per cent. This

was the background of cheap money for Goschen's conversion of the 3 per cents. into new Consols yielding 2¾ and then 2½ per cent. There followed a rise of Bank rate to 5 per cent. in the autumn of 1888, and a fall to 2½ per cent. in April, 1889 ; a rise to 6 per cent. at the end of 1889 and a fall to 3 per cent. in April 1890 ; a renewed rise to 6 in November, 1890 (on the occasion of the Baring crisis), and a fall to 3 in January, 1891.

There were still occasional traces of a reflux attracted by dear money. In the nine weeks following the rise to 5 per cent. on the 3rd October, 1888, there was a reflux of £1,965,000. On the other hand from the rise to 5 per cent. on the 26th September, 1889, to the 1st January, 1890, interior demand took £2,134,000. The rise to 6 per cent. (30th December, 1889) was followed by a big reflux amounting to £4,678,000 in seven weeks, but this was mainly seasonal. And the dear money at the end of 1890 was accompanied by an interior demand of £2,251,000.

On the other hand with the return to cheap money at the beginning of 1892 there began a swollen interior demand which persisted up to the middle of 1893. In the twelve months ending with the first Wednesday in June, 1893, the interior demand amounted to £7,340,000. By that time the recession in trade had become severe. The unemployment percentage for 1893 was 7·5, the worst during this depression. The wage index remained practically stationary at the high level of 162, and the lag of wage earners' cash balances, referred to above in connection with the interior demand in 1867 and 1874–5, may have contributed to it. But it is probable that there still survived some tendency to accumulate idle currency in the provincial banking system under the influence of unremunerative discount rates.

The Baring Crisis, 1890

The Baring crisis of 1890 has been referred to above. What is really noteworthy about that event is that there was *no* crisis. Everything had been arranged before any

public announcement of the embarrassments of the historic firm was made.

The trouble arose from the discredit into which Argentine securities had fallen. Barings, like the other leading merchant bankers, combined the functions of an accepting house and an issuing house. In the latter capacity they had launched a number of Argentine loans. An issuing house does not necessarily or ordinarily participate in its own flotations or even underwrite them. But Barings had entered into commitments appropriate to underwriters in connection with some of their loans, and, when the market for Argentine securities suddenly dried up altogether, they found that they had undertaken more than they could perform.

Since January, 1885, the Argentine Republic had had an inconvertible paper currency and gold had been at a premium. For some years vast borrowings in Europe, Federal, Provincial and others, artificially sustained the balance of payments and kept down the premium. The total indebtedness showed signs of exceeding all reasonable bounds, and by 1889 European investors, becoming aware of the precariousness of this situation, displayed a growing unwillingness to take any more Argentine securities. The gold premium rose, and that increased the discredit. In the course of 1890, after civil disturbances, a change of Government and an abortive attempt to arrange a moratorium, matters came to a head. Argentine securities were unsaleable. On Saturday the 8th November, 1890, the Bank of England received from Barings a confidential intimation that they were about to suspend payment.

Had Barings been merely an issuing house, concerned with the flotation of loans, the repercussions would have been limited. But they were also responsible for a very large accepting business. That is to say, they accepted bills on behalf of traders who were thus enabled to get their purchases of goods financed by bills drawn on what was reputed to be a first-class name. Barings, like other merchant bankers, did most of their acceptance business on

behalf of foreign merchants, so that goods purchased for importation into foreign countries were financed by bills on London, the purchasers undertaking to supply money to the acceptors in London in time for the maturity of the bills. The trade bill, accepted by the trader who purchased goods himself, had for long been the prevailing instrument of credit in British trade both domestic and foreign, but it was gradually falling into disuse. In domestic trade the purchasers of goods were tending more and more to obtain bank advances and pay cash. In foreign trade the practice of arranging for bills to be drawn on accepting houses or banks instead of on the importing merchants was growing. The discount market therefore handled a great volume of the acceptances of a limited number of first-class names of world-wide repute. The failure of one of these names would strike at the foundation of the credit system. The crisis of 1866 had shown how great a shock would be caused by the failure of a discount house. The failure of Barings would have worked havoc among the discount houses. It was fortunate that the Governor of the Bank of England, William Lidderdale, was a man of wisdom and decision. A preliminary investigation satisfied him that there was a reasonable expectation that the firm, if given time to realise its assets without forced sales, would prove to be solvent.

He made up his mind that what was wanted was a guarantee of Barings' liabilities sufficiently solid to satisfy the money market while the firm's assets were being realised. But whatever his opinion of the ultimate adequacy of the assets might be, there was undeniably a risk of a heavy loss. The total liabilities exceeded £20,000,000. The capital of the Bank of England, though large, is limited, and its shareholders could not afford to throw millions away. Here was a case where a privately-owned institution could not assume unaided the full responsibilities of the lender of last resort. Lidderdale approached the Chancellor of the Exchequer, Goschen, and asked for a Government guarantee. That Goschen could not give.

He promised in case of need to authorise the suspension of the fiduciary limit, but the prospect of asking the House of Commons to vote a supplementary estimate to meet the losses of a private firm he would not face.[1] Lidderdale was driven back on the resources of the City to supplement those of the Bank of England, and by the 15th November, a week after he had first learned of the threatened disaster, he had formed a syndicate of the principal banks and financial houses to share the burden of the guarantee.

He also took steps to safeguard the Bank's reserve position against a possible panic. The reserve was at the respectable figure of £11,000,000, but he borrowed £3,000,000 of gold from the Bank of France and £1,500,000 from the Imperial Bank of Russia. The arrival of the French gold, along with other movements, raised the reserve to £14,552,000 on the 19th November. Bank rate had been raised to 6 per cent. on the 7th November. By the 3rd December the reserve was £16,673,000 and the rate was put down again to 5 per cent.

The assistance thus given by foreign central banks marks an epoch. International co-operation in dealing with a financial crisis was no new thing. The credits of £2,000,000 opened in Paris and of £900,000 in Hamburg, gave opportune assistance to the Bank of England in 1839. But in 1890 what was given was in the form not of credits but actual gold. It was the growth of gold reserves that had made that possible. The gold in the Bank of France had risen to 1¼ milliards or £50,000,000 in 1889, and at the end of 1890, after the loan of gold to the Bank of England, was £44,800,000. A reserve on such a scale was no longer a mere working balance, but was a hoard from which considerable sums could be drawn without any appreciable loss of safety.

The hoard was not easily drawn upon by the ordinary mechanism of the market. Though the free coinage of silver had ceased in France, five-franc pieces remained unlimited legal tender. The Bank of France was legally

[1] See *Life of Goschen* by Arthur Elliot, Vol. II, pp. 169–74.

entitled to pay its notes in these coins, which had been reduced by the depreciation of silver to the standing of token coins worth much less as bullion than their face value. It was therefore possible for gold to rise to a premium, up to the limit at which it became profitable to collect gold coin from circulation for export. The limit was not very high. But the prospect of a premium even of something less than 1 per cent. was sufficient to give rise to an exchange risk which would counterbalance a large difference in discount rates between London and Paris. And in fact the Paris Bank rate remained unaltered at 3 per cent. from the 7th February, 1889, to the 19th May, 1892, through all the zigzags in which the London Bank rate indulged.

If Lidderdale's measures in November, 1890, were open to criticism it was perhaps as going unnecessarily far. But the fault, if it was one, was on the right side. And it was impossible to say *a priori* how far it was necessary to go to prevent a panic. As it turned out, Barings paid all their liabilities in full, and were left with a handsome balance to restart business with as a private limited company a few years later. But the public could not know this beforehand, and for all they knew the guarantors might have suffered serious loss.

It is interesting to compare the Baring crisis with that of 1866. Overend, Gurney and Company asked for assistance from the Bank of England, and after an examination of their position it was refused. The Bank can hardly be blamed. The formation of a guarantee syndicate, had it been thought of, would hardly have been possible among the crowd of banks and financial institutions, much more numerous and smaller than in 1890, and less inclined to co-operate.

Nevertheless it is worth recording that Overend, Gurney and Company did eventually pay all their creditors in full ; the loss fell entirely on the shareholders. If assistance had been forthcoming in May, 1866, the business might have been preserved as a going concern, and the shareholders, even though they would certainly have had to pay up heavy

calls on the shares, would at any rate have maintained in being an extremely valuable goodwill.   On the other hand, quite apart from Overend, Gurney and Company, there was so much unsound business in being in 1866 that something like a crisis was probably in any case inevitable ; the trouble could hardly have been got over with such smoothness as that of 1890.

The Baring crisis did not play a decisive part in the trade cycle.   The following year, 1891, was still one of activity, though the unemployment percentage rose to 3.5. Nor was it one of cheap money, for Bank rate rose to 5 per cent. for three weeks in May.   It was in 1892 that depression definitely took hold.   Bank rate was reduced to 3 per cent. in January and 2 in April, 1892, and did not rise above 3 till May, 1893.   But in spite of cheap money unemployment rose to 6·3 per cent., and the wholesale price index, which had still been at 72 in 1891, fell to 68.

AMERICAN EXPORTS OF GOLD AND CHEAP MONEY, 1893–6

The year 1893 was one of intensified depression and crises.   Unemployment rose to 7·5 per cent.   In the early part of the year crises broke out in Australia and Italy, and in August, 1893, came the great American crisis.

The circumstances of the American crisis were such that it did not greatly aggravate the trade depression in Great Britain and Europe.   The crisis arose out of the silver policy.   Since 1878, though the free coinage of silver had not been restored, a prescribed annual amount of coinage of standard silver dollars had been required by statute. For a time room had been found for this additional currency by the redemption of a part of the national bank notes, but from 1890 onwards this compensating process ceased.   And as trade recession began in Europe a corresponding contraction became necessary in the United States. There were heavy exports of gold from the United States, and then for a short time the need for further exports was postponed by the chance coincidence of an abundant

harvest in the United States with scarcity in Europe. Before the end of 1892, however, the exports of gold began again, and in the year ending June, 1893, the net outflow amounted to $87½ millions (£18 millions). For a time the deflationary effect of the crisis reversed the flow, but it was soon resumed and continued till 1896. In fact in the eight years from July, 1888, to June, 1896, the net ·exports of gold from the United States amounted to $323 millions (£66 millions). At the same time the output of gold from the world's mines was increasing. In 1892 for the first time since 1853 the year's output exceeded £30,000,000. In 1895 it passed £40,000,000, and in 1899, when the further increase was interrupted for a time by the outbreak of the South African War, it reached £63,000,000.

It was this flood of gold that permitted an uninterrupted spell of cheap money of unusual length in London. Bank rate fell to 3 per cent. on the 5th October, 1893, and did not rise above 3 again till the 22nd October, 1896. And from the 22nd February, 1894, to the 10th September, 1896, more than two years and a half, the rate remained unchanged at 2 per cent.

During this period the wholesale price index continued to fall. In 1893 it was still 68, and in the three following years was 63, 62 and 61. But it would be a mistake to infer that they were years of deepening depression. On the contrary the unemployment percentage fell steadily, and the wage index, after having been stationary since 1892, showed signs of moving upwards in 1896. And it may be mentioned that the fall of prices was entirely in the category of foodstuffs. The index for materials of industry remained unchanged at 60.

When Bank rate was reduced from 2½ to 2 per cent. on the 22nd February, 1894, the reserve was £22,602,000 and just exceeded the figure reached in September, 1876, which till then had been the highest recorded. Two years later it was £40,997,000 (26th February, 1896). Bank rate was ineffective, and for the greater part of the time the market rate of discount was below 1 per cent.

And it is noteworthy that, far from making Bank rate effective by sales of securities in the open market, the Bank of England actually *increased* its holding of securities, which had fallen to £31,000,000 in the second quarter of 1894, to £44,000,000 in 1896. This was partly for the purpose of offsetting an exceptional deposit held idle at the Bank for a considerable period by the Japanese Government out of the war indemnity received from China. But such an exceptional deposit, if not offset by a purchase of securities, would itself have tended to make Bank rate effective.

BANK RATE AND GOLD 1896–1904

In 1896 the United States began to import gold, and Great Britain lost on balance £5,655,000 in that year. By the 9th September, 1896, the Bank of England's reserve had fallen to £32,380,000. By all earlier standards that was a fantastically high figure ; nevertheless Bank rate was raised to 2½ per cent. and a fortnight later to 3. On the 21st October, 1896, the reserve had fallen to £25,920,000 and Bank rate was raised to 4 per cent.

Bank rate had once more regained its significance. In 1897 the reserve rose to £28,000,000 and brought fourteen months more of cheap money (2 to 3 per cent.). But there were still no net imports of gold, and as business improved, the demands for currency for internal circulation grew. In April, 1898, the reserve had fallen to £18,351,000, and Bank rate went up to 4 per cent.

A new standard of reserve requirements had come into vogue. Up to 1890 a fall of the reserve to £10,000,000 or thereabouts had been the normal signal for a high Bank rate. After 1896 the critical point was somewhere about £20,000,000. Even so Bank rate remained relatively lower. In the years 1896 to 1900 trade activity was at a high level. By 1899 the unemployment percentage had fallen to 2, and the price level was rising rapidly. Yet the Bank rate did not rise above 4 per cent. till the eve of the South African War in October, 1899. At the end of November,

1899, the reserve fell to £19,336,000 and the rate was raised to 6 per cent. for the first time since 1890. But that was as much the result of unfavourable prospects in South Africa as of monetary exigencies, and early in the new year the rate came down by steps to 4 per cent.

There are still traces in this period of the short-period effects of cheap and dear money on interior demand. In the 2½ years of 2 per cent. from 1894 to 1896 interior demand amounted to £17,812,000. That might with some plausibility be attributed to the gradual recovery of economic activity, but when at last in October 1896 Bank rate went up to 4 per cent., there was a reflux of £2,809,000 in six weeks, which cannot be interpreted as seasonal.

In the years of growing activity that followed there is no definite evidence of a recurrence of this effect. Interior demand expanded, reaching £10,361,000 in 1899 and £10,072,000 in 1900. The unemployment percentage fell to 2 per cent. in the former year, and the wage index rose to 179 in the latter. In 1901, though the wage index remained at 179, there were signs of reaction. The unemployment percentage rose to 3·3, and the wholesale price index, from 75 in 1900, fell to 70. Interior demand declined to £2,975,000. On this occasion the transition from activity to depression was not accompanied by any acute financial crisis. But in Germany, where the activity had been greater than elsewhere, a series of failures both of banks and of industrial concerns began at the end of June, 1901, with the suspension of the Leipziger Bank.

The prosperity which then reached its turning point had been, so far as British industry was concerned, unusually prolonged, and solidly founded. Bank rate was only put up to 5 per cent. or more on two occasions, first from October, 1899, to January, 1900, and then in January, 1901. The violent zigzags, which had been a striking feature of the years 1871–4, and in a less degree of the years 1888–91, were almost absent. Between the two spells of dear money Bank rate did fall, it is true, to 3 per cent., but only for a short time. In fact except for eight weeks at 3 or 3½ per

cent. it was at 4 per cent. or more from the 3rd October, 1899, to the 6th June, 1901. The pressure was more sustained, and so had not to be either so intensified or so often repeated.

Of the attraction of currency to London from the provinces there is little trace. From the 4th October, 1899, when Bank rate was raised to 5 per cent., to the 6th December there was a reflux of £220,000. But the reflux in the quarter from the 6th December to the 7th March, 1900, was only £665,000, and was the least recorded among corresponding quarters since 1875, though Bank rate was at the high average of 4·88 per cent.

The rise to 5 per cent. on the 3rd January, 1901, was followed, it is true, by a heavy reflux amounting by the 20th February to £7,152,000. But a great part of this was seasonal. The interior demand in the four weeks from the 5th December to the 2nd January reached the unusually high figure of £2,917,000, and this, being mainly due to the cash movements at the turn of the year at a time of exceptional trade activity, was naturally followed by a bigger reflux than usual. (The Bank return happened to come close to the 1st of January.) There was probably a residue of reflux due to dear money, but how great it was it is impossible to say. It may be remarked that from the 20th February, 1901, when the reflux ended, to the 5th June interior demand reached the high total of £5,497,000 though Bank rate remained up at 4 per cent. the whole time.

For the whole year (5th December, 1900, to 4th December, 1901) interior demand was, as we have seen, at the relatively low level of £2,975,000. On the other hand in the following year (to 3rd December, 1902) it rose to £7,920,000. This is hardly to be explained as a result of cheap money, for Bank rate averaged 3·33 per cent. The second half of the year, with an average Bank rate a fraction higher than in the second half of the preceding year, yet experienced an interior demand of £5,821,000 as compared with £1,714,000.

Whatever the causes of this rather anomalous increase of interior demand may have been, it did not last. The total for 1903 was £2,559,000, and for 1904 it became a negative quantity, there being a net reflux of £2,126,000. That was the first time there had been a net reflux in any complete twelve months since 1887. ·

The year 1904 corresponded to the worst point of the depression. The unemployment percentage for the year however was only 6, and, if that is to be taken as the criterion, it was the mildest depression that had occurred since the statistics began. On the other hand the wage index fell from 179 in 1900 and 1901 to 176 in 1904.

BANK RATE AND GOLD, 1905–8

The reflux of currency in 1904 combined with substantial imports of gold to raise the reserve to £30,856,000 on the 8th March, 1905, and Bank rate, having been 3 per cent. since April, 1904, was reduced to 2½. In fact it did not rise above 3 per cent. till the 28th September, 1905, when there had been seventeen months of uninterrupted cheap money. The year 1905 was marked by the first evidences of recovery, the unemployment percentage falling to 5, and the wholesale price index showing a slight upward tendency. Interior demand was £4,332,000.

The next year, 1906, was one of activity. For the first nine months Bank rate was at 3½ or 4 per cent. The seasonal interior demand in the summer months reached a high figure, but it was covered by substantial imports of gold. In September, 1906, however, there arose an intense demand for gold for exportation to the United States, the exports thither in the months of September and October being £7,171,000. In four weeks the reserve fell from £24,762,000 to £18,290,000 (12th September to 10th October), and Bank rate was raised to 5 and then to 6 per cent. (19th October). Large imports of gold followed, and in the early months of 1907 Bank rate was gradually reduced, reaching 4 per cent. on the 25th April, 1907, the reserve then being £25,905,000.

As in 1906, the seasonal interior demand in the summer months of 1907 was met by imports of gold and, as in that year, the equilibrium was eventually disturbed by exports of gold ; in the four weeks to the 16th October, 1907, the net exports were £2,942,000. But meanwhile a change had begun to be felt in the state of business. The wholesale price index had risen almost continuously from 72 in the middle of 1905 to 82·4 in May, 1907. But that was the turning point ; it started to fall and in October 1907, was 78·8. The unemployment percentage gave the same warning. Having fallen to 2·8 in May, 1907, it began to rise. In July it was a shade higher than it had been twelve months before, and in October it had risen to 4·2, compared with 3·9 in October, 1906. The tendency, though it was not very pronounced, was unmistakable.

Business in Great Britain, though active, was in a sufficiently sound condition. But that was not so in the United States. Inflated speculative positions had grown up in that country, and the fall in commodity prices found out their weaknesses.

On the 22nd October came the failure of the Knickerbocker Trust in New York, which heralded one of the greatest of American crises. Then quickly followed not only other important failures, but a general suspension of cash payments by the entire American banking system. There appeared a premium on gold, which at times rose as high as 4 per cent. And, in consequence of the peculiarly rigid system of statutory reserve proportions then obtaining in the United States, there was an insistent demand for gold even at the price so augmented. In fact the exchange quoted in New York on London *in terms of gold* fell to 4·78, whereas the normal gold import point may be put at 4·84 or a little less.

Enormous exports of gold from England to the United States followed. The net exports in the week ending the 6th November were £6,265,000. Bank rate was put up to 5½ per cent. on the 31st October, 6 on the 4th November and 7 on the 7th November. That was the first time it had

risen above 6 per cent. since 1873. The reserve on the 6th November was £17,695,000. In that critical week there had been a reflux of no less than £3,126,000 to set against the loss of gold by export. At first sight that might be thought to be a renewed experience of the power of dear money to attract money from the country. But there was no preceding period of cheap money, for Bank rate had been at 4½ per cent. since the middle of August, 1907, and had not been below 4 since September, 1906. It is more likely that this reflux was the result of deliberate action by the joint-stock banks, and sprang from a desire to enable the Bank of England to avoid a further rise of Bank rate. If so, it was evidence of the growing spirit of solidarity and co-operation in the English banking world. The division of any London bank's cash between cash in hand and cash at the Bank of England is largely a matter of custom, and the latter portion can be strengthened substantially at the expense of the former without any serious risk of inconvenience. It would not be difficult in the conditions of 1907 for the principal banks between them to transfer £3,000,000 from their own vaults to the Bank of England, and, if an advance of Bank rate was thereby avoided, it would be well worth while. Even in 1866 the London banks had co-operated in this way to enable the Bank of England to avoid exceeding the fiduciary limit.

The 7 per cent. Bank rate was the signal for an inflow of gold from all quarters. The Governor of the Bank, when giving evidence before the American Monetary Commission in 1908, said that gold was attracted from twenty-four different countries (including British possessions). An analysis of the gold imports of November and December, 1907, shows however that the number of countries which made any considerable contribution was really very limited. Of £19,000,000 imported £6½ millions came from the gold producing countries in Australia and Africa, £7 millions from Germany and £3½ millions from France. All the others together only contributed £2,000,000, though it must not be forgotten that gold to the amount of

£2,500,000 released by India was equivalent to a further import.

Germany, France and India were the principal sources from which the gold came. Germany had a higher Bank rate than England, but a state of things approximating to a flight from the currency developed there. The exchange on London rose at one moment to 20·60, being well above the gold export point. That implied a reluctance to part with gold, though it was stated that the Reichsbank placed no obstacles in the way, and the reluctance was on the part of the commercial banks. However that may be, enough gold was allowed to be taken for export to bring down the exchange to 20·53 by the beginning of December, 1907.

In the case of France the discount rate of the Bank of France was kept down to 4 per cent., and the high Bank rate in London might reasonably have been expected to attract French funds. But the Bank of France did not leave the matter to the free play of the market; it proceeded to buy bills on London on its own account to an amount which at one time reached 81 millions of francs (£3,200,000) thereby in effect releasing an equivalent amount of gold.

The release of gold by India was occasioned rather by the need for contracting the Indian currency in sympathy with the deflationary tendency in England than by any flow of funds from India to England. The American crisis itself, giving rise to extensive forced sales of goods and securities, was a powerful deflationary influence.

By the 1st January, 1908, the Bank of England's reserve had risen to £21,473,000, and Bank rate was reduced to 6 per cent. In eleven weeks successive reductions had brought it down to 3 per cent. (19th March), and the reserve was £31,279,000.

BANK RATE AND GOLD 1908–14

There followed eighteen months of cheap money. There were wide variations in the reserve, which fell at one time

below £20,000,000 in consequence of heavy exports of gold, but rose again to nearly £31,000,000 in March, 1909, without Bank rate rising above 3 per cent. A renewed fall of the reserve to £22,950,000 (13th October, 1909) was due mainly to interior demand. Bank rate was raised to 4 and 5 per cent. (21st October), and the reserve was restored by net imports of £3,591,000 in the succeeding seven weeks.

This rise of Bank rate to 5 per cent. in 1909 is by no means to be compared with the spells of dear money imposed in the years 1876–8 or 1884–6. Recovery had already begun. The unemployment percentage fell from 7·9 in July, 1909, to 7·1 in October, whereas in October, 1908, it had been 9·5. The wholesale price index was rising and was 75·2 in October, 1909, comparing with 72·2 in October, 1908. Seven weeks of dear money might slow down the revival a little, but would not check it. And the experience of the succeeding years suggests that on the whole it had a salutary effect.

In 1910 the improvement was accelerated. Till October Bank rate oscillated between 3 and 4 per cent. In August, 1910, however exports of gold began on a large scale. By the end of October the outflow had reached £9½ millions, and the reserve had sunk to £22,018,000. Bank rate was raised to 4 per cent. (29th September) and 5 (20th October), and as in the previous autumn an inflow of gold followed. Unemployment in 1910 averaged no more than 4·7 per cent., the percentage in October being 4·4.

Interior demand was noticeably less in the years from 1903 to 1913 than it had been from 1889 to 1902. In 1907 it was only £4,517,000 and in the three years 1905–7 averaged only £3,956,000. In 1908 it fell to nothing, and in the years of recovery, 1909–11, it averaged only £5,270,000. Unemployment did not fall as low in 1906 or 1907 as in 1898–1900, and in 1908 and 1909 it was higher than in 1893. The rise in wages from 1890 to 1900 was 10 per cent., whereas from 1900 to 1907 it was only 6 per cent. Professor Bowley has estimated the national wage-bill

year by year from 1880 to 1914, and shows the following
results for years of maxima :

	£ millions.
1883	486
1890	586
1900	726
1907	779

Thus the increase from 1890 to 1900 was £140 millions
or 23·9 per cent., while from 1900 to 1907 it was only £53
millions or 7·3 per cent.   His estimate for 1913 was £857
millions, showing an increase of 10 per cent., and for 1913
we have the big interior demand of £9,246,000.   The wage
index had risen to 197 and unemployment had fallen to
2·1 per cent.

After the brief rise to 5 per cent. in October, 1910, Bank
rate reverted to 4 per cent. (26th January, 1911) and
remained at 3 to 4 per cent. till October, 1912.   By that
time activity had reached its full extent.   Unemployment
was 2 per cent., and the wholesale price index was 85·8.
Though the reserve was high, £27,388,000, Bank rate was
raised to 5 per cent. on the 17th October, 1912.   That was
due perhaps rather to the outbreak of the Balkan War
than to a far-sighted intention to prevent the expansion of
business from going too far.   But, whatever the motive,
the results were highly beneficial.   There followed a period
of steady and solidly founded activity free from any
inflationary tendency, and Bank rate remained at 4½ or 5
per cent. for fifteen months.   For the first time since 1825
a period of active trade was kept in control without a rise
of Bank rate above 5 per cent.

The reserve continued to show wide fluctuations.   Seasonal movements had become very great, the difference
between the maximum reserve and the minimum in a year
sometimes exceeding £10,000,000.   Not only did the big
seasonal reflux of currency in January and February
regularly recur, but from about 1890 a marked seasonal
fluctuation in the exports of gold becomes distinguishable.

There was a regular tendency towards increased exports in the autumn, the months September to November usually showing a substantial net loss by export, though a net loss on the whole year was very exceptional. There was a corresponding tendency towards a seasonal rise in Bank rate. This may seem rather irrational, for if the decline in the reserve was merely seasonal a recovery would follow and there was no need to correct it. But the seasonal movements might become so great as hardly to be manageable consistently with the system of a fixed fiduciary issue, and, if there was a danger of that, an adjustment of Bank rate to counteract them would be a prudent measure. From 1899 onwards an autumnal rise of Bank rate (occasionally as late as the early winter) becomes a regular institution. Only in the two years of depression, 1904 and 1908, did no such rise occur. Both in 1912 and 1913 the rate rose to 5 per cent. in October, but in between the rate only fell to 4½.

These seasonal applications of dear money could only take effect by attracting foreign money, for the attraction of currency from the country to London had ceased to have any importance. The seasonal drain of currency was an international matter ; it was partly attributable to crop-moving and partly to the turn of the year. In so far as the demand for gold in London was associated with a demand in foreign centres the rise in the Bank of England's rate would be met by a corresponding rise in foreign rates. But that did not mean that the rise was of no effect at all. There would usually be some foreign centres that could spare gold, and would acquiesce in exports or (more probably) in a suspension of imports. For it was a time of superabundant gold, when many countries were accumulating reserves, and gold might be temporarily diverted from some of them with very little strain.

And it would be possible to justify the seasonal variations of Bank rate on broader grounds. The whole basis of credit regulation was empirical ; it was determined by the gold position. Now it was difficult to judge of the gold position in the midst of a big seasonal movement. A mere

comparison with previous years at the same time of year would throw little light on the problem, for the rate of progress of seasonal movements may vary greatly from year to year. It is when a seasonal movement has exhausted itself that the situation becomes comparatively clear. Apart from the cash movements concentrated at the actual turn of the year, the main part of interior demand was usually about completed early in the autumn. So it was possible to judge towards the end of September or the beginning of October whether the state of the reserve was such as to require a turn of the screw. The interior demand at the end of December always had to be allowed for, but it was limited and compressed into a short period. Though the reserve usually fell lower at the turn of the year than in October or November, this did not necessitate a further rise of Bank rate because it had already been taken into consideration.

When the seasonal reflux in January and February seemed satisfactorily large and rapid, Bank rate would be reduced. The seasonal maximum of the reserve was usually reached about the beginning of March, but the time of seasonally lowest Bank rate varied much more than that of the seasonally highest. The reflux in the early months of the year was rather in the nature of a reaction from the interior demand in the preceding year than an indicator of conditions in the future. Consequently the reductions of Bank rate were more tentative and less guided by policy than the subsequent rises.

The year 1914 opened with a big seasonal reflux of currency, which with substantial net imports raised the reserve to £33,884,000 (28th January). Bank rate, which had stood at 5 per cent. since the 2nd October, 1913, was brought down in the space of three weeks to 3. This reversion to cheap money was a sign of slackening business. Unemployment was still at a low figure, but a little higher than in 1913. By June, 1914, the last complete month before the crisis which accompanied the outbreak of war, the setback to business had made but slight progress, unemployment in that month being only 2·4 per cent.

CHAPTER IV

BANK RATE AND DEFLATION, 1914-32

THE WAR CRISIS, 1914

BANK rate had been at 3 per cent. for six months, when the Austro-Hungarian ultimatum to Serbia began to disturb markets at the end of July, 1914. As the crisis developed, the source of trouble turned out to be the position of Great Britain as an international short-term creditor, in virtue of the London acceptance business. Bills on London had been accepted on behalf of traders all over the world, who had assumed the obligation to remit funds to the accepting houses or banks in London in time to meet the bills. The approach of war caused a sudden fear that the delicate exchange mechanism on which these remittances depended might be interrupted. There was a rush to acquire funds in London, and on the 28th July, the day when hostilities actually began between Austria-Hungary and Serbia, the demand for sterling exchange, especially from the United States, attained such a magnitude that the foreign exchange market broke down. An important contributory cause of the breakdown was the danger of transporting gold by sea under war conditions and the impossibility of arranging insurance against war risks, which had become imminent.

This failure of the foreign exchanges hit the London credit system in a vital part. The great merchant bankers depended on punctual remittances from their oversea clients for the means of meeting their acceptances. Their capital was ample to provide a guarantee fund against any occasional default, but was quite inadequate to cope with a complete breakdown. The City was suddenly confronted with the prospect of a general suspension among the very names which were regarded by the discount market as the most unexceptionable.

The pick of the bills on which the call money, the

second line reserve of the joint-stock banks, was secured, were suddenly brought under suspicion. The banks began to safeguard themselves against loss by calling in their loans, and the discount houses were driven to the Bank of England. The Bank continued to discount the bills without demur, and at first, on Thursday, the 30th July, merely raised its rate from 3 to 4 per cent. It was the next day, Friday, the 31st July, that saw crisis grow into panic. The urgent need for sterling had led to a flood of sales on the Stock Exchange at a time when the jobbers, bewildered by the imminence of war, had no idea how far to mark down prices, and were unwilling to buy anything on any terms. On the Friday morning it was hastily decided that the Stock Exchange should be closed. The two markets in which the banks lent money at call or for short periods and on which they depended for raising cash, the discount market and the Stock Exchange, were thus both in a state of prostration.

So long as the Bank of England would discount bills, it was still possible to call money from the discount houses. The pressure on the Bank for discounts suddenly became overwhelming. On the Friday afternoon Bank rate was raised from 4 to 8 per cent. The next day, Saturday the 1st August, the Bank received a letter from the Government promising indemnifying legislation if the fiduciary limit was exceeded, and requiring as a condition a 10 per cent. Bank rate. No public announcement of the existence of the letter was made at the time, but Bank rate was raised to 10 per cent.

But something more than the traditional crisis lette was needed. The greatest names known to Lombarc Street were threatened with default and failure. The breakdown of the foreign exchange market was a temporary difficulty, but, even when that market was revived, who could say what the effect of war on the accepting houses would be, or how many of their clients in countries with which Great Britain might soon be at war would be either able or willing to remit money in discharge of their obligations?

For such an emergency there was no precedent. The whole body of accepting houses could not be relegated to insolvency like Overend, Gurney and Company in 1866. The entire resources of the City would have been inadequate to give a collective guarantee such as was accorded to Barings in 1890. Special measures by Government and Parliament were unavoidable.

The first step was the declaration of a moratorium for acceptors of bills of exchange on Sunday the 2nd August. It took the form of an Order-in-Council, which had no legal validity, but it was of course assumed that validating legislation would follow immediately, and it was in fact passed on Monday, the 3rd. Next three extra bank holidays were declared. Legally a bank holiday is simply a day on which bills do not mature. The 3rd August, being the first Monday in August, was an ordinary bank holiday, and the Government, having standing power under statute to declare any day a bank holiday at its discretion, declared the 4th, 5th and 6th to be bank holidays. The suspension of all banking business for these four days gave a breathing space to devise measures of relief.

The banks were in a state of panic. Acutely aware of their own insecure position, they expected their depositors to be equally panic-stricken, and they thought they must be prepared for a universal demand for currency. This danger could be guarded against either by extending the moratorium which had already been announced for bills of exchange to cover bank deposits, or alternatively by placing a sufficient supply of additional currency at the banks' disposal.

It was decided to do *both*. A general moratorium was instituted, which covered bank deposits (except savings bank deposits). And a special issue of currency notes by the Government was authorised.

The issue of currency notes was provided for by the Currency and Bank Notes Act, which became law on the 6th August, 1914. The Act included a section (with retrospective effect) empowering the Government to

authorise the issue of Bank notes in excess of any limit prescribed by law, thereby giving covering authority to the letter addressed to the Bank of England on the 1st August. It might have been supposed that the power thus given to the Bank of England to issue its notes without regard to the fiduciary limit ought to have sufficed for all purposes. But the kind of emergency imagined by the bankers would have required a drastic change in the practices of the Bank of England. They conceived of demands for cash that would exceed their own holdings of bills and securities, which the Bank would regard as eligible. The banks would have to depart from their long-established practice of never borrowing or selling bills, and would have to borrow direct from the Bank of England. Moreover there might be a demand for currency such as notes for denominations of five pounds and upwards would not satisfy. On the 31st July and the 1st August there had been enormous demands for gold coin, a crowd attending at the Bank of England to turn notes into sovereigns. This demand was mainly due to the action of the banks themselves in paying depositors in Bank of England notes when currency was genuinely needed for the payment of wages or holiday travelling, but it was interpreted as an indication of the character of the panic demand that was feared.

Account had also to be taken of the position in Scotland and Ireland, where the banks of issue were unwilling to see Bank of England notes of small denomination, with the advantage of being legal tender, put in circulation in competition with their own one-pound notes. They were more easily reconciled to the issue of Treasury notes.

Accordingly the Currency and Bank Notes Act authorised the issue by the Treasury of legal-tender currency notes of one pound and ten shillings. The issue was made at first by way of advances to any bank to an amount not exceeding one-fifth of the bank's deposit liabilities. The banks were to be direct borrowers, but from the Treasury, not from the Bank of England.

What rate of interest was to be charged on these advances ? Bank rate had been raised to 10 per cent. on the 1st August.   It was a principle generally accepted that the provision of any emergency currency in addition to that permissible under the Bank Charter Act should be subject to a deterrent rate of interest as a safeguard against inflation. The advances of currency notes were in substitution for the advances that would otherwise have been made by the Bank of England, and there was no reason why they should not be made at the same rate.   It was decided that they should be made at Bank rate.

But at the same time the imposition of so high a rate as 10 per cent. was questioned.   The letter of 1st August had simply followed precedent.   But the policy and the reasoning which had gone to make the precedents of 1857 and 1866 had faded from memory.   It was decided to reduce Bank rate to 6 per cent. on the 7th August when the banks re-opened, and then on the next day to 5 per cent. The 10 per cent. rate had been in operation only for one working day.

As it turned out, there never was a time when safeguards against inflation were more urgently needed.   But it by no means follows that the continuance of a 10 per cent. Bank rate would have been the right measure to rely on. The danger of inflation arose at that stage not from the issue of currency notes but from certain other financial operations.   Of these the most important were those for dealing with the bills of exchange out of which the crisis had arisen, the pre-moratorium bills.   The moratorium which gave the acceptors of these bills a temporary relief was the cause of great dislocation of business and could not be indefinitely prolonged.   Something had to be done to provide for the bills before the moratorium could be withdrawn.   It became clear that nothing less than a Government guarantee could meet the situation.   This was given at first in the form of a guarantee of the bills when discounted by the Bank of England.   That committed the Government to ensuring that the bills would be

met on maturity, and there followed an arrangement by which the Bank of England was to advance to acceptors the funds for paying off the bills on maturity, and the Government guaranteed these advances. The acceptors were to pay interest on the advances but the principal was only to become due a year after the end of the war. The effect was to extinguish the bills with all the contingent liabilities attaching to drawers and endorsers, and leave outstanding only the liabilities of the acceptors to the Bank of England, and the Government guarantee of those liabilities. As a measure for relieving business from an intolerable embarrassment this was effective, but it had the incidental effect of swelling the assets and therefore the liabilities of the Bank of England to an unprecedented volume. From £33,600,000 on the 22nd July securities, other than Government, held by the Bank rose to £121,800,000 on the 2nd September. The Government was borrowing from the Bank for the initial expenses of the war, and the total of private deposits at the Bank rose from £42,200,000 to £133,800,000. Securities and deposits both continued at a high level and the 5 per cent. Bank rate became completely ineffective. In the early months of 1915 the market rate of discount even fell below 2 per cent. As mentioned above (pp. 57–60), it is the practice of the joint-stock banks to base their charges for loans and overdrafts on Bank rate, but had Bank rate remained at 10 per cent in 1914 it is hardly conceivable that they would have charged 10½ or 11 per cent. to their customers when they were flooded with redundant cash ; a penal Bank rate at such a level would soon have become inoperative.

On the other hand if inflationary financial expedients had been avoided, and the 10 per cent. Bank rate had been effective, it would not have been needed long. Even as it was there was a big inflow of gold. Up to the outbreak of war business had been tending towards depression, and dear money would have accentuated that tendency. Eventually, even if the loading up of the Bank of England with pre-moratorium bills had been avoided, the strain of

Government borrowing would probably have given rise to some degree of inflation, but at a later stage.

There was no trace of panic among bank depositors, but the interior demand for currency in the first two or three weeks of the war was enormous. That was partly due to the precautions of the banks themselves, and partly to real additional needs for currency arising out of mobilisation and warlike preparations. The reserve fell from £26,875,000 on the 29th July to £9,967,000 on the 1st August (the last working day when the return was issued on Thursday, the 6th August), and practically the whole of this reduction of £16,908,000 may be attributed to interior demand. On the 7th and 8th of August the fiduciary limit was exceeded by an amount at the maximum of £3,043,000. Currency notes to an amount exceeding £4,000,000 were already available, and big imports of gold were arriving, so that at that time the interior demand since the 29th July must have been nearer £40,000,000 than £30,000,000. By the 19th August, when the first formal return of currency notes disclosed a net issue of £16,696,000, the interior demand since the 29th July had been £33,797,000, and had fallen a little.

Currency notes had already begun to come back from circulation. But it was not reasonable to insist that the advances by which the currency notes had been issued to the banks should only be repaid in currency notes. Repayment could hardly be refused from a bank which had a credit balance available at the Bank of England, but which might find it exceedingly difficult to collect an adequate sum of currency notes from circulation among the public. Repayment in such circumstances was accepted, and as the rediscounting of pre-moratorium bills was placing enormous sums of superfluous cash at the disposal of the banks, the original advances were soon extinguished, and the currency notes left outstanding in circulation.

In April, 1915, steps were taken by the Government and the Bank of England to make Bank rate effective. The Government was borrowing enormous sums which, in the

intervals between the great War Loans, were raised by additions to the floating debt. The Bank proceeded to borrow at call in the discount market (like a bill-broker) all sums offering at a fixed rate of interest and relent the money so raised to the Government. At the same time the Government, instead of putting Treasury bills up to competitive tender offered them without any limit of total amount to the market at a fixed rate of discount. The effect was to prevent the rates quoted in the discount market for call money and bills falling below these fixed rates. If the rates offered failed to attract as much money as the Government needed, the deficiency was made good by advances from the Bank of England (Ways and Means advances) which injected a fresh supply of money into the market and made it more disposed to lend. Thus the market was really governed by the Treasury bill rate, and Bank rate was practically superseded by it. This system continued (with one or two short interruptions) throughout the war and till April, 1921.

At first the Treasury bill rate was low, 2¾ per cent., but after the big 4½ per cent. War Loan of July, 1915, the Treasury bill rate was raised to 4½ per cent.

But while the war lasted the short-term rate of interest had but little significance. Other forces were at work on the one hand aggravating and on the other limiting inflation. The industries supplying war needs and financed by the Government eventually formed a large proportion of the entire economic activity of the country. They generated a volume of demand which would have kept the other industries busy even if they had been absolutely precluded from supplementing their working capital by borrowing at all. Bank rate remained at 5 per cent. except for one experimental advance to 6 per cent. in 1916–7.

THE POST-WAR INFLATION

The transition of the money market to peace conditions may be placed at the end of March, 1919, when the advances

from the United States Treasury ceased, and with them the pegging of the exchange on New York at 4·76½. The prohibition of the export of gold on the 1st April, 1919, marked the formal abandonment of the gold standard and opened the way to renewed inflation. Bank rate was still 5 per cent., but the market was governed by the Treasury bill rate which was 3½ per cent. In June, 1919, with the idea of floating the Victory and Funding loans in a tide of cheap money, the sale of Treasury bills was suspended, and for the time being the day to day financial requirements of the Government were met with money borrowed at call through the Bank of England at 3 per cent.

Nothing was being done to stem the flood of inflation. It was becoming clear that inflation was not due exclusively to the embarrassments of Government finance. There was an enormous expansion of bank advances. Here was the same problem that had led Horsley Palmer to prescribe a rise in Bank rate in 1832, but with a difference, in that the disorder had gone past the stage of a mere loss of gold and shortage of reserves, and had taken the form of a depreciating currency and a rising price level.

Somehow or other the too lavish creation of the means of payment had to be stopped. The Cunliffe Committee had recommended a limitation of the issue of currency notes. But currency notes were drawn out by the banks against their balances at the Bank of England, and, so long as those balances could be replenished by credit operations, there was no way of preventing the issue of whatever amount of currency notes the banks chose to take.

The banks did not even have to call money from the discount market to replenish their balances ; all they had to do was to buy less Treasury bills. It was not the discount houses but the Government that was then driven to borrow from the Bank of England. It was the advances from the Bank to the Government on Ways and Means that supplied the cash foundation on which the inflationary superstructure of bank credit was being built up. Here

the rationing of credit, which had formerly been the alternative to a rise in Bank rate, and had been superseded by it after 1847, was inapplicable.

It became clear that after all Bank rate was still the clue to the problem. That did not mean that the banks could be induced to take more Treasury bills by the offer of a higher rate of discount and so to diminish the need of Ways and Means advances. However attractive Treasury bills might be, the banks would still have to keep up their cash reserves, and would not apply for more bills than would be consistent with that essential condition. But if Treasury bills were made more attractive relatively to advances to traders, the banks would raise their charges for loans and overdrafts as well as for discounts, and so discourage trade borrowing.

In October, 1919, the Treasury bill rate was raised from 3½ to 4½ per cent., Bank rate remaining at 5 per cent. ; on the 6th November it was raised to 5½ and Bank rate to 6 per cent. In December, 1919, a Treasury Minute appeared limiting the fiduciary issue of currency notes.

DEFLATION, 1920–2

There was perhaps a pause in the progress of inflation, but no more than a pause. In March, 1920, the pace was as great as ever. In April Bank rate was raised to 7 per cent. and the Treasury bill rate to 6½. And then at last the corner was turned. The inflated prices of commodities began to subside, and presently the feverish activity of industry began to abate. By November, 1920, the symptoms of trade depression became clearly visible. Horsley Palmer's corrective had been applied, and the appropriate sequence of events occurred, the limitation of transactions, the fall of prices, the disemployment of labour—but not the recovery of the foreign exchanges, at any rate of the exchange on the one remaining gold currency, the American dollar. For the United States had simultaneously had recourse to Horsley Palmer's remedy, and the rediscount

rate of the Federal Reserve Banks had been raised to 6 and 7 per cent., close in the wake of the Bank of England's rate.   The compression of the consumers' income in Great Britain failed to raise the dollar value of the pound, because the compression of the consumers' income in the United States was proceeding even faster.   Each country seemed to be waiting for the other to reduce its rate first.   The 7 per cent. rate remained in force in London till April, 1921, and in New York till the following month.   So high a rate for an uninterrupted period of twelve months was a departure from all precedent.   On all previous occasions, as soon as dear money had clearly done its work, the rate had been rapidly reduced.   Often, it is true, the rate had been reduced prematurely, when a reflux of currency to the reserve had been too easily brought about, and on such occasions a further dose of dear money had been found necessary, as in 1873.   In 1920 it was justifiable to keep up Bank rate so long as there was any uncertainty whether inflation had been successfully checked.   But even in the late summer of 1920 there was no real doubt that this was so, and by November, 1920, it was abundantly clear that the danger was in the opposite direction, and was that of excessive deflation.

Even when the rate was lowered from 7 per cent., it was only by slow and cautious steps of ½ per cent. at a time at considerable intervals, and the 3 per cent. level, which may be regarded as the upper limit of cheap money, was not reached till the 13th July, 1922.

This tremendous measure of deflation was imposed at a time when wages were more or less fluid, being based in many industries on a cost of living index.   The compression of the consumers' income took effect in reductions of wages to an extent that had never before been practicable. The average reduction of wages was eventually 36 per cent. Nevertheless the percentage of unemployment among trade unions far outstripped all previous records, rising to 15·2 per cent. in 1922.   The percentage among work people insured against unemployment (which becomes

available at the end of 1921) rose in January 1922 to 17·7. In the summer of 1922 revival became perceptible, and by March, 1924, the unemployment percentage among insured work people had fallen below 10 per cent.

THE GOLD STANDARD AND DEAR MONEY

But meanwhile cheap money had come to an end. Bank rate had been raised to 4 per cent. in July, 1923. It had not been made effective, and revival, though it had slowed down, had not stopped. In July, 1924, however, the 4 per cent. Bank rate was made effective, and what was perhaps a graver threat to revival, the prospect of a return of the pound to gold parity came clearly into sight. The expectation of this happening was itself a deflationary influence. Revival stopped. At the beginning of March, 1925, Bank rate was raised to 5 per cent. With an unemployment percentage of eleven this imposition of dear money was another startling departure from earlier practice. A 5 per cent. rate had ordinarily been imposed only at times of high activity. An exception, and not an encouraging one, is to be found in the years of gold scarcity from 1875 to 1886, when the rate was several times raised to 5 per cent. under conditions of depression, and when the depression became all the more protracted and intense. The rise of Bank rate to 5 per cent. in 1925 was the beginning of a continuous regime of dear money lasting with little relief for five years. There was an interval of nine weeks at 4 per cent. in the autumn of 1925, but otherwise the rate remained at either 4½ or 5 per cent. till still higher rates were imposed in 1929.

The gold standard was re-established at the end of April, 1925, by the removal of the prohibition on the export of gold, that had been in force since 1919. Credits had been arranged in favour of the Bank of England in New York to guard against a possibly excessive outflow of gold. As it turned out, there was in the first instance no considerable outflow, and soon there was an inflow which raised the

gold in the Bank of England from £154,000,000 on the 29th April to £162,600,000 on the 5th August.

Bank rate ceased to be effective, the market rate of discount on three-month bills falling gradually from 4⅝ per cent. in May to under 4 per cent., and Bank rate was reduced to 4½ (6th August). In spite of some loss of gold the market rate slipped down further, and on the 1st October, 1925, Bank rate was reduced to 4 per cent.

Sir Ernest Harvey had something to say as to the course of events in November, 1925, in the evidence he gave before the Macmillan Committee. (Question 7590.) " The market," he said, " decided, so it appeared, to leave the Treasury bills rather severely alone. We had difficulty for a week or two, the Bank had to come to the rescue to cover the amounts required, efforts were made to reassure the market, but without success, and eventually at the end of the month, the last week, the amount which the Bank had to provide in order to cover the required amount of tenders was very substantial. . . .

"Finally we were compelled, simply in order to get the bills taken up, and to avoid our being driven into a very difficult position by reason of the large additions of credit that we were having to create, to raise the rate from 4 per cent. to 5 per cent."

The only explanation that Sir Ernest Harvey gave of the reluctance of the market to take Treasury bills was that gold had been lost, and " there were apprehensions of a rise in the New York rate." The implication is, no doubt, that the market expected on these grounds that the discount rate in London would rise, and bills could then be obtained on better terms.

But the Bank of England had not been leaving the market alone. It reduced its holding of Government securities to an unusually low level in October, 1925 (£28·8 millions on the 14th) and the market was compelled to borrow from it. The effect is seen in the weekly returns of Treasury bill tenders :

TREASURY BILL TENDERS, 1925

	Offered £ millions	Applied for £ millions	Average Rate
2nd October	... 45	65·9	3·36
9th October	... 40	66·4	3·32
16th October	... 35	41·9	3·63
23rd October	... 40	48·4	.3·74
30th October	... 40	49·2	3·81
6th November	... 45	47·9	3·91
13th November	... 40	44·8	3·87
20th November	... 40	43·1	3·92
27th November	... 45	47·4	3·95

The Bank in fact had been following the traditional procedure in reinforcing the tendency of an outflow of gold to make Bank rate effective by reducing its holding of securities. This procedure was always interpreted by the market as the prelude to a rise of Bank rate. But in any case, when the Bank succeeded during October in forcing the market to borrow from it, it was most natural that the discount houses should " leave Treasury bills severely alone " rather than borrow at a half per cent. above Bank rate (the rate charged for advances) in order to take them.

The return to the gold standard, with the attendant reimposition of dear money, had interrupted the progress of recovery from the severe depression of 1922. It may well have been the case that a continued relaxation of credit at the end of 1925 would have meant continued exports of gold. And the banks and the money market had the power of maintaining their cash in spite of the losses of gold by abstaining from buying Treasury bills.

But it is not to be inferred that deflationary measures were unavoidable. We explored above (Chapter II) the different ways in which a rise of Bank rate may strengthen the reserve position. One of these, the attraction of currency from the provinces, had ceased to be relevant ; even had it

occurred, it would only have strengthened the reserve in the Banking Department, whereas in 1925 attention was concentrated on the gold holding. The attraction of funds from abroad for temporary investment was still operative, and indeed the Bank appear to have placed too much reliance on this result. Over short periods the movements induced may well be considerable,· and it is not unlikely that the inflow of gold up to August, 1925, was caused in this way. But the relief so obtained is delusive, because as soon as Bank rate is reduced the foreign funds will be withdrawn, and that, no doubt, was the explanation of the loss of gold that troubled the Bank in October and November, 1925.

The true efficacy of dear money as a support to the gold position was to be found first in the deflationary effect on this country, which made the balance of payments favourable by compressing the consumers' income, and eventually, when the deflationary tendency spread to other countries, in the general reflux of gold coin from active circulation. But this second process no longer worked when the active circulation of gold coin had been almost everywhere abandoned. London's power as an international centre was not quite so unchallenged as in the nineteenth century, for New York had gained in importance as a rival centre. Yet the power of London remained great, and when the Bank of England restricted credit and adopted dear money, deflation still tended to sp ead to other countries. But deflation abroad no longer brought additional supplies of gold to the surface ; instead it would simply reduce the note circulation and improve a reserve ratio to which in most countries very little significance was attached.

In fact deflation on an international scale, instead of bringing a general relief of tension, *counteracted* the favourable effect of deflation in Great Britain on the British balance of payments.

The advance of Bank rate to 5 per cent. in March, 1925, supervened on a condition of things which promised to

bring the pound sterling gently and smoothly to par with the dollar without any effort at all. Credit was expanding and the price level in the United States, which may be taken as indicating the price level in terms of gold, was rising. This expansive tendency came abruptly to an end. The rediscount rate, it is true, was raised in New York, but only to 3½ per cent., and till 1928 the American Federal Reserve Bank adhered to moderate rediscount rates and a policy of credit relaxation. The deflationary tendency in the gold standard world was due to the continuance of dear money in London. In British industry unemployment remained practically undiminished, fluctuating about a mean of 10 or 11 per cent.

In 1927 two new developments opened up some prospect of relief. In the first place the acquisition of an enormous volume of bills on London and New York by the Bank of France in connection with the stabilisation of the franc tended to make Bank rate ineffective, and secondly the American Federal Reserve Banks intensified their policy of credit relaxation, reinforcing a low rediscount rate by open market purchases of securities. In April, 1927, the market rate of discount fell to 4 per cent. and Bank rate was reduced to 4½ (having been at 5 for sixteen months).

In that month the Bank of France repaid to the Bank of England the balance, amounting to £33,000,000, of the advance that had been made by the latter to it during the war. The sudden extinction of securities to that amount in the Bank of England's balance sheet enabled the Bank to gain control of the market, and for the remainder of the year 1927 the 4½ per cent. Bank rate was made effective, the market rate of discount varying between 4·29 and 4·38 per cent.

In the early part of 1928 the effect of accentuated credit relaxation in the United States began to be felt. The Bank of England's gold increased from £149½ millions in December, 1927, to £172 millions in July, 1928, and the market rate dropped to 3·8 per cent. (June, 1928).

But by that time there had already been a change of

policy in the United States. The rediscount rate in New
York was raised to 5 per cent. (13th July, 1928). There
was an end of easy credit. And soon there followed a
change in the policy of the Bank of France. Having
accumulated foreign exchange to an amount of no less than
£260 millions, in the years 1927 and 1928, the Bank of
France early in 1929 transformed £50 millions of this into
gold, and thereafter ceased to accumulate foreign exchange
and accumulated gold instead.[1]

By the beginning of February, 1929, the gold in the
Bank of England had fallen below £150 millions. Bank
rate rose to 5½ per cent. " We were forced to go up," said
Sir Ernest Harvey to the Macmillan Committee. (Question
7597.) " We were partly actuated by the need for protecting our own immediate position, and I will not say that
there was not a hope in our minds that possibly our action
might have some effect on sentiment in Wall Street." " I
think," he added, " that the action which the Bank
took then in making it evident to everybody that they were
prepared to go to whatever rate was necessary to protect
this market was certainly a contributory factor in breaking
the speculative boom which was doing so much damage,
not only to us but to all other European countries."

This sounds as if it meant co-operation in the policy of
stopping speculation by stopping prosperity. And, whatever the motive may have been, the effect of dear money
could not fail to be in that direction. For a deflationary
policy in the United States there was at the time every
justification. An orgy of speculation, such as had been
raging in Wall Street ever since 1926 was only too apt to
cause inflation. There was a speculative supplement to
the resources of the investment market, involving a release
of cash, and the credit restriction imposed by the Federal
Reserve Banks in 1928 was really needed to prevent a
dangerous vicious circle of inflation developing.

Throughout these years the existence of depression in
England had been a moderating influence in America. And

[1] See my *Art of Central Banking*, pp. 30–40 and 213–20.

after February, 1929, the intensification of that depression reinforced the moderating influence.

But British industry could ill afford to undergo this further ordeal.

John and Sam kept house together. John was in bed with pneumonia; Sam had a slight head-ache after a debauch. John volunteered to go out in a snow-storm to the druggist to get some aspirins for Sam.

But in view of the attitude of the Bank of England's representatives before the Macmillan Committee, when they regarded the deflationary effect of dear money as a very secondary matter, Sir Ernest Harvey's statement must rather be interpreted to mean that the high Bank rate in London was intended to attract away funds that would otherwise have been used for speculation in New York. Indeed in the course of the statement from which the foregoing quotations come Sir Ernest Harvey said : " We were contending not with an official rate normally below our own, but with a real effective rate in New York which was always higher, and sometimes very much higher, than our own rate."

As a matter of fact the idea, so prevalent at the time, that the high rates on call money and time money lent to the New York Stock Exchange were attracting large sums from Europe for temporary investment was as baseless as the idea that the speculation was resulting in a vast inflow of funds from European speculators and investors for the purchase of American shares. Whatever the magnitude of these operations may have been, the available statistics show that both in 1928 and in 1929 the United States was on balance an exporter of capital, alike for long-term and for short-term investment.

The United States did nevertheless absorb gold in 1929 on a considerable scale. But the principal strain on the gold position was attributable to France. France absorbed no less than £75,000,000 in the year. The French absorption, being due to the re-stocking of the country with currency after the inflation which culminated in 1926,

was quite insensitive to credit conditions in London. The American absorption was due to the measures of credit restriction resorted to by the Federal Reserve Banks. By July, 1929, their " open market assets " (Government securities and acceptances) had been reduced to $222 millions in comparison with $702 in the preceding January, and the amount of rediscounts had been high ever since the rate was raised to 5 per cent. in July, 1928. This restrictive policy was taking effect on American industry, which showed a slackening tendency from July, 1929, onwards. There was little hope of making any appreciable impression on the American absorption of gold in these circumstances.

The conclusion to be drawn is that the Bank of England ought to have been willing *to let gold go*. It ought in fact to have been willing to do so at any time since the return to the gold standard. If it could only retain its gold by a recourse to deflationary measures, and could not otherwise maintain the gold standard, then either the return to the gold standard was premature or the restoration .of the former parity was a mistake. It is, I think, not unreasonable to hold that a policy of cheap money and credit relaxation from the beginning would have had a favourable effect on economic activity throughout the world in 1925, and would have made the task of retaining the Bank of England's gold quite easy. But even if that had not been so, and credit relaxation had been found to involve a serious outflow of gold, an acquiescence in that outflow would have afforded the best prospect of maintaining the gold standard.[1]

Even in 1929 it was not too late. Though the revival of activity that had been interrupted in 1924 had never been really resumed, British industry in the years 1927–9 had been in a state of uneasy equilibrium. It was free from the devastating effects of a vicious circle of deflation, and would probably have been as amenable to measures of relaxation as it proved to be to those of restriction.

[1] See my evidence before the Macmillan Committee (Questions 4166–70, 4207–15, 4249–88 and 4355–68), and my *Art of Central Banking* (pp. 233–40).

The decisive part played by gold at that time was recognised by the Bank of England. The Governor of the Bank, in giving evidence before the Macmillan Committee (Questions 3490-3), advocated international co-operation "to pursue a common monetary policy and do away with the struggle for gold." Asked by Lord Macmillan how that would help our internal position, he explained that " had it not been for the struggle for gold over the last few years . . . we would not have had anything like the difficulties in maintaining the exchange that there have been," and " I think the internal situation would have been much easier over the last few years if the rate had been x per cent. instead of y per cent., say 4 per cent. instead of 6 per cent."

" You mean there would have been less unemployment? "

—" I think there would."

Like James Morris in 1848 Mr. Norman found himself agreeing that the disemployment of labour might be the price paid for the convertibility of the currency.

For a time after the advance of Bank rate to $5\frac{1}{2}$ per cent. in February, 1929, there was an inflow of gold. The gold in the Bank reached £163 millions in June, but there followed a renewed and rapid outflow which brought it down to £129 millions at the beginning of October, 1929.

As in November, 1925, the loss of gold made Bank rate effective. " The market," said Sir Ernest Harvey, " which often displays not unnaturally a rather nervous disposition at such times, applied very sparingly for new [Treasury] bills. In three successive weeks we were faced with the necessity of taking up substantial amounts of bills because the tenders were deficient. . . . At the same time in order to hold the position, and in order to withdraw again some of the credit that we had been forced to create, we had been under the necessity of selling other assets very heavily."

And so the rate went up to $6\frac{1}{2}$ per cent. (26th September, 1929).

The seeds of disaster had already been sown. As I have said, a reaction from the industrial activity which had prevailed in the United States had already become per-

ceptible in July, 1929. The Wall Street crisis in October, 1929, at once accelerated the movement towards depression. In England, where industry had been persistently impervious to the contagion of American activity in the preceding years, the prospect of a depression redoubled by the contagion of depression in America was ominous in the extreme.

Yet it was only by slow steps that Bank rate was reduced. It was lowered, as in 1921 and 1922, by ½ per cent. at a time, and the transition from 6½ to 3 per cent. took six months. Three per cent. is cheap money, and perhaps the difference between 2, 2½ and 3 per cent. is not very material. But at a time of depression and unemployment and falling prices far transcending all previous experience, Bank rate was held for a year at 3 per cent. or 1 per cent. above the rate that had been thought suitable for long periods in 1894–6, 1876–7 or 1867–8.

THE CRISIS OF 1931

On the 14th May, 1931, Bank rate was reduced to 2½ per cent. By that time the strain was near breaking point. Unemployment in Great Britain was 20 per cent. Shrinking demand and falling prices had undermined the solvency of Continental industry. In the same month of May, 1931, occurred the failure of the Austrian Creditanstaldt, the beginning of the financial crisis which brought down the German banking system in July, and culminated in the suspension of the gold standard by Great Britain in September.

In the middle of July, 1931, the gold holding of the Bank of England, which had been rising for six months and was at a high level, suddenly began to fall. Bank rate was raised to 3½ per cent. on the 23rd July and to 4½ on the 30th. To raise the rate when unemployment among insured work people had risen to 22 per cent. was surely to gild the lily. If, in the language of 1848, the price of the convertibility of the note was to be a further disemployment of labour, the position had become untenable. And in fact it had.

But it was not mainly this dilemma that was the proximate cause of the flight from the pound and of the collapse of the gold standard ; it was rather the financial embarrassments of the Government. There was a section of opinion in Europe which held that the right course for the Bank of England would have been a more drastic advance of Bank rate. But the advocates of that view were thinking of a high Bank rate rather as a device for attracting foreign money than as one for compressing the consumers' income. And in face of the utter inadequacy of even the highest rate of interest that could be contemplated, reckoned over a period of a few months, to counteract the exchange risk involved in the fear of a depreciation of the pound, that could hardly be anything but a secondary influence.

The equilibrium of the budget had been destroyed by the combined effects of a growing expenditure on unemployment relief and a shrinking national income. The source of the trouble was the rise in the purchasing power of gold in world markets, or in other words the fall in the prices of commodities in terms of gold. When the purchasing power of gold rose by a half, the purchasing power of every currency unit that was convertible into gold had to be raised in that proportion.

A given volume of economic activity would therefore represent one-third less in money. A compression of the consumers' income on this scale was more than Great Britain, starting from a state of depression in 1929, could compass. Unemployment and the decline of taxable capacity were merely the two most conspicuous symptoms of a condition of things that was bringing the whole economic system to the verge of a breakdown.

The National Government which came into office at the end of August, 1931, made strenuous efforts to balance the budget, but it was too late to stem the flight from the pound. On the 21st September the convertibility of the currency into gold was suspended. On that day Bank rate was raised to 6 per cent. Once the gold standard was

suspended, there could be no doubt of the purpose of that step. In face of the exchange risk the high rate could not possibly attract foreign money.   It could only be intended as a safeguard against inflation.   Fantastic fears of inflation were expressed.   That was to cry, Fire, Fire, in Noah's Flood.   It is *after* depression and unemployment have subsided that inflation becomes dangerous.

The 6 per cent. Bank rate did not altogether prevent the rebound of industry when released from the gold standard.   But the depreciation of the pound was so restricted that the net gain was no more than to relieve the British economic system from the further deflation arising from the continued appreciation of gold in terms of commodities after September, 1931.

The 6 per cent. rate was kept in force for five months. When it was reduced in February, 1932, the return to cheap money was effected quickly.   The slow gradations of 1921–2 and 1929–30 were not repeated.   Three per cent. was reached in nine weeks.   At the end of June the rate was reduced to 2 per cent., where it has now remained for six years.

But it was too late ; cheap money by itself was insufficient to start revival.   The vicious circle of deflation, broken for a moment by the suspension of the gold standard, had been joined again.

CHAPTER V

BANK RATE AND CONSOLS

LONG-TERM AND SHORT-TERM RATES OF INTEREST

In the foregoing chapters there has been no reference to the long-term rate of interest. In view of some recent theories, which regard Bank rate as producing its effect mainly or even exclusively through the long-term rate of interest and investment in fixed capital, this side of the subject calls for examination, and the present chapter will be devoted to an investigation of some of the statistical material bearing upon it.

It may be taken as axiomatic that the short-term rate of interest has *some* reaction on the long-term rate. Long-term and short-term loans sometimes present themselves as alternatives both to borrowers and to lenders. Banks place part of their resources in long-dated or funded securities. Traders who extend their fixed capital often have the choice of providing the funds either on the one hand through the long-term investment market, whether by an issue of shares or debentures in the capital market, or by selling securities, or by contracting a mortgage, or on the other hand through a bank advance. Banks also advance money to stock jobbers, investors, and speculators for the purchase of securities, and the sums advanced become available through the stock-market for capital purposes on the same footing as savings.

When the short-term rate of interest rises, the tendency is to deter people from resorting to bank advances for these purposes, and to induce those who have to raise funds to have recourse to selling securities or to long-term borrowing instead. But when we come to measure the inducement, we find that it is very slight. When Samuel Gurney was being examined before the Parliamentary Committee of

1848,[1] James Wilson pressed him in regard to this matter.

" Are not the prices of public funds," he asked, " both foreign funds and home funds, in a great degree regulated by the rate of interest ? "

" Much less than is supposed," was the answer.

" As money becomes scarce and dear," pursued Wilson, " does not the price of Consols and of Dutch stock and other foreign stock fall ? "

" It has its effect," conceded Gurney, " but it is by no means the only ground for variations in this matter ; for instance we have had periods when money on Consols has been worth 10 per cent. What is the effect of that ? It amounts for six weeks perhaps to 25s.[2] only in the £100. If the value of money becomes permanently high in the country it affects the value of Consols heavily ; but if it is only for a particular period it does not affect it much."

Still Wilson was not satisfied : " Last spring had not the raising of the rate of interest and the scarcity of money an immediate effect in reducing the price of all public stocks ? "

" A very slight effect," was the reply ; " if the Bank raises the rate of interest from 3 per cent. to 4 per cent., it does not affect the price of Consols many shillings in the £100, but if the value of money permanently increases, it affects prices very materially."

What Gurney meant was that the effect depended on the *time* for which the dear money was expected to last.

Suppose that at a centre where the normal short-term rate is 3 per cent. it rises to 7 per cent. If it could be foreseen that the rate would remain at 7 per cent. for three months and then drop to 3 per cent. again, the extra cost of holding a long-dated security with borrowed money would be offset by a fall of price equal to 1 per cent. (the equivalent of 4 per cent. per annum for a quarter of a year). A trader who had intended to raise a bank advance to cover some expenditure might be led by a rise of the interest on the advance from 3 to 7 per cent. to sell Government

---

[1] Questions 1867–9.

[2] 5s. in the printed report of evidence is obviously a misprint for 25s. The interest at 10 per cent. for 6¼ weeks would be 25s.

securities instead. But if the price of the Government securities fell from 100 to 99, he would not gain by doing so. A similar calculation would apply to anyone who has to choose either between long-term and short-term borrowing or between long-term and short-term lending. In practice many uncertainties have to be allowed for. A speculative element enters into the price of a security, and when the price falls some people may interpret that as a presage of a further fall rather than as a temporary movement to be recovered in the course of a few weeks or months. Nor does any one know how long a high short-term rate is going to last.

THREE-MONTHS AND SIX-MONTHS BILLS

With regard to this last matter, however, the discount market itself gives some guidance, for it quotes different rates for three-months and six-months bills. Under conditions of normal quiescence six-months bills would command a higher rate than three-months bills. To all holders of bills, especially to banks and discount houses, liquidity is a valuable quality. When a bank's deposits are payable on demand, that does not merely mean that sums to an unpredictable amount may be drawn out in currency across the counter, but that sums which are equally unpredictable and are in practice very much larger have to be met day by day through the clearing house. To meet these irregular outgoings, banks find it advisable to hold assets which turn into cash at short intervals. Short bills meet this need. Call loans to the discount market have the same function, and their liquidity depends on that of the discount houses. Six months bills are, therefore, distinctly less desirable as assets either of banks or of discount houses than three months bills. Moreover, over and above the natural disadvantages of six months bills was the circumstance that the Bank of England did not take them.

Consequently there was usually an appreciably higher rate of discount on six months bills than on three months

bills, the difference ordinarily being from ¼ to ½. But when Bank rate was high and both rates went up in sympathy with it, the three-months rate was often much more affected than the six-months rate. It was quite common for the latter rate actually to be the lower at such times. Evidently that meant that the high rate was not expected to last long. We find an extreme example of this in November, 1873, when at one time the three-months rate was 8¼ per cent. and the six-months rate 6¼. That might be interpreted to mean that the market expected the rate to be 4½ per cent. in the second half of the six months, and so, with 8¼ for the first half, to make an average of 6¼. Bank rate was then 9 per cent., and the circumstances were exceptional. But a margin of ½ per cent. was not uncommon. It was close to 1 per cent. in the autumn of 1906, and again in the autumn of 1907.

On both these occasions the variations in the price of Consols were remarkably slight. In 1873 for example, when Bank rate was reduced from 3½ to 3 per cent. on the 21st August, the price of 3 per cent. Consols was 92¾ ; on the 7th November, when Bank rate was raised from 8 to 9 per cent., Consols were at 92⅝, and on the 20th November when the rate was reduced again to 8 they were at 92⅞.

Common Causes affecting Long-term and Short-term Rates

We shall find a number of instances in which the long-term and short-term rate do move together, but we cannot invariably infer that this is the *result* of the short-term rate influencing the long-term rate. For often both rates are affected by the same cause. War or the threat of war would bring about both a rise of Bank rate and a fall of Consols. Trade activity stimulates the demand both for working capital and for fixed capital, in order that output may be extended to meet a growing consumption demand. Bank rate is put up to prevent the demand for working capital causing an undue expansion of credit. At the same time the prices of fixed-interest securities fall, not

only or principally as a direct effect of the rise of the short-term rate of interest, but because traders sell securities held in reserve in order to raise capital, investors and speculators are attracted by the good prospects of industrial shares, and banks sell securities to make room for increased advances and discounts. To describe the tendency more broadly, we may say that the expansion of demand raises the level of profits on commercial and industrial investments and makes them more attractive competitors with fixed-interest bearing securities. At a time of depression profits decline, and there is a diminished demand for working capital, and both long-term and short-term rates of interest fall. There is, it is true, a falling off of savings, which would tend to raise the rate of interest with a given demand for long-term capital. But at a time of depression the resources of the long-term investment market are reinforced by the proceeds of liquidation of a mass of redundant working capital (above, p. 51). That is partly because traders who find themselves encumbered with idle cash balances invest their surplus funds, and partly because banks, finding their advances and discounts shrink more than their deposit liabilities, buy securities to fill the gap. These matters are considered in greater detail below (pp. 159 and 203–5).

CONSOLS AND BANK RATE, 1844–65

We turn next to a survey of the actual movements of the long-term and short-term rates of interest since 1844. (See Appendix I.) We take as a measure of the former the yield of Government securities, Consols being quoted for the purpose except in the period from 1879 to 1888 when their price was tied close to parity by the Government's option of repayment. In those years the 2½ per cent. annuities take the place of Consols.

The year 1844, when the Bank Charter Act was passed, was still under the shadow of depression. The 3 per cents. rose above par, and the 3¼ per cents. were successfully converted to a 3 per cent. stock (yielding 3¼ for a prelimi-

nary period of years). In the years 1845 and 1846, though Bank rate did not rise above 3½ per cent., growing activity, manifested especially in railway construction, had a depressing effect on Consols. When Bank rate rose in January, 1847, from 3 to 3½ per cent., Consols stood at 93½. With the rise to 5 per cent. in April, 1847, they fell to 87⅞, and the crisis of October brought them down to a low point of 78¾ (19th October, 1847).

This was a very heavy fall, and may, I think, be attributed mainly to forced sales. That would be particularly so in April, 1847, when the Bank of England restricted its lending. And in October, though the Bank did not stint its discounting facilities, there must have been many traders who could not raise cash on discounts, either because the bills they held were of too long maturity to be eligible at the Bank of England, or because the names of acceptors and endorsers had lost credit. In those days, when joint-stock companies were few, there was legally no boundary line between the resources of a trading concern and the private fortunes of the partners who owned it. If the concern got into difficulties in raising cash, securities would be sold from the private fortunes.

As the strain of the crisis passed away, Consols rose, and by January, 1848, when Bank rate was reduced from 5 per cent. to 4 they were at 89. Political troubles, particularly the revolutionary outbreaks on the Continent, depressed Consols during 1848 in spite of further reductions of Bank rate. The price even fell to 80 (6th April, 1848). But in the years of cheap money 1849–52 the price steadily recovered and actually rose above par.

The year 1853 saw increased trade activity, dear money, and the beginning of war between Russia and Turkey. Even before Great Britain became involved in the war, Consols had fallen from 98½ (22nd July) to 91 (4th September, 1853), and in the spring of 1854, when this actually occurred, they dropped to 85¼ (30th March). The return of peace in 1856 brought Consols to 96½ (2nd July), but renewed trade activity and credit pressure caused a

reaction. In July, 1857, when Bank rate was reduced from 6 per cent. to 5½, Consols were at 91½. On the 8th October when Bank rate was put up to 6 per cent. and the financial crisis was rapidly developing, the price had fallen to 90. The strain was not so great as in 1847, and the lowest price touched was 86½. On the 24th December, 1857, when the pressure was over, and Bank rate was reduced from 10 per cent. to 8, Consols had already risen to 93⅝. In the course of 1858 they touched 98⅞ (8th October), and remained high till the spring of 1859 once again brought a threat of war. This was the war between France and Austria, which was destined to gain Lombardy for Piedmont. Great Britain was not involved, but it happened at a time when the London stock market was in a somewhat unsound condition, and the sudden fall in securities caused a long string of failures. Consols fell in a week from 95¼ to 88¼ (28th April, 1859) and Bank rate rose from 2½ to 4½ per cent. On this occasion it was the pressure in the stock market that caused the rise of Bank rate, and, when the pressure passed, Consols rose to 95¾ and the rate was lowered again to 2½ per cent. (14th July).

The year 1858 had been one of intense depression, but in 1859 revival was already making itself felt. In 1860 came an end of cheap money, Bank rate being between 4 and 5 per cent. from February till November, but Consols kept up and varied little. The end of the Franco-Austrian war was a favourable factor, and outweighed the growing activity of business.

In the autumn of 1860, however, came the approach of civil war in the United States, with the resulting drain of gold and dear money. Early in 1861 the civil war actually began ; Consols fell at one time to 89⅛ (25th June, 1861). But under such conditions it is remarkable that the fall was no greater. Even when the " Trent " affair, which occurred on the 8th November, 1861, threatened to involve Great Britain in war with the Northern States, the lowest price touched was 89⅝ (6th December).

The year, 1862, was one of cheap money. Bank rate was

at 2 to 3 per cent. from the 7th November, 1861, to the 15th January, 1863. Yet Consols varied little, the highest and lowest prices of the year 1862 being 94¾ and 91½ (the latter ex-dividend). There followed a period of dear money, Bank rate being from 5 to 9 per cent. from the 2nd November, 1863, to the 2nd March, 1865. Yet Consols kept up above 90, till the late summer of 1864, when the pressure of a number of big mercantile failures, along with a Bank rate of 8 and 9 per cent., depressed the price for a time to 87.

When we examine the movements in more detail, the reactions of Bank rate on Consols during these years seem to be extremely slight. When Bank rate rose from 2 to 3 per cent. at the end of October, 1862, Consols were at 93⅜. The rise to 5 per cent. at the end of January found them at 92⅛, and when 3 per cent. was reached again in April, 1863, they were at 93⅛. In May, 1863, the rate rose to 4 per cent. and Consols were still at 93⅛, and on the 2nd November, when an advance to 5 per cent. came, at 93¼. On 3rd December, 1863, Bank rate was raised from 7 to 8 per cent. and Consols fell to 90½. That was *ex-dividend*, and as the interest in those days was paid half-yearly the real drop since November was very small. There followed oscillations of Bank rate, which were accompanied by very slight movements of Consols till there came the drop from 90⅞ on 15th July, 1864, to 87⅛ on the 8th September, a period in which Bank rate rose from 6 to 9 per cent.

Consols and Bank Rate, 1865–78

The year 1865, was one of moderate rates till October, and Consols varied from a little above 90 to a little below. From the 5th October, 1865, when Bank rate rose to 6 per cent., till the failure of Overend, Gurney and Company in May, 1866, the rate was high. With the growing tension Consols fell. When Bank rate was raised from 6 to 7 per cent. on the 3rd May, 1866, they were at 86½. The lowest point touched during the crisis was 84 (corresponding to an ex-dividend price of about 83). When Bank rate was reduced from 10 per cent. to 8 on the 16th August,

1866, the price had recovered to 88⅛. The further rise was slow. When Bank rate came down to 3 per cent. on the 7th February, 1867, the price was still no more than 90⅞. There was then a rapid rise, the maximum price of the year 1867 being 96¼ on the 1st June (immediately before the deduction of the July dividend). When the long spell of sixteen months at 2 per cent. came to an end in the autumn of 1868, Consols weakened a little, and on the 13th July, 1870, just before the Franco-German war crisis, the price was 92⅞. The outbreak of war brought Bank rate up to 6 per cent. and Consols down to 88½, but both effects were transitory, and, when Bank rate was reduced to 3 per cent. on the 15th September, 1870, Consols were at 92⅛. Cheap money then prevailed for a year, and the price of Consols showed very little change. Nor did the rises to 5 per cent. first in October, 1871, and again in May, 1872, have any visible effect ; the price remained persistently between 91½ and 93¾, and, if the dividend be allowed for, the range was even less.

As we have already seen (above, p. 94), trade and industry were becoming extremely active and prosperous, and in November, 1872, Bank rate was for a short time at 7 per cent. Yet Consols never fell below 91¼ (3rd December, *ex dividend*). And the same state of things continued through 1873 and 1874, the range of variation in the former year being 94¼ and 91¾, and in the latter 93⅝ and 91¼.

Probably the steadiness of the long-term rate of interest in the years 1871–4 was the resultant of two conflicting forces. On the one hand the activity of trade and the high level of profits tended to raise the long-term rate, because shares became attractive competitors of fixed-interest securities in the eyes of investors. On the other hand the political situation had passed through the stormy period which ended with the Franco-German war, and had reached a state of tranquillity which favoured a rise of fixed-interest securities. But whatever the underlying causes may have been, the violent oscillations of Bank rate between 3 or 3½ per cent. and 5, 7 or 9 per cent. left the

market in long-term investments completely undisturbed. In the years of growing depression 1875–8 Consols rose, reaching 98 on the 3rd June, 1878. Cheap money on the whole predominated, but its continuance was interrupted on several occasions by advances of Bank rate to 5 per cent. or more, without interfering with the progress of Consols. When the rate rose from 4 to 5 per cent. on the 6th January, 1876, Consols were at 93⅝, and three weeks later when the rate fell again to 4 Consols had risen to 94¼. The rate was reduced by steps to 2 per cent. (20th April) and Consols rose further to 94⅞. There followed a year at 2 per cent. in the course of which Consols rose to 97½ (21st July, 1876) and fell again to 94, when Bank rate at last rose to 3 per cent. (3rd May, 1877). Another spell of dear money began with a rise to 4 per cent. on the 4th October, 1877, and 5 on the 11th. Consols on the former date were at 95¾ and by the 29th November, when the rate was lowered again to 4, had risen to 96⅞. Seven months later, when Bank rate passed above the 3 per cent., which may be regarded as the upper limit of cheap money, Consols were at 95⅞ (4th July, 1878), which was just about equivalent to the price on the 29th November, 1877, if accrued dividend be deducted from the latter. Thus perversely enough a considerable proportion of the rise in Consols had taken place in the short periods of dear money.

The dear money that began in the summer of 1878 led up to the crisis associated with the failure of the City of Glasgow Bank on the 2nd October. It is an astonishing fact that Consols never fell below 93¾, and in the period from 14th October to the 21st November, when Bank rate was 6 per cent., actually rose from 94½ to 96¼.

Bank Rate and the 2½ per cents., 1879–88

From the end of January, 1879, when Bank rate was once more 3 per cent., to the 13th January, 1881, cheap money reigned. Consols rose to 100¾ (December, 1880). From this time till the conversion of 1888 Consols, being repayable at par at the option of the Government, ceased

to give a reliable guide to the long-term rate of interest, for
when the rate fell below 3 Consols could never rise far above
100. A suitable measure is supplied however by the 2½
per cent. annuities created in 1855. The amount in existence up to 1884 was, it is true, so small as not to constitute
anything like a free and active market. Nevertheless the
quoted price was adjusted at sufficiently frequent intervals
so as to correspond with the prices of more active securities,
and is a reasonably trustworthy guide. In 1884 the
amount was increased by Childers' conversion from
£3,750,000 to £32,810,000, and the market in the annuities
became itself relatively active.

The 2½ per cents. rose from 78 in January, 1879, to 81¼
in January, 1881, and in May, 1881, jumped up to 90.
So violent a rise was a vagary, and can have had little to
do with the return to cheap money. Bank rate had only
risen to 3½ per cent., and fell to 3 per cent. on 17th February and 2½ on the 28th April, 1881. A reaction followed,
bringing the price down to 87¾ in August, when Bank rate
rose to 4 per cent., and to 86 in October, when Bank rate
rose to 5. But though Bank rate rose to 6 per cent. in
January, 1882, and reacted to 3 in March, the 2½ per cents.
remained almost without alteration at 85½ to 86. And
then twenty-one weeks of 3 per cent. (March to August,
1882) saw the price drop to 83½, the result, no doubt, of
political complications particularly the campaign in Egypt.
The battle of Tel-el-Kebir in September, 1882, settled the
trouble for the time being, and to that event can be
attributed the rise from 83½ to 86½ in spite of a 5 per cent:
Bank rate (September, 1882, to January, 1883).

The year 1883 and the first three months of 1884 were
a time of moderate Bank rate (3 to 4 per cent.), and the 2½
per cent. annuities rose once more to 90⅞ (3rd April, 1884).
Depression and cheap money brought the price to 93⅛
in September, 1884. But then twelve weeks at 5 per cent.
interrupted the rise, and in the early part of 1885 political
complications once again depressed the price. At the end
of March, 1885, it fell to 85 as a consequence of the danger

of war with Russia over the Penjdeh incident on the Afghan
frontier.   The Army Reserve was called up, and a vote of
£11,000,000 taken for naval and military preparations.
But in May the dispute was settled, and the 2¼ per cents.
recovered to 88.   Bank rate fell to 2 per cent., and cheap
money, 2 to 3 per cent., continued, except for five weeks at
4 at the turn of the year, till August, 1886.   When Bank
rate was raised from 2½ to 3½ per cent. on the 26th August,
1886, the 2½ per cent. annuities were at 89⅜, and they varied
little while Bank rate rose to 5 per cent. (16th December,
1886) and fell again to 3 (24th March, 1887).   On the latter
date the price was 89.

There followed a very pronounced rise which brought
the price up to 97¼ in March, 1888.   This was not a time
of exceptionally cheap money.   In fact Bank rate was at
4 per cent. for 4¼ months.   And it was a period of reviving
activity, the unemployment percentage falling from 8·3
in August, 1887, to 5·7 in March, 1888.

It was this rise in the prices of Government securities
that afforded the opportunity for Goschen's conversion of
the 3 per cents.   The new Consols into which the old were
converted yielded 3 per cent. for one year, then 2¾ per cent.
for fourteen years (to April, 1903), and thereafter 2¼.
The present value of the interest in excess of 2¼ was about
3¼, so if the 2¼ per cents. were worth 97¼ the conversion
yielded a capital gain of ½ per cent. to the holder.

CONSOLS AND BANK RATE, 1888–99

The conversion was a great success, but as soon as it was
completed the 2½ per cents. fell, and the new Consols
were below par.   By October, 1888, the latter had fallen to
97, and though there was some recovery in 1889, the Baring
crisis brought the price down to 93½ (14th November,
1890).   This fall in Consols, so far as not due to forced sales
when the crisis was pending, must be attributed mainly to
the activity of business, and the favourable opportunity for
investment in industry that resulted.   In the years 1888
to 1890 there were three successive doses of dear money, but

it was not under their influence that the fall in Consols mostly took place. There was some recovery in 1891, then a relapse to 94¼, and a somewhat more consistent rise in 1892 and 1893, which were definitely years of depression. When Bank rate was reduced from 2½ to 2 per cent. on the 22nd February, 1894, Consols were at 99½. There ensued a period of 2½ years memorable alike for the continuance of Bank rate unchanged at 2 per cent., and for the rise of Consols to prices far above all previous records. When Bank rate was at last raised to 2½ per cent. on the 10th September, 1896, Consols were at 112$\frac{9}{16}$, and shortly before had actually touched 114 (1st July, 1896). If allowance be made for the fall of interest to 2½ per cent. in 1903, and for the Government's option to redeem at par in 1923, the yield was barely 2 per cent.[1]

Was this a manifestation of the power of the short-term rate of interest over the long-term rate? I should say that that is certainly not an adequate account of the matter. There had been a persistent fall in the yield of Government securities ever since 1874, interrupted by periods of active business, of financial crisis or of political disturbance, and this fall had by no means been confined to times of cheap money. The rise in Consols in the years 1894–6 may be regarded as a continuance of this tendency, and, even if it was favoured by the exceptionally low discount rates, we must seek for a cause for the entire movement.

Now the years 1874–96 are remarkable for the heavy fall in the prices of commodities. Sauerbeck's wholesale price index, after reaching 111 in 1873, only reached 88 in the active years 1880–2 and 75 in the active years 1889–91. In 1896 it fell to 61. This fall in prices was undoubtedly a monetary movement. It may be directly traced to the scarcity of gold resulting from the adoption or restoration of the gold standard by a number of countries. A fall of prices arising from such a cause would be felt in a shrinkage of profits, which would make investments in industrial

---

[1] Discounted at 2 per cent. the extra ¼ per cent. of interest up to April, 1903, was worth 1½, and the extra ½ per cent. up to April, 1923, was worth 10¼. So the price on a 2 per cent. basis would have been 111¾.

enterprises less attractive in comparison with gilt-edged securities. Estimates of prospective profits are largely empirical, the future being expected to resemble the past, and, when realised profits have been low, the standard of yield anticipated from industrial investments tends to be correspondingly low.

That is why any trade depression is likely to result in a rise of the prices of fixed-interest-bearing securities. And when there is super-imposed on the cyclical alternations of activity and depression a protracted tendency towards declining demand and falling prices of commodities, this rise in securities becomes more persistent. Here we have a tendency which goes far to explain the fall in the long-term rate of interest as measured by a yield of Consols of $3\frac{1}{4}$ per cent. in 1873 and of 2 per cent. in 1896.

But there were circumstances in the years 1894–6 which may well have reinforced the tendency. At a time of depression there is, as we saw above (pp. 51 and 150), an extensive liquidation of working capital; goods are sold off and replaced by cash. This cash is received from *consumers*, for the transfer of goods from one trader to another does not diminish working capital. The cash received is applied partly to extinguish bank advances or bills, partly to swell traders' cash balances and partly to the purchase of securities. The banks find their deposits and advances shrinking, while their cash is swollen by the currency extracted from the consumers ; they seek to restore the normal proportion between their earning assets and their cash reserves by inducing their customers to borrow. But it may be difficult to stimulate borrowing to the extent desired, and, when discount rates have fallen very low, the banks will have recourse to buying securities. Thus, either through the traders themselves or through the banks, the proceeds of liquidation of working capital come into the investment market and constitute an additional demand for long-term or funded securities, over and above the demand emanating from savings.

Now one of the underlying causes of this demand for

securities is the disturbance of the normal proportion of cash to deposits in the banks. And in the years 1894–6 this disturbance was accentuated by the exceptionally large influx of gold, aggregating from the 1st January, 1894, to the 30th June, 1896, £30,792,000. This was due partly to the increased output from the mines, which exceeded £40,000,000 in 1895, and partly to the outflow of gold from the United States. Interior demand for currency could only absorb a small part of the gold, and the rest accumulated in the Bank of England, where the deposits were swollen far beyond any former amount. These deposits represented to a great extent idle reserves in the hands of the commercial banks. The growth of discounts and advances could not possibly be rapid enough to maintain the customary proportion of earning assets, and so the banks were driven to buy securities.

The effect was much more pronounced than when a somewhat similar situation occurred in 1867–8, partly perhaps because the credit structure had become bigger in proportion to the currency foundation, and partly because the available amount of Government securities had diminished. In fact the shortage of trustee investments was acutely felt, and the Colonial Stock Act, 1900, was devised to relieve it. It is a remarkable fact that in the three years from the end of 1893 to the end of 1896, the banks which published balance sheets increased their investments by £30,000,000, but entirely other than Government securities.

The fact that the prices of gilt-edged securities had been pushed up to an unduly high level was recognised at the time. The fixed debt charge was reduced by £2,000,000 in the budget of 1899 on the ground that it was a waste of public money to buy Consols at 111.

Consols and Bank Rate, 1899–1914

It was in that year however that this abnormal situation was brought to an end. The threat of war in South Africa culminated in the actual outbreak of hostilities in October, 1899, and by the end of the year Consols had fallen to 98

(21st December, 1899). But it would be a mistake to attribute the whole of this fall to the war. For the revival of business had been making steady progress, and a state of full employment and activity had been attained. Prices and wages were rising, and interior demand for currency had reached unprecedented dimensions. The causes to which the abnormal rise of Consols had been due had thus been removed. Not only had the demand for securities on the part of the banks to make good an insufficiency of discounts and advances come to an end, but the long ordeal of deficient profits to which industry had been subjected was likewise a thing of the past. Consols fell to 91 in November, 1901, rose to $97\frac{7}{8}$ in June, 1902, after the restoration of peace in South Africa, but fell again, and even dropped below 90 in the autumn of 1903.

The Russo-Japanese war brought the price down to $85\frac{1}{4}$ in March, 1904, and seventeen months of cheap money (April, 1904, to September, 1905) failed to raise the price above $91\frac{1}{2}$. When Bank rate rose to 4 per cent. in September, 1905, Consols were at $89\frac{11}{16}$. By that time the revival of business was well started, and on the 11th October, 1906, when the first spell of dear money began, Consols were at $86\frac{3}{8}$. The price varied little up to the spring of 1907, but between the 25th April, when Bank rate was reduced from $4\frac{1}{2}$ to 4 per cent., and the 15th August when it was raised again from 4 to $4\frac{1}{2}$, Consols fell from $85\frac{13}{16}$ to $81\frac{11}{16}$. On the 10th August, the price fell to $80\frac{1}{8}$.

It is curious that in the period of increasing tension that culminated in the American crisis at the end of October, 1907, and the rise of Bank rate to 7 per cent. (7th November) there was no appreciable further fall of Consols. The lowest price quoted was $81\frac{1}{2}$ on the 9th November. The crisis over, Consols rose as Bank rate fell, reaching $87\frac{5}{16}$ when Bank rate was reduced to 3 per cent. on the 19th March, 1908. Eighteen months of cheap money followed. Consols remained up at a little above 87 for some months, and were at $88\frac{1}{8}$ in the middle of July, 1908, but in August they began to fall away, and by the end of

the year were at 83½. When cheap money came to an end with the advance of Bank rate to 4 per cent. (14th October, 1909) Consols had fallen to 82⅝. While the rate rose to 5 per cent. and fell again to 3 (10th February, 1910) the price of Consols varied little.

In interpreting these movements we must not forget that the Stock market may put the price of Consols up or down *in anticipation* of a fall or rise of Bank rate. It is the essential function of the jobber to anticipate events, and a change in Bank rate is usually foreshadowed by movements of gold or of the foreign exchanges. But after every allowance has been made for that, the relation between Bank rate and the price of Consols in the years 1900 to 1910 seems to have been very slight and capricious.

In the autumn of 1910 there was a spell of dear money and Consols fell to 78⅝ (15th November), and then as Bank rate came down step by step Consols recovered to 81. In 1911 notwithstanding six months at 3 per cent. they fell to 76¾ (21 September) and after recovering to 78¾ (8th November, 1911) had fallen again to 73 when Bank rate rose to 5 per cent. (17th October, 1912). After some recovery in 1913 they fell to 71 (19th December, 1913), and on the 8th January, 1914, when Bank rate was reduced from 5 to 4½ per cent. the price was 71⅝. The combined effect of a slackening of business and further reductions, which brought Bank rate down to 3 per cent. (29th January, 1914), raised Consols to 77½ (4th February).

A reaction followed, and on the 22nd July, 1914, the day before the presentation of the Austro-Hungarian ultimatum to Serbia, the price was 75½. Thereupon the development of the war crisis brought a rapid fall, and the last price of Consols before the Stock Exchange closed was 70 (30th July).

CONSOLS AND BANK RATE, 1914–32

We need hardly look for any relation between Bank rate and the long-term rate of interest under war conditions. Under the pressure of war-time borrowing and unfavourable

developments in the progress of the war Consols fell below
52 (February, 1917) and the big war loan of that time was
brought out on a 5¼ per cent. basis.

The approach of peace brought Consols momentarily
above 63 a few weeks before the Armistice. After a
reaction the price rose to 61½ at the actual date of the
Armistice, only to fall away again. At the end of May, 1919,
Consols being then at 55, it was decided to issue the Funding and Victory loans, in order to effect some reduction in
the floating debt, the rapid growth of which was bound
to cause inflation. Too ready a reliance was placed on the
conventional City view that cheap money favours gilt-
edged securities. It was decided to suspend altogether the
sale of Treasury bills (which had been on offer at a fixed
rate of 3½ per cent.), and to supply the deficiency with
money borrowed at call through the Bank of England at
3 per cent. or less. The result was to accentuate the
tendency to inflation, and to strengthen the competitive
power of industrial investments with the new loans. The
loans produced very modest results, and Consols fell below
51 (September, 1919).

Even when Bank rate was raised to 6 per cent. (6th
November, 1919) the progress of inflation was hardly
retarded, and when at last the rate became 7 per cent. on
the 15th April, 1920, Consols had fallen to 45⅝. At the
end of 1920 they fell to 43⅞.

Probably in this period the most powerful influence
affecting the price of Consols was the depreciation of the
pound, as measured by the exchange on the United States.
In fact dear money itself was intended to induce a recovery
of the pound, and, if it raised hopes of this object being
attained, would actually cause a rise in Government
securities. A favourable movement of the exchange in the
early months of 1921 was associated with a rise of Consols
to 48⅝ at the beginning of April. Bank rate began to be
reduced by slow gradations, but there was a setback in the
exchange in the summer, and Consols fell below 46 in June.
From September, 1921, there followed a steady improvement

in the exchange, and Consols ended the year at 50⅜. In 1922 there was again a concurrent improvement in the exchange and in Consols up to April, Consols reaching 59¾ on the 22nd April. For a long time that was the high-water mark. Bank rate fell, and in July, 1922, was down to 3 per cent. But the revival of economic activity was beginning to be felt. The exchange moreover was within 10 per cent. of parity with the dollar, and there was much less room for any reaction of the prospect of a return to parity upon the prices of securities. Early in 1923, when the exchange was within 3 per cent. of parity, Consols rose above 59 again, but there followed a setback both to the pound and to Consols, and when the gold standard was actually re-established in May, 1925, Bank rate had gone up to 5 per cent., and Consols were no more than 56. In the years of dear money and depression that followed Consols fluctuated but little, varying between 54 and 57 till the end of 1929, when, under the influence of still dearer money and of the pressure and unsettlement resulting from the Wall Street crisis, they fell below 53.

In the course of 1930 there supervened conditions of depression and cheap money such as had not been experienced since 1922, and in June, 1931, in spite of the financial crisis in Austria and Germany, Consols rose above 60 for the first time since 1918.

The suspension of the gold standard in September, 1931, once again linked both the long-term and the short-term rates of interest with the depreciation of the pound. Bank rate rose to 6 per cent. and Consols fell heavily, touching 49½ on the 25th September. But in the first half of 1932 Bank rate was rapidly reduced, and Consols rose. Depression had reached an unparalleled intensity, and the possibility of a further depreciation of the pound had lost its terrors. It was in the countries that were making desperate efforts to adhere to the old gold parities that distrust of currency units was rife. Great Britain and others which had accepted depreciation were in relatively calm water. The effect on the market in gilt-edged securi-

ties was about to receive a sensational and dramatic illustration. By June, 1932, Consols had risen to 63½. The 3½ per cent. Conversion loan stood at 90. For the first time since 1914 Government securities of the funded type were yielding less than 4 per cent. The 5 per cent. War Loan, amounting to £2,085,000,000, was due to be repaid in 1947, but had become redeemable at the option of the Government at any time since 1929. The fall in the yield of Government securities afforded an opportunity, through the exercise of this option, for a great conversion operation. And on the 30th June, Consols being then at 67⅛, and 3½ per cent. Conversion Loan at 94, this was announced.

A notable and courageous feature of the proposal was that the new security to be offered to the holders of the war loan stock was to yield only 3½ per cent. The holders were to get a substantially lower yield than they could have obtained by buying Government securities in the open market immediately before the announcement was made. Even for a few days afterwards this was still possible. But the prospect of a demand for the reinvestment of £2,000,000,000 to be liberated by the repayment of the loan soon forced up the prices of other securities, and within a few days Consols stood at 73 and the 3½ per cent. Conversion Loan at 99.[1] The conversion was a great success, an unconverted residue of £164,000,000 being redeemed without difficulty along with some maturing Treasury bonds by the issue of the 3 per cent. and 2½ per cent. Conversion loans.

The success attained was due partly to the sheer magnitude of the operation. The amount of money seeking reinvestment was so great as to overwhelm the market. It could not find anything like a sufficient outlet, and the prices of all eligible securities were forced up so violently as to drive the money back into the new War Loan stock offered by way of conversion. But the success was also greatly assisted by the trend of the market. The rise in Government securities, which had been in progress for

---

[1] As there was a bonus of 1 per cent. paid to holders who signified their agreement to convert before the end of July, the 3½ per cent. at 99 ceased to be more attractive than the new War Loan stock.

some months before the conversion, was the beginning of
a movement which was soon to carry their yield far below
3½ per cent.   In fact 2½ per cent. Consols actually touched
94 in January, 1935.   The rise from 49½ in September, 1931,
to 94 in January, 1935, far surpasses that recorded in the
years up to 1896.   On that occasion the lowest price
touched since the conversion of 1888 had been 93½ in November, 1890, and the rise to 114 in July, 1896, was thus 22
per cent.   The rise from September, 1931, to January,
1935, was 90 per cent.

CHAPTER VI

LONG-TERM AND SHORT-TERM RATES OF INTEREST

CYCLICAL FLUCTUATIONS AND THE LONG-TERM RATE OF INTEREST

WHAT inferences can we draw from this statistical material? Since we are looking for the effect of Bank rate, we are concerned with short-period tendencies.

There is quite clearly a cyclical movement. Consols rise in times of depression. They rose to par in 1852, to 98½ in 1858, to 96 in 1868, to 98 in 1878, whereas in the intervals of active business (even apart from the special pressure of crises) they were much lower. In the period from 1879 to the conversion of 1888, when the 2½ per cents. rose from 78 to 97¼, the association of the rise with depression is not so certain. The advance from 81¼ to 90 in 1881 and that from 89 to 97¼ in 1887-8 both occurred at times of growing activity, though in both cases, as the activity gathered way and approached its maximum, the price fell again.

After 1888 the association once more becomes evident. The active period, 1889-91, brings Consols down from 99 to 94, and the depression from 1892 onwards starts a rise which carries the price up to 114. Even on this occasion, however, the rise continued after the depression was over. Before the end of 1895, when Consols were still at about 107, revival was well started and making visible progress. At the beginning of 1899, when revival was complete and activity had achieved its limit, Consols had fallen very little below their highest quotation and were at 111. There was then a heavy fall, but the approach of the South African War makes any apportionment of causes of the fall impossible.

The period from 1899 to 1914 was marked by a persistent fall in Consols, and the effect of the mild depression which

prevailed from 1902 to 1904 was rather to retard the fall than to cause an actual rise. But both the depression of 1908 and the recession that was beginning in the early months of 1914 were accompanied by noticeable rises in Consols.

In the post-war period we find a marked recovery of Consols first in the depression of 1921-2, and later in the period from the end of 1929 to June, 1931, and then comes the sensational rise in 1932-5.

Now depression is *also* associated with a low Bank rate, and in many of the instances referred to the rise in Consols and the low Bank rate synchronised. But it cannot be inferred that the rise in Consols was *caused* by the low Bank rate. For as has been pointed out above, there is good reason to believe that they were the effects of a common cause. Depression diminishes the demand both for working capital and for fixed capital.

When, as is usual, cheap money and depression go together, we cannot distinguish their relative effects. But, as we have seen, there have been periods of depression in which the general tendency to cheap money has been interrupted by spells of dear money, and during which there has been no consistent response of the long-term rate of interest. Indeed on several occasions Consols rose while Bank rate was high (see above, pp. 155 and 157).

DEAR MONEY AND CONSOLS

If we turn to periods of activity, we find a predominant tendency to dear money, but sometimes wide fluctuations between high and low short-term rates. And the price of Consols is curiously insensitive to these changes. When there is a drop of more than a point or two in the price, that is because there is some special cause, such as a war or a financial crisis, at work. In the years 1871-4 such slight movements as occurred in Consols seem hardly to have been affected at all by the violent movements of Bank rate. In 1881-2, it is true, we find a big rise of the 2½ per cents. from 81½ to 90 concurrent with cheap money, and a

reaction to 85½ when Bank rate rises to 6 per cent. But the price had already fallen to 87¾ before Bank rate rose above 2½ per cent., so the real extent of the reaction was not very great.

The long spell of 2 per cent. from 1894 to 1896 was followed by several years of growing activity, with Bank rate oscillating between 2 and 4 per cent. A rate of 4 per cent. at that time, when Consols hardly yielded 2 per cent., might be regarded as dear money. Yet, when 4 per cent. was in operation, Consols tended rather to rise than to fall.

The big drop in Consols came with the South African crisis in 1899, before the actual outbreak of war and before the rise of Bank rate. Consols fell from 111⅝ in January, 1899, to 102¾ in October with Bank rate at 3 to 3½ per cent., and when Bank rate, after going up to 6 per cent. was reduced to 4 in January, 1900, Consols were still as high as 101½ in spite of the unfavourable course of the war.

The next period of activity was in 1906-7. Consols fell from 90⅝ in April, 1906, to 80⅛ in August, 1907. But the fall was not especially associated with dear money. The price had already fallen to 86⅜ when Bank rate was raised from 4 to 5 per cent. in October, 1906, and was 85¾ when, after having been as high as 6, it was reduced to 4 per cent. again in April, 1907. The lowest price, 80⅛, was reached while Bank rate was still 4 per cent., and it had recovered to 83¾ when the 7 per cent. rate that followed the American crisis was reduced to 6 in January, 1908.

In the years 1912-3 Consols fell from 78 to 71. Yet in the six months of 5 per cent. Bank rate from October, 1912, to April, 1913, they actually rose from 73 to 75. Too much stress should not be laid on that, for the time was one of great political unsettlement on account not only of the Balkan wars but of the Irish question. But nowhere in these successive phases of activity do we find evidence of any considerable effect of Bank rate on the long-term rate of interest.

It might be that a fall of the short-term rate of interest

below the average would have a more noticeable effect on the long-term rate than a rise above the average. For a high Bank rate is not usually expected to last more than a few weeks, whereas in conditions of depression a low rate might conceivably be expected to last for years. But even if cheap money (with a market rate down to, say, 1 per cent.) were expected to last for as long as two years, the effect on the price of 3 per cent. stock would not exceed 4 points. And that is an extreme assumption.

In the case of dear money, even though it is not expected to last long, the effect may be reinforced by a direct restriction of credit, a refusal on the part of the banks to lend for the purchase and holding of Stock Exchange securities. Even if the refusal applied only to speculative shares, it would affect the resources of the investment market as a whole, and would so react on the long-term rate of interest. But whatever effect there may have been is *already* reflected in the statistics of the price of Consols which we have been using.

PROMOTIONS AND THE RATE OF INTEREST

On the whole I think we may infer that Bank rate and measures of credit restriction taken together rarely, if ever, affected the price of Consols by more than two or three points, whereas a variation of ⅛ per cent. in the long-term rate of interest would correspond to about 4 points in the price of a 3 per cent. stock.

Now a variation even of less than ⅛ per cent. in the long-term rate of interest ought, theoretically and in the long run, to have a definite effect for what it is worth on the volume of capital outlay. That is to say, if the rate of interest operates as a criterion of all projects for capital outlay, separating those which promise a sufficient yield to be remunerative from those which do not, then any rise, however small, in the rate ought to transfer a corresponding slice of projects from the remunerative to the unremunerative class. But there is in reality no *close* adjustment of prospective yield to the rate of interest. Most of the

industrial projects offered for exploitation at any time promise yields ever so far above the rate of interest. But they have to wait till promoters combining the necessary qualifications of technical, commercial and industrial ability and knowledge, with access to money, become available. The limited number of people composing this inner ring of specialised promoters will want to be satisfied that the projects they take up will yield them a commensurate profit, and the rate of interest calculated on money raised will probably be no more than a very moderate deduction from this profit. It is not even true that the most profitable projects are dealt with first. It is a matter of chance which project a promoter will select from among those which are becoming ripe for exploitation within the sphere of his competence. It may easily happen that an exceptionally profitable project has to wait a long time, while money is being spent by those qualified to take it up on much less remunerative openings, or even wasted on enterprises that turn out complete failures.

The idea of the possible openings for investment forming a series in order of remunerativeness, so that all promising a yield in excess of the rate of interest prevailing at the moment have already been filled, and a fall in the rate will bring into exploitation a nicely calculated segment of the remainder, as a slice is cut off a sausage, is an academic fiction. The boundary between the eligible and the ineligible projects is not a mathematical line ; it may rather be compared, say, to the northern limit of tropical vegetation than to the tropic itself. A small change in the long-term rate of interest, though it may be assumed ultimately to give a bias to the calculations of some at any rate of the promoters, could not be expected to have any quick or measurable effect.

Where the project takes the form not of a new enterprise but of an extension of the capacity of an existing concern, the procedure is simpler. The difficult task of establishing the business and creating a goodwill has already been accomplished, and presumably the extension is needed

because the selling power which constitutes this goodwill is outstripping the concern's productive capacity. Sometimes such an extension can be financed out of accumulated reserves, in the form of marketable securities, which are sold ; sometimes bank advances are obtained in anticipation of future reinvested profits ; or, if these resources are insufficient, additional permanent capital may be raised either privately or by a public issue.

It is true of these extensions, as much as of the new enterprises, that they are undertaken in the expectation of a profit in comparison with which any variation in the long-term rate of interest is small. Selling power and expectation of profit are really the same thing, for selling power means power to sell without an undue sacrifice of price and therefore at a reasonable profit.

Transport and public utility undertakings differ somewhat from industrial enterprises in the methods of raising capital. The individual undertaking is usually on a large scale. Its prospects of profit depend on local conditions, amounting often to a local monopoly, and the rate of profit is probably subject to some public control or limitation. The profit is more moderate and at the same time more assured, and a preliminary period of trial under the auspices of specialised promoters is not so necessary. The goodwill of the concern is almost ready made, for it is required to meet the needs of a growing population or of a population with a growing standard of living. The capital is therefore probably raised by a direct public appeal in the first instance.

In consequence of the amount of capital being large in proportion to the value of the services produced, interest forms a relatively considerable proportion of the charge to the consumer. But in view of the special character of the demand and the tendency to local monopoly, the charge to the consumer has but little influence on the rate of development.

In fact the charges for transport and public utilities affect the consumer to some extent as incidental to the cost

of housing. In the case of house rent likewise a considerable proportion of the charge to the consumer arises from the long-term rate of interest. A *large* rise or fall in the long-term rate of interest should materially retard or hasten the progress of housing development and with it the progress of public utilities and transport undertakings. But even house rent has to provide a margin of profit. The rents the occupiers of residential property are prepared to pay form part of consumption demand, and the property owners and builders, like any other traders who set out to satisfy a portion of consumption demand, are seeking profit. The difference between residential property and capital installation in industrial enterprises is one of degree and not of kind. The effect upon house building of such changes in the long-term rate of interest as were traceable to the direct influence of the short-term rate in the nineteenth century and up to 1914, changes which rarely amounted to as much as ⅛ per cent., can hardly have been other than trifling.

POSTPONEMENT OF CAPITAL ENTERPRISES

Now, as we have seen, the reason why the effect of the short-term rate on the long-term rate was so small was that the market could never foresee the continuance of the former for more than a very limited time. But within that limited time the short-term rate might affect the action of the promoters of capital enterprises very materially, for a high short-term rate might afford grounds for *postponement*. It is not merely that promoters will probably raise a part of the necessary funds by way of short-term bank advances. But even the apparently small effect of the high short-term rate on the prices of securities acquires importance when it is a question of choosing a favourable moment for an issue or sale of securities.

If the charge for bank advances rises from 3 to 7 per cent., a promoter might be led to avoid such advances, and to raise all the funds required for a project by a sale of securities. But if the rise in the short-term rate has had its due effect

on the prices of securities, he will lose just as much by selling or issuing securities as by obtaining a bank advance. If the high short-term rate is expected to last six months, and the prices of securities have thereby been depressed by 2 per cent., he will in effect have to pay the equivalent of 7 per cent. per annum for the use of the money for the first six months. For that is what he would save by deferring the sale of the securities till the return of cheap money.

Consequently the promoter would really be paying the equivalent of 7 per cent. per annum for six months on the *whole* of the capital raised. If he postpones the project for six months, he presumably postpones for that time the moment at which the full ultimate yield of the project will accrue to him. That yield, including as it does profit, may be much more than 7 per cent. on the capital ; he may expect 10 per cent. or even 20 per cent. But whereas the 7 per cent. is a definite and immediate loss, the anticipated yield has to be heavily discounted for uncertainty and risk.

In the case of transport and public utility undertakings, promoted to meet the growing needs of the communities they are destined to serve, postponement for a period at any rate of a few weeks or months is usually possible. The precise time at which the needs have to be met is not definitely marked, and, unless there has already been such delay as to make the undertaking overdue, it is probably possible to choose the moment for raising capital within fairly wide limits. That is so whether the undertaking is in the hands of a concessionary company or of a public authority. Undertakings of this kind, offering a more moderate profit on a relatively large capital, should be more susceptible to the motives for postponement than ordinary industrial enterprises.

The Equalising Function of the Investment Market

The postponement of promotions and flotations relieves the demands on the investment market. Dealers in the

market find themselves buying a smaller amount of securities. But to measure the true effect of dear money on capital outlay, we must take account of the behaviour of the investment market *as a whole.*

The function of the market is to equalise the demand for capital funds with the supply. The demand consists of the capital outlay represented by the promotions and flotations. The supply of capital funds will in the long run simply consist of the savings of the community. But over any short period the savings may be supplemented by a release of cash either from balances or from bank advances, or may be diminished by an absorption of cash either into balances or into the repayment of advances.

This release, or absorption of cash may be effected by various groups of people. As we have seen, the promoters themselves may raise money by bank advances. The jobbers and dealers[1] in the stock market will be regular borrowers, as the securities in the hands of each will be a very fluctuating quantity. And then outside the market is a crowd of speculators and speculative investors, who are ready to buy securities with borrowed money whenever they see a favourable opportunity, but lapse into quiescence when no such opportunity is in sight. Banks also may release cash by buying securities or absorb cash by selling them.

The equalising function devolves primarily upon the stockjobbers. They aim in general at keeping their holdings as near as may be to a normal constant. They therefore react quickly to any excess of purchases or sales by the public. They make it their business as far as possible to *anticipate* any such excess. Any occurrence which is likely to stimulate purchases of securities by the public is the signal for a marking up of quotations before the purchases begin, and any occurrence of a kind to cause sales will be accompanied by an immediate marking down of

---

[1] To the stock-jobbers, whose practice it is to be ready to buy and sell the securities they deal in, and to make a price whenever asked, must be added a number of regular dealers, investment companies and others, who are practically stock and share merchants.

quotations. The stock-jobbers, assuming as they do the responsibility of making prices, must in fact act as professional speculators. And they will sometimes depart from the normal practice of counteracting the fluctuations of their holdings, and become speculators in a more positive sense. When they take a favourable view of prospects, they will deliberately acquire an additional supply of securities with borrowed money ; or alternatively, when prospects seem unfavourable, they may reduce their holdings, and even go short, effecting forward sales of the securities they distrust in excess of their existing holdings. In such cases the investment market itself is in the position of releasing cash through an increase of its indebtedness to the banks or absorbing cash through a decrease.

This procedure applies to transactions in securities which are already dealt in and quoted in the market. But the demand for capital funds which the market has to meet, includes the new flotations by which securities not previously dealt in or quoted are placed on the market. New flotations are of course influenced by the existing level of prices of securities. A fall of prices in the market makes the prospect of an issue of given yield less favourable, or requires a concession on the price to make it equally acceptable. And we have just seen how this may lead to postponement where the fall of prices is traceable to some temporary cause such as a rise of Bank rate.

But the price level of securities (the inverse, that is, of the long-term rate of interest) is not found to give the market adequate control over the volume of new flotations. Postponement is not easily practicable for projects for which the preparations are far advanced, and for those in an early stage the market cannot foresee how soon or to what extent the effect of postponement will be felt in its operations. The persuasive effect of an adjustment of price is not enough. In practice the equalising function of the investment market depends on its power to *refuse* to supply funds in excess of its resources.

When a new issue of a security is brought out, it is offered

on terms which it is hoped will attract enough subscriptions. If there is a deficiency, either the issue must be curtailed or withdrawn, or the deficiency must be made good from some other source. It is to provide for the contingency of a deficiency that the practice of getting an issue of securities underwritten has grown up. Every issuing house is in touch with a number of individuals and concerns, who are willing to undertake this service for a commission. The underwriters bind themselves to take whatever portion of the issue is not subscribed for by the public.

That means that a deficiency of subscriptions does not prevent the issue. But it does not mean that new flotations escape from the limitation imposed by the capacity of the market. For the resources of the available underwriters are themselves limited. If flotations outrun the capacity of the market, those in a position to act as underwriters become loaded up with securities which they can only sell, if at all, at a sacrifice of price, and which they probably have to carry with borrowed money. Under such conditions flotations begin to be completely held up ; promoters are *forced* to acquiesce in a postponement or abandonment of their projects.

When the investment market thus resists an excess of new flotations, it accomplishes its equalising task with a smaller rise in the long-term rate of interest than would otherwise be necessary. And it accomplishes it more promptly and certainly than would be possible by means of the long-term rate of interest.

The power of the investment market to limit new flotations in this way facilitates its equalising task only in one direction. It can guard against an excess of new flotations, but not against a deficiency. The modern economic system, as the world has hitherto known it, has required for its smooth working a continuous pressure of projects for capital outlay upon the resources of the investment market. Only occasionally at times of depression, when there has been a falling off of consumption demand, has this pressure been relaxed. Even at such times

it would probably be going too far to say that there has been an actual deficiency of projects, involving an involuntary absorption of cash by the investment market. As is explained below (pp. 202–6) the apparent excess of unemployed savings during a depression is at any rate partly due to the liquidation of working capital.

BANK ADVANCES TO SPECULATORS

The bank advances to stock-jobbers and to underwriters of new capital issues may be regarded as within the investment market itself. They are incidental to professional dealings in securities, and are parallel to the bank advances to traders in commodities. The advances to speculators and speculative investors on the other hand, even though they are often made through stockbrokers, are outside the confines of the market ; they increase the resources with which the market has to equalise the demands upon it.

The speculator buys shares with a view to reselling them after a short interval and making a capital gain ; the speculative investor buys shares at what he regards as a low price with a view to holding them and enjoying a high yield on his money in the form of income. The speculator borrows money in order to buy, and repays it when he resells ; the speculative investor borrows money in anticipation of his future savings or other receipts. The speculator is usually attracted by existing securities with an active market ; the speculative investor more often, though by no means exclusively, turns to new issues.

Now the prospects of shares in any concern depend above all on the demand for the goods and services which the concern produces. What provides the speculator with his opportunity is the expectation of an increase in the demand for the product of some company of which the shares are dealt in in the market. Increased demand will mean increased sales or higher prices or both, and the consequent prospect of higher profits and dividends will mean a rise in the price of the shares.

Both speculators and speculative investors hope to be more far-seeing than the market ; if they are not mere gamblers, they will proceed on some special knowledge of the shares they buy. In tranquil times, free from any considerable fluctuations of general demand, the volume of speculation will, no doubt, vary from time to time, but there is no reason why its movements should have any pronounced trend. They are fortuitous, depending on the prospects of particular industries or of particular companies. But an expansion of general demand will make the prospects of *every* industry better than before. As soon as a knowledge of the increased sales and growing activity of particular industries spreads among the public, there will be an intensified motive for the speculative purchase of shares, and the proceeds of bank advances obtained for the purpose will form a supplement to the resources of the investment market. When the prices of shares have been fully adjusted to the state of demand, the speculation will die away, and the resources of the investment market will be diminished by the repayment of the bank advances. Thus when speculation is increasing, it adds a supplement to the resources of the investment market, and, when it is falling off, the supplement gives place to a deplement.[1] It should not be overlooked that when the amount of advances to speculators remains unchanged, a condition consistent with a high degree of speculative activity, there is no supplement.

The speculative supplement involves a release of cash, and enlarges the demand for capital outlay beyond the amount of current savings. And the deplement involves an absorption of cash, and reduces the demand for capital outlay below the amount of current savings. The former is a source of inflation, the latter of deflation.

Speculators are not directly sensitive to changes in the short-term rate of interest. They hope for relatively big capital gains in a short space of time, compared with which

[1] No apology is necessary for introducing this word to fill a gap in the language, the contrary of " supplement."

the burden even of a very high rate of interest for a few weeks is negligible. If therefore we suppose the short-term rate of interest to be raised at a time of expanding demand for commodities, when the resources of the invest-ment market are being supplemented by bank advances to speculators, the rise of the rate will not directly cause any appreciable reduction in the speculative supplement, or in the aggregate resources of the investment market. And so long as the investment market discharges its function of equalising the inflow and outflow of investible funds, the amount of capital outlay will continue to be adjusted to the resources of the market. Even if the rise in the short-term rate of interest causes the postponement of flotations, that will not be allowed to interfere with the equalising pro-cess. The postponement depends not on the short-term rate of interest alone, but on the fall in the prices of securities in sympathy with the rise in the short-term rate. If the market, having undiminished resources, does not *require* any postponement of capital outlay, the fall in the prices of securities will not occur, and there will be little post-ponement or even none.

There would then, it is true, be some tendency for pro-moters to avoid temporary borrowing, and to resort to increased sales of securities instead. Bank advances to promoters, like bank advances to speculators, are outside the market, and any reduction in them is a reduction in the resources of the market. But the temporary borrowings of promoters are likely to be governed rather by considera-tions of prudence than by the charge for interest, and a rise in that charge, when not associated with a fall in the prices of securities, is a very minor item of expense.

For the promoter, as for the speculator, the principal incentive to strain his resources by temporary borrowing is in the prospect of profit. When general demand is high and growing, there will be an inflationary supplement to the resources of the investment market. If the growth of this supplement is to be checked by a high Bank rate it will not be through the deterrent effect upon the borrowings of

speculators or promoters, but through the effect on more amenable forms of temporary borrowing, and the consequent check to demand.

The amount of capital outlay depends partly upon the amount of current savings, partly upon any absorption or release of cash arising in the course of the flow of current savings through the investment market into the hands of those undertaking the capital outlay. The amount of savings will be determined by the resources and the motives of the recipients of incomes, and of those who have the responsibility of distributing or reinvesting the profits of business. The volume of savings may be affected by many different causes, but ovet short periods the most powerful cause is the state of profits. Most of the large and variable or precarious incomes are derived from profits, and it is from those incomes that the power and the motive for saving are both greatest.

Thus an expansion of general demand enlarges the resources of the investment market both by expanding profits and savings and by holding out inducements to promoters and speculators.

CAPITAL OUTLAY AND THE ACCELERATION PRINCIPLE

A considerable part of capital outlay is ordinarily undertaken for the " widening " of capital,[1] that is to say, for extending the capacity of industries in response to a growth of the demand for their products. If a contraction of consumption demand as a whole is super-imposed on the normal growth of demand for the product of each particular industry, the result is to diminish the extensions of capacity and very likely in some industries to suspend them altogether.

Capital outlay is also incurred for what may be called the " deepening " of capital, that is, an increase in the amount of capital employed for a given output. The deepening of capital is less dependent on the growth of

---

[1] For a further discussion of the distinction between the widening and the deepening of capital see my *Capital and Employment*, particularly Chapters III to V.

demand than the widening, for its purpose is a reduction of costs which may still be advantageous when no increase of output is called for, or even in an industry of which the output is diminishing.

Nevertheless the practical application of the deepening process does often involve a concurrent increase of output, or at any rate is often most conveniently carried out along with some extension of capacity. Consequently the fluctuations of consumption demand do affect the deepening as well as the widening of capital.

The reaction of consumption demand upon capital outlay has recently attracted attention among economists under the name of the "acceleration principle,"[1] as playing an important part in the theory of the trade cycle.

For example, as I wrote many years ago, " it may be that in a particular industry the output increases, taken over a long period, at an average rate of 1 per cent. per annum, and that the fixed capital requires renewal after twenty years' use. Then 5 per cent. of the capital requires renewal each year, and the demand for new plant will be 6 per cent. of the total amount of plant when the increase of 1 per cent. is allowed for. But if there is an expansion of trade which increases the output of this particular industry in a particular year by 4 per cent. instead of 1 per cent., the new plant needed will be 9 per cent. of the existing plant or no less than 50 per cent. more than the average ; while if during a depression the output falls off by 2 per cent. instead of increasing by 1 per cent. the new plant needed will be only 3 per cent. of the existing plant or half the average."[2]

The excess of capital outlay over replacements in any industry thus tends to be proportional to the *rate of increase* of demand for the product of the industry. And when there is a monetary expansion causing a substantial increase in consumption demand all round, then, as soon as the existing capital is fully employed, there will naturally be great

[1] See Professor G. Haberler's *Prosperity and Depression*, pp. 30 and 80–98.
[2] *Good and Bad Trade*, 1913, p. 207.

pressure on the investment market to provide the means of extending the capacity of all industries at the same time. The same principle applies to the demand for new houses and other durable instruments of consumption. But it is not to be inferred that the expansion of capacity will take place to the full extent desired. The equalising function of the investment market will come into play to limit the amount of capital outlay to the available resources. And those resources will be composed of current savings together with any inflationary supplement derived from bank advances.

It is through the inflationary supplement that the amount of capital outlay is expanded in response to the acceleration principle. And that occurs because the expansion of consumption demand offers, in the prospects of increased profits, an inducement to speculators and speculative investors as well as to promoters to make a special effort to extend their operations. They supplement their available cash with bank advances.

The inflationary supplement thus added to savings becomes a source of additional income and so of additional consumption demand. But it is not an *originating* cause of activity. It is a consequence of an increase of activity which has already occurred and is in fact one aspect of the vicious circle of inflation.

And the banks will not acquiesce in an unlimited expansion of credit for this purpose. They may intervene in two ways. In the first place they may directly discourage borrowing for speculative purposes. They may be more exacting in regard to the character of the security or in the amount of margin required, and they may refuse to lend altogether in some cases. So long as all the banks are equally restrictive, no one bank will lose custom by this attitude, and in face of a credit stringency the banks are likely to take common if not concerted action.

Secondly, in the circumstances assumed the danger of inflation would be met by a rise of Bank rate and so of short-term rates of interest on advances generally.

Though this would make no impression on the speculative borrowers, the deterrent effect would be felt on commercial borrowing ; the expansion of general demand would be checked, and with it the source of the speculation would be stopped.

General demand for all products is composed of consumption demand, and the demand for capital goods. If the demand for capital goods is determined by the prospective profits in the industries in which the capital goods are to be used, it follows that the fundamental factor is simply consumption demand. It is an expansion of consumption demand that gives rise to increased profits from the industries satisfying that demand ; and thereby it stimulates both those industries themselves and also the instrumental industries which supply them with capital goods.

It may perhaps be said that the relation between the consumption industries and the instrumental industries is reciprocal. The demand for the products of either group can be supplemented by the proceeds of bank advances or by cash released from balances. Increased activity in either group will induce increased activity in the other, for the additional incomes generated by such activity will be devoted partly to consumption and partly to savings which will become available, through the medium of the investment market, for capital outlay.

But, over and above these symmetrical relations, there is a special characteristic of the instrumental industries in that, as their ultimate purpose is to be the means of supplying consumable goods, they are stimulated by an increased demand for the latter. And if capital outlay is swollen beyond current savings by an inflationary supplement, that is usually the cause.

Long-term and Short-term Rates of Interest

In the foregoing pages I have been proceeding on the assumption that the effect of the short-term rate of interest on the prices of securities is limited to the gain or loss from holding securities with borrowed money for the relatively

short period for which the market would forecast the continuance of the existing short-term rate. From that assumption follows the inference that the prices of securities are only affected to the extent at most of two or three points, and that the effect on the long-term rate of interest is limited to a small fraction. That inference the statistical material from 1844 to 1914 supports.

Mr. Keynes in Chapter 37 of his *Treatise on Money* (pp. 352–63) contests any such calculation : " One might suppose," he says, " that whilst it is reasonable that long-term rates of interest should bear a definite relation to the prospective short-term rates, quarter by quarter, over the years to come, the contribution of the current three-monthly period to this aggregate expectation should be insignificant in amount. . . . It may, therefore, seem illogical that the rate of interest fixed for a period of three months should have any noticeable effect on the terms asked for loans of twenty years or more. In fact, however, experience shows that, as a rule, the influence of the short-term rate of interest on the long-term rate is much greater than anyone who argued on the above lines would have expected " (p. 353).

The experience he relies on is that of the years 1919–29 in England and America. But he is content to accept the correlation disclosed between the long-term and short-term rates, without ever considering whether it may be due either to the long-term rate influencing the short-term rate, or to both being influenced by a common cause. Especially must the latter possibility be taken into account in a period which saw the reaction from the exceptionally high rates of interest, both long-term and short-term, which had been attained at the end of the war and during the post-war inflation. We shall turn in the next chapter to a further consideration of these years.

Meanwhile, so far as the years 1844–1914 are concerned, Mr. Keynes explains that " for the period before (say) 1894 the extreme insensitiveness of Consols . . . disqualifies it as an index of the price at which current long-term

borrowing could be arranged." " There was no year
between 1867 and 1894[1] in which the yield on the average
price of Consols varied more than 1s. 6d. per cent. from one
year to another."

Of the years following the rise of Consols to par in 1880
it is undoubtedly true that the insensitiveness of the price
disqualifies it as an index, for the Government's option of
repayment prevented the price from rising far above par.
But there is no reason for rejecting the price of Consols as
an index for earlier years, and statistics of railway debentures show them to have been not less insensitive at that
time.[2]

For the years 1880–8 the 2½ per cent. annuities, to which
I have had recourse above, do not differ materially in their
fluctuations from the railway debentures.

Mr. Keynes deduces from the years 1919–29 the conclusion that " short-period fluctuations in Bank rate are four
times as wide as those in the yield on Consols (*i.e.* a 4 per
cent. fluctuation in the former corresponds to a 1 per cent.
fluctuation in the latter) " (p. 355). And he produces the
following table for the years 1906–13 " corrected for trend
and with the fluctuations of Bank rate damped down to a
quarter."

	Bank rate	Yield on Consols
1906	110	104
1907	113	105
1908	100	100
1909	100	100
1910	104	102
1911	102	103
1912	103	104
1913	109	104

Here there are three years of high Bank rate, 1906, 1907
and 1913, showing respectively " damped down " per-

---

[1] Misprinted " 1924."
[2] See the tables appended to a paper read by Mr. R. A. Macdonald to
the Royal Statistical Society (*Journal* for March, 1912, pp. 376–9).

centages of 10, 13 and 9 above the level of 1909, while for Consols they show percentages of 4, 5 and 4 only. Since the former percentages before being damped down would be 40, 52 and 36, one-tenth would give a better correlation than a quarter.

The following is a similar calculation for Consols and Bank rate in the years 1919–29, the period from which Mr. Keynes's estimate of a ratio of one to four was derived :

	Actual Index	*Bank Rate Index Damped down*	*Yield of Consols*
1919	147·9	112·0	107·2
1920	190·3	122·6	123·2
1921	175·6	118·9	120·9
1922	106·3	101·6	102·5
1923	100	100	100
1924	115·0	103·7	101·9
1925	131·6	107·9	103·0
1926	143·7	110·9	105·6
1927	133·6	108·4	105·8
1928	129·3	107·3	103·7
1929	158·0	114·5	106·7

It looks as if the ratio of one to four was based on the years immediately following the war, when both long-term and short-term rates had been raised to exceptional levels, first by the war and then by the post-war inflation. For the years from 1924 to 1929 the ratio averages very nearly one to eight.

But in any case statistics of annual averages cannot throw much light on the question. Conditions of activity, with rising prices and high profits, send up both long-term and short-term rates. To isolate the effects of changes in Bank rate, it is necessary to examine movements over shorter periods, as has been done in the preceding chapter. The upshot is to show that the effects of the short-term on the long-term rate are very small, and to that extent to confirm the theoretical calculation given above.

The Macmillan Committee stated that " changes in the level of bank rate affect the price and therefore the yield of investment securities. In periods of low bank rate the price of fixed-interest-bearing securities tends to rise and their yield to fall. The supply of such securities is therefore gradually encouraged, because the cost of borrowing is lower, whilst at the same time the demand for them is increased once confidence has returned in any degree. Long-term funds are thereby placed at the disposal of Government and entrepreneurs and the process of real capital formation is stimulated, with the result that a general rise of prices is engendered."[1] It is not clear on what grounds this statement is based. Is it anything more than a reflexion of the prevalent view of the average stockbroker or City editor, who is accustomed to expect an adjustment of ½ or ¼ of a point in the price of Consols whenever there is a change in Bank rate ? That is all that our statistical investigations would support. The Committee seems to have made the assertion without considering the probable *magnitude* of the effect on the long-term rate of interest, and unfortunately no Samuel Gurney was there to correct their misconception (see above, pp. 146–7).

When it is argued that the effect of changes in the rate of interest is much greater on the instrumental industries than on the industries producing consumable goods, because the effect must be proportional to the time destined to intervene between the operations of the industry and the sale to the consumer of the ultimate product to which the operations contribute, there is again a confusion between long-term and short-term rates of interest. If the change were *in the long-term rate*, the effect would be disproportionately great on the instrumental industries, since their ultimate consumable output is spread over the lives of the instruments which are their immediate product.

If the rate of interest were to rise from, say, 4 to 5 per cent.

---

[1] Report of the Committee on Finance and Industry, 1931. (Cmd. 3897), para. 48.

for all terms, long and short, the additional cost to a trader who holds goods in stock for three months would be ¼ per cent., whereas the present value of an instrument with a life of thirty years, and rendering services worth £10 a year, would be reduced from £173 to £154 or by 11 per cent. But if the rise to 5 per cent. were only expected to last for three months, the effect in the second case would be precisely the same as in the first, ¼ per cent. The time for which some goods are expected to be held in stock may be substantially less than the time for which the existing short-term rate of interest is expected to last. A rise in the rate will not bear so heavily on such goods as on an instrument. But in any case the pressure is slight, and if we want to compare the relative effectiveness of Bank rate operating through working capital and through instrumental capital, we must consider their responsiveness to this slight pressure.

Relative Responsiveness of Fixed and Working Capital to Bank Rate

We have already seen how relatively subordinate is the part played by the short-term rate of interest in the investment market. It has little influence on the temporary borrowing of speculators and promoters, or therefore on the resources of the investment market. And as the market is so organised as to adjust the volume of capital outlay to its resources, the short-term rate of interest has but little direct influence on capital outlay.

But even when great pressure is applied to the investment market, for example when the banks, finding it insufficiently amenable to dear money, endeavour to cut down advances to speculators and promoters by directly restrictive decisions, the response of capital outlay is bound to be tardy.

The promotion of an enterprise involving the raising and installation of capital is a substantial undertaking and involves much planning and preparation, first in the financial field, then in the technical. The preparatory stage,

once it is in train, can only be suspended or prolonged at some cost and inconvenience. If, on the other hand, the preparatory stage has not started, the moment at which the work of installation is to be entered upon, and financial operations on a large scale become necessary, will still be a long way ahead.

Moreover a capital installation usually involves a long period of production, six months or a year or more. At any moment a considerable proportion of the capital outlay in progress is under contracts or commitments entered into months or years before, and the part which has been affected by a recent change in the conditions of the investment market is correspondingly restricted.

It follows that even the effects of causes which do predominantly determine the amount of capital outlay are subject to a considerable time lag. The equalising function of the investment market works tardily, and the adjustment of capital outlay to the fluctuations in the resources of the market over any short period is imperfect.

On the other hand when a trader borrows from his bank in order to purchase goods, either for resale or for use in manufacture, his outstanding indebtedness will depend on the quantity he chooses to get delivered at a time. He will not let his stock fall below the minimum which he judges necessary to guard against its being depleted by unexpected demands, but when the minimum is reached, and he has to replenish the stock, he is free to buy a week's supply or a month's or three months'. If he suddenly finds that he is charged 8 per cent. for an overdraft instead of 4, he can reduce the amount he has to pay in interest at very little cost of inconvenience by obtaining the goods at shorter intervals and in smaller quantities. That does not necessarily mean buying smaller supplies ; he can order the goods far ahead, if he thinks the moment favourable for a forward purchase, and can nevertheless stipulate for a series of deliveries at short intervals, so that at no time during the period over which his order extends will his stock be inconveniently large.

This is much the easiest way by which a trader can keep down his floating indebtedness. He may have a reserve of marketable securities, but if he sells them he must pay commission, and must choose a favourable moment to sell. In regulating his purchases of goods he is dealing with a business in which he neither pays commission nor needs outside advice, for he is himself an expert and a professional trader. In selling securities he needs the services and the advice of a broker, and he must pay commission, which, even though only a fraction of 1 per cent., is a substantial offset to a saving of interest for a short period.

He may try to strengthen his cash out of current receipts, restricting the distribution of profits and withholding the surplus and any unappropriated depreciation allowance from investment. But over a short period that is likely to be a very limited amount, especially for a dealer in commodities with relatively little fixed capital.

A trader who happens to be on the point of undertaking an extension of plant can postpone this, but that course is subject to the disadvantages attaching to the postponement of any capital project. And when a trader has obtained a bank advance for an extension of plant and has gone too far for postponement, the most convenient way of reducing that advance, at any subsequent moment when it is still outstanding, is by postponing the acquisition of goods for stock, even though that was not the original purpose of the advance.

The effect of a rise in the interest charge for bank advances on the purchase of goods by traders will be quick. No preparatory period intervenes. From the very outset there will be some traders arranging purchases and deciding the amount they will add to their stocks. The effect begins at once, and, by the time the great majority of traders have turned over their stocks at least once, the effect will be completed.

Its operation may, it is true, be deferred for a time if producers have an accumulation of orders already on hand. They will be kept busy till the orders are worked through,

and the traders who gave them will be bound by their contracts to take delivery. This is an important cause retarding the restrictive effect of dear money at a time of great activity. But it affects the production of fixed capital as well as that of consumable goods. The producers of the former are quite as likely as those of the latter to find their capacity strained at such a time.

And not only is capital outlay for these reasons less sensitive to the changes in the short-term rate of interest, but it offers a far narrower field for the influence of such changes than the goods in various stages of manufacture which are bought by traders. In any given interval of time the latter may be something like twenty times the former.

Thus many reasons combine to lead us to the conclusion that the primary effect of Bank rate is not on capital outlay, but on traders' stocks of goods. A rise of Bank rate makes traders " less disposed to buy and more disposed to sell," and a fall has the contrary effect. In the latter case production is stimulated, and the resulting increase in incomes generates an increase of demand ; in the former production declines, and income and demand are reduced.

This conclusion merely confirms the assumptions universally made in the early days of the Bank rate tradition, when the working of Bank rate was thought of in terms of bills, and bills were regarded as the means of financing transactions in commodities. And it seems strange that it is not invariably accepted at the present day. If it is doubted and even rejected, the principal explanation seems to be that the reasoning on which it was based has been forgotten. Economists, called upon to explain why a rise in Bank rate has deflationary effects, have sometimes supposed, like Wicksell, that the influence of Bank rate must be looked for in its effect upon costs as a whole. On discovering how minute that effect is, they have jumped to the conclusion that the whole doctrine of the deterrent or deflationary effect of Bank rate is a baseless superstition. Others have penetrated further into the matter, and have

at any rate considered the relation between temporary
borrowing and stocks of commodities. Mr. Keynes dealt
with this aspect in his *Treatise on Money* (Chapter 29, and
p. 363) and argued that the cost of interest on bank advances is so small in comparison with carrying costs and
with expectations of price changes, that it can be neglected.
Mr. Harrod (in *The Trade Cycle*, p. 122) and Mr. A. T. K.
Grant (in *A Study of the Capital Market in Post-War
Britain*, pp. 26–30) take the same view. Mr. Grant even
perpetrates the surprising statement that " the one thing
which is inflexible in the short run is the amount of working
capital required by the community." As well might he
describe a cushion as inflexible, or the ink in a fountain pen
as unvarying. He regards the amount of working capital
as depending " on the rate at which goods are being taken
up by the final consumer in the case of consumption goods,
and by the final owner in the case of new capital goods,"
and has apparently forgotten that traders may delay replenishing their stocks.[1]

Now there is no doubt that *in certain cases* expectations
of price changes will far outweigh the influence of the rate
of interest. In fact whenever the price changes anticipated are so considerable as to provoke speculation, the
speculators in commodities are likely to be as indifferent
to the charge for interest on bank advances as speculators in
securities.

But speculation in commodities is confined to those the
supply of which cannot be readily adapted to fluctuations
in demand. It does not extend outside the range of
primary products except very occasionally, when a new
and unexpected demand springs up for some finished product and for the time being surpasses the capacity of the
industry that supplies it. So far as primary products are
concerned, the same insensitiveness of supply to demand

[1] It is of course true that when traders restrict their purchases general
demand falls off, and owing to the decline of sales the reduction of stocks
of goods is less than they intend. But that only makes the effect on
activity *greater*. It is in fact the principle of the vicious circle.

that gives rise to big fluctuations of price makes productive activity in any case unresponsive.

It may be mentioned that dealers in primary products are not all speculators. The carrying of stocks of wheat or cotton is itself a business. There tends in the most highly organised markets to be a division of function between the dealers who buy and sell forward, and those who actually hold stocks of the commodity. The latter can eliminate the risk of price changes by hedging, that is to say, by effecting forward sales whenever they buy. They derive their profit from the margin between spot and forward prices, and from the turn between buying and selling prices, and this has to cover the cost of handling, transporting and storing the commodity.

For some commodities the cost of storage is high. It may be as much as 10 or even 15 per cent. per annum, of their value. But even where the cost exceeds the charge for interest, it is absurd to suppose that the latter is *negligible* in comparison with the former. In any case such high charges only apply to a few products, such as wheat, cotton or hides, which are bulky in proportion to value, or to perishable or fashionable goods which lose value by keeping. The majority of finished products cost relatively little to store, and, where accommodation does not have to be hired, cost nothing.

Traders and industrialists when consulted as to their practice in regard to holding and replenishing stocks of commodities are apt to thrust the matter aside, and to say that they never consider the charge for bank advances in connection with it. But of course both aspects of the business are in their eyes of very slight consequence and make a very slight impression on their minds. If pressed, they can usually be brought round to the admission that what they have to pay in interest is not absolutely negligible. Indeed in certain moods they are quite ready to make vehement protests against a high charge on bank advances, without any pressing or persuasion at all.

If it were a question not of interest but of a tax varying

from 4 to 8 per cent. per annum on the holding of stocks of goods, no economist would be put off for a moment by the practical trader's argument that it would have no effect on business. And the practical traders' argument itself would probably be the direct contrary.

A high Bank rate is imposed as a deterrent upon short-term borrowing. If a rate of, say, 6 per cent. were found to be negligible, the rate could be raised indefinitely. No one would regard a rate of 60 per cent. as negligible. Some rate could undoubtedly be found far short of that which would affect trading operations perceptibly. Few people would deny the efficacy of 10 per cent. But whatever the critical level is, as soon as the rate is high enough to call for the trader's consideration, the burden is bound to be felt in the special region of working capital long before it is felt as an item in costs as a whole. And with a little care and at very slight inconvenience most traders can escape the greater part or even the whole of the extra burden by keeping their stocks of goods within narrower limits.

There is nothing to prevent Bank rate from being raised to 10, 15 or 30 per cent., if business is insensitive to any lower rate. The only reason why it has stopped short at 10 per cent. or less in the past is that business has in fact responded.

MR. KEYNES'S THEORY OF INTEREST

Mr. Keynes's theory of interest, in his *General Theory of Employment, Interest and Money*, is a theory of the long-term rate. Yet he makes the long-term rate depend on the action of the monetary authorities. The theory is built on the existence of idle balances, representing savings that are withheld from active employment, that is to say, are not devoted by the holders to any permanent income-yielding use. The motive for so withholding them he finds in uncertainty regarding the future long-term rate of interest, and the consequent fear of a capital loss for which even an actuarially equivalent hope of a capital gain is insufficient compensation. He reasons that so long as the

long-term rate of interest prevailing in the market is below what is regarded as a " fairly safe rate," this motive will operate and there will be some idle balances of money in addition to the active balances required for current transactions.

Mr. Keynes concludes that the long-term rate of interest and the amount of money available for the idle balances are mutually related in such a way that either can be regarded as a function of the other. The monetary authority is in a position to determine the long-term rate of interest, because it can decide what amount of money is to be created, and therefore what surplus is to be available to constitute the idle balances.

New money is issued " by a relaxation of the conditions of credit by the banking system, so as to induce someone to sell the banks a debt or a bond in exchange for the new cash." (*General Theory*, p. 200.) He points out that, even when currency is introduced in other ways, such as the coining of gold or the printing of notes, this process of credit relaxation will still become necessary to bring about the requisite adjustments.

To employ the new cash in active balances, there must be an increase in incomes, and an increase in incomes must be brought about by a fall in the long-term rate of interest, to permit of which a part of the new cash must be placed in idle balances.

Mr. Keynes does not specifically say that the fall in the rate of interest must be in the *long-term* rate. And more than once he says that by the rate of interest he means the complex of the various rates of interest current for debts of different maturities (pp. 143 and 167). " It is not difficult," he says, " to re-state the argument so as to cover this point " (p. 143). " We can draw the line between ' money ' and ' debts ' at whatever point is most convenient for handling a particular problem." A " debt " may be limited to money that cannot be recovered within three months, " or we can substitute for ' three months ' one month or three days or three hours or any other period ;

or we can exclude from *money* whatever is not legal tender on the spot " (p. 167).

But it is *not* possible " to restate the argument so as to cover this point." To explain the interest on a debt maturing within three months or less as compensation for the " risk of a loss being incurred in purchasing a long-term debt " is self-contradictory. Mr. Keynes assumes " as a rule . . . that money is co-extensive with bank deposits," and if, as we must surely suppose, the idle balances are placed on time deposit, then money itself *earns interest*, and at a rate depending on the short-term rate.

When the banks " induce someone to sell them a debt or a bond," the debt may, it is true, be a short-term advance and the inducement may be a low short-term rate of interest. But this will not involve any increase in idle balances ; in fact the fall in the short-term rate of interest will actually make the holding of idle balances *less* attractive.

Now the short-term rate of interest is determined by the money market, which is entirely in the hands of the banks. The central bank is in a position to dictate the rate. On the other hand, the long-term rate is determined by the investment market, in which the banks can only intervene as competitors with the other buyers and sellers. Their power of influencing the market is limited and usually, though not invariably (see p. 265), slight.

It would be natural to infer that it is through their power over the short-term rate that the banks would be able to influence the creation of money. And that is the way the Bank of England reasoned a hundred years ago. Mr. Keynes, however, is precluded from following the same path because he believes that borrowing for the holding of stocks of goods is wholly insensitive to the short-term rate of interest. It follows that the short-term rate of interest can only affect activity through its influence over capital outlay, and that practically means through its influence on the long-term rate.

With his complete disbelief in the influence of the short-term rate of interest on stocks of goods, Mr. Keynes combines a naïve faith in the influence of the long-term rate on capital outlay. There is a determinate relation between consumption and the consumers' income as a whole, and the consumers' income can only expand so far as provision exists for applying the excess over consumption to capital outlay. If capital outlay is regulated by the long-term rate of interest and the long-term rate of interest is determined by the amount of idle balances, then it is upon the regulation of the idle balances that the consumers' income ultimately depends and with it the degree of economic activity.

It follows that when the banks proceed to create money by inducing people to sell debts or bonds, it is the effect on the long-term rate of interest that matters. " If the monetary authority were prepared to deal both ways on specified terms in debts of all maturities, and even more so if it were prepared to deal in debts of varying degrees of risk, the relationship between the complex of rates of interest and the quantity of money would be direct. The complex of rates of interest would simply be an expression of the terms on which the banking system is prepared to acquire or part with debts. . . . Perhaps a complex offer by the central bank to buy and sell at stated prices gilt-edged bonds of all maturities, in place of the single bank rate for short-term bills, is the most important practical improvement which can be made in the technique of monetary management " (*General Theory*, pp. 205–6).

Mr. Keynes contemplates the central bank itself affecting the rate of interest by buying and selling securities. But according to his own theory that is not the way to do it. The central bank by buying securities does, no doubt, create new deposits, but they are deposits to the credit of the commercial banks, not to the credit of individuals with savings to dispose of. Unless the commercial banks create new deposits to provide their customers with additional idle balances, the long-term rate of interest will not

fall. Thus it is not the intervention of the central bank in the investment market that raises the prices of securities, but the further action taken by the commercial banks in creating credit. It does not matter whether they buy securities or make additional advances, provided the additional idle balances come into existence. Nor does it matter by what process the central bank creates credit ; it need not buy securities, but might with equal effect make additional advances or discounts or buy gold. Similarly, when activity has to be checked, the central bank must contract its deposits and the commercial banks must pass on the pressure to their customers by contracting their deposits in turn. Neither need actually sell securities.

It may be said, perhaps, that if the banks increase or decrease their advances instead of buying or selling securities, there is no immediate effect on the prices of securities, and the proceeds of the advances may go into active balances and leave the idle balances unchanged. But according to Mr. Keynes's theory active balances will only increase or decrease if the total of incomes increases or decreases, and that will only occur if the long-term rate of interest falls or rises.

What would be the function of Bank rate in this analysis? The central bank has to induce the commercial banks to expand or contract their deposits by itself expanding or contracting their cash reserves. If it relies on purchases or sales of securities to effect this object, it may find, as the Bank of England found in 1839, that its operations are counteracted by contrary movements of its discounts. If it tries to force the commercial banks to contract credit by selling securities, they may fill the gap in their cash by getting bills rediscounted. In that case, if the central bank is to fulfil its function as lender of last resort, it must have recourse to some method of deterring borrowers. In other words it must raise its discount rate.

The commercial banks can pass on the pressure to their customers. So long as they can charge a sufficiently high rate on their own advances and discounts, the high Bank

rate is no burden to them. The deterrent effect is felt, if at all, by the customers who borrow from the banks.

The banks may sell securities. If so, that is simply a part of the general tendency to sell securities under the influence of dear money, a tendency which will depress the prices of securities to the level at which the inducement to sell is compensated, and will then stop. The rise in the long-term rate of interest involved in this fall of the prices of securities will not lead to any diminution of idle balances, because the idle balances themselves will be earning a higher rate of deposit interest.

The deflationary power of the rise of Bank rate will be confined to the deterrent effect of the rise in the long-term rate of interest on capital outlay. If the banks, by selling securities, reduce active balances below the level corresponding to the consumers' income, their customers will restore their active balances by obtaining additional advances.

Surely the power of Bank rate so limited is negligible. If this picture is a true one, the system of credit regulation pursued for the past hundred years has been one long practical joke. It has been founded on "psychological" reactions which have had no basis in reality.

This presentation of the central bank's regulation of credit is based on two assumptions : that working capital is insensitive to the short-term rate of interest, and that capital outlay is sensitive to the long-term rate. Both of these I have given reason to reject.

Mr. Keynes's theory of the long-term rate is based on the principle that the growth of capital[1] will be pushed to the point at which the " marginal efficiency " of capital is brought to approximate equality with the rate of interest. The sausage theory of capital equates the marginal yield of capital, in the sense of the cost-saving capacity of the marginal or least remunerative instrument, to the rate of interest ; it is an approximation to the truth, in that the

---

[1] By the growth of capital I mean here what Mr. Keynes calls " investment," the aggregate increment of the equipment of entrepreneurs.

deepening of capital does have a tendency, vague and slow though it be, to be adjusted to the limit of remunerativeness set by the rate of interest. But Mr. Keynes's marginal efficiency is not the cost-saving capacity of the marginal *instrument*, but the expected profit-earning capacity of the marginal *enterprise*. It is unnecessary to indicate the theoretical objections to this usage,[1] but what we have to take account of is the fact that, as marginal efficiency is based on the expectation of profit-earning capacity, there enters into it a psychological element, and a psychological element which is essentially a forecast of the state of demand.

Mr. Keynes's theory does not preclude these expectations being modified by a credit policy which affects general demand. His rejection of the influence of changes in the short-term rate of interest on stocks of commodities is expressly subject to the qualification : " unless these changes create an expectation of changes in prices " (*Treatise on Money*, Vol. II, p. 363). In the language of his later work, the *General Theory*, this might be described as a modification of the marginal efficiency of capital. It is to such changes of " current expectations as to the future yield of capital goods " that Mr. Keynes attributes the fluctuations of the trade cycle (*General Theory*, p. 315). If we imagine a change in Bank rate to create an expectation of a change in prices, an increased or decreased demand for stocks of commodities will also result, and so there will be a corresponding increase or decrease of activity, independent of the long-term rate of interest.

But this is not the only qualification to which Mr. Keynes's scepticism of the sensitiveness of working capital is subject. He also regards the " fringe of unsatisfied borrowers " as affording the banking system a means of influencing investment in stocks of commodities independently of mere changes in the short-term rate of interest (*Treatise on Money*, Vol. II, p. 365). That is to say, the banks can and do restrict credit by refusing to lend, instead

[1] See my *Capital and Employment*, pp. 181-6.

of imposing a deterrent rate of interest, and they can induce a creation of credit by relaxing their refusal.

Now I have suggested above (p. 61) that the reason why a moderate Bank rate has often proved unexpectedly effective as a deterrent is that it produces changes in traders' expectations, which reinforce its effects, and also that a high Bank rate leads the commercial banks, not merely to charge correspondingly high rates to their customers, but to keep down the volume of credit by refusing to lend to the less eligible borrowers. If Bank rate worked in no other way, these results would be adequate by themselves to achieve the regulation of credit.

seems to follow that Mr. Keynes's rejection of the traditional view of Bank rate is by no means so uncompromising as a superficial survey of the pronouncements on the subject contained in his more recent works would suggest. And I may add that his view of Bank rate does not really depend on the theory of liquidity preference and idle balances expounded in his *General Theory of Employment, Interest and Money*. All that that theory involves is that the volume of credit should carry a load of idle balances corresponding to the prevailing long-term rate of interest. The quantity of currency and the quantity of bank credit, to maintain full employment at a given level of wages, must be adequate to provide the requisite active balances after allowing for this load.

The Proceeds of Liquidation of Working Capital

There still remains the question whether the idle balances of Mr. Keynes's theory exist, or rather whether they exist on a considerable enough scale to give significance to the theory.

We have referred above to the inflationary supplement that may be added to the resources of the investment market by bank advances to speculators and promoters. But that does not exhaust the possibilities of an inflationary supplement. People may contribute to the same result by drawing on existing cash balances to buy securities,

without obtaining any bank advances. And those who do obtain bank advances will first use up their existing cash, and will limit their borrowing to the remainder of what is needed.

Idle balances in Mr. Keynes's sense will be a source of a supplement when they decrease or of a deplement when they increase. Like the speculator, the holder of an idle balance is guided by a view as to the prices of securities ; the view however is not as to the prices of any particular securities but as to the long-term rate of interest, which enters into the prices of all. He is not influenced by an improvement in the prospect of profits and dividends as such, but only by the rise in the long-term rate of interest resulting from an increased marginal efficiency of capital in which that improvement of prospects would be reflected.

The idle balances are withheld from the purchase of securities on account of the " risk of a loss being incurred in purchasing a long-term debt." When I was writing *The Economic Problem* in 1925, I took for granted that " in a community where there is social security, and where the practice of investment is developed, nearly all the people who have a surplus of any considerable amount will invest all beyond a moderate working balance of money."[1] In doing so I was following the opinion then accepted both among economists and among the public generally, and, so far as I know, neither Mr. Keynes nor any one else has furnished any evidence that the current savings in course of being accumulated out of income are to any considerable extent held up in idle balances by the motive indicated.

Nevertheless there is a class of funds which would be placed in securities in suitable conditions but would be withheld if there were a serious risk of a loss through capital depreciation. Reference has been made above (p. 159) to the proceeds of liquidation of working capital, arising when demand is shrinking, and the goods traders sell are replaced by smaller quantities at lower prices. Money coming from that source is liable to be required

[1] *The Economic Problem*, p. 50.

at short notice for an expansion of working capital as soon as business revives, and the gain in interest from placing it in securities for a short time may be easily wiped out by a small capital depreciation.

The liquidation of working capital is one manifestation of the vicious circle of deflation. It means that the orders given to producers fall short of the amount of sales to consumers, and that the shrinkage of economic activity is greater than the shrinkage of demand. At the same time the mere fact that for the moment demand is in excess of the consumers' income is an alleviation of the tendency towards depression. If consumers maintained their cash balances unchanged, and rigidly limited their outlay to their income, traders would find that they could not obtain any cash resources from the liquidation of their working capital. They could indeed get rid of redundant stocks by selling them at lower retail prices, but they would not on balance receive any additional cash. If some traders received more cash, others would receive less. It is because consumers release cash that traders absorb cash.[1]

The release of cash by consumers is in fact an inflationary supplement of general demand in mitigation of the assumed predominant tendency to deflation. But the absorption of cash by traders is a counteracting deflationary influence or deplement. If traders, instead of absorbing the cash, buy securities with it, so that it becomes available through the investment market for capital outlay, they are no longer undoing the original release of cash by the consumers. To that extent they are a channel for the release of cash from the consumers to the investment market, a release of cash which constitutes an inflationary supplement to the resources of that market.

Thus, when at a time of depression the investment market seems to be flooded with a superfluity of savings, it is not to be inferred that current savings are in excess of capital outlay, and that remunerative openings cannot be found

---

[1] It is of course possible, however, that one set of traders may accumulate idle cash by selling goods to another set of traders who, failing to resell the goods, have to incur increased bank advances.

to employ them. Savings are supplemented by the proceeds of liquidation of working capital, and it is the total thus swollen that the investment market fails to employ. It should be noted that Mr. Keynes, in expounding his doctrine, takes for granted that the market can always find a use for whatever resources it may receive, so long as marginal efficiency does not fall (as it never has) to zero. That is to say, subject to that condition, the investment market never fails to apply to capital outlay any part of the funds placed in it.

As at times of depression the liquidation of working capital causes an accumulation of idle funds, so at times of activity the need for increased working capital draws on balances, and occasions an increase in bank advances. And whereas in the former case a part of the idle funds will be placed in the investment market either directly by traders or by the banks which find their deposits growing and their advances shrinking, so in the latter case there will be sales of securities both by traders and by banks. At times of depression the inflationary supplement derived by the investment market from speculators shrinks and may turn into a deplement, but this shrinkage is partly offset by the entrance of a part of the proceeds of liquidation of working capital into the market. At times of activity the inflationary supplement derived from speculators is partly offset by the sale of securities to provide increased working capital. There is clear evidence that on the whole the resources of the investment market are increased by activity and diminished by depression. So far as British statistics are concerned there is a tendency for external investment to grow to a maximum at a time of activity and to shrink again at a time of depression.

Mr. C. K. Hobson, in his *Export of Capital*, made estimates of the net export of capital from the United Kingdom year by year from 1870 to 1912. Maxima are revealed for the years of activity 1872, 1881, 1890 and 1907. For 1900 the figure is so far a maximum that it is higher than that for any of the three preceding or four succeeding years.

It is still low for a year of activity, but no doubt the explanation is that the Government borrowing for the South African War absorbed savings that would otherwise have been available for external investment. Now external investment is evidence of surplus resources in the investment market. The need for investment at home is likely to be met first, and only the residue to be placed abroad. And the need for investment at home is likely to be greater at a time of activity than at a time of depression. Therefore we can infer that the resources entering the investment market rise at times of activity and fall at times of depression.

INFLUENCE OF THE LONG-TERM RATE OF INTEREST ON THE SHORT-TERM RATE

Allusion has been made above (p. 185) to the long-term rate influencing the short-term rate. That occurs because the two rates are in competition with one another at various points. The short-term lenders, mainly banks, invest a part of their resources in long-term or funded securities, and increase this part if they find difficulty in placing short-term money at adequate rates. The short-term borrowers have the alternative open to them of raising additional capital on a long-term basis.

If the long-term rate is low relatively to the short-term rate, and traders can get a favourable rate on time deposits, they will tend to raise more permanent capital. They avoid paying a high rate for bank advances, and suffer little loss or actually make a gain on their idle cash. If the disparity of rates is expected to last a long time, the effect may be appreciable. But what the traders gain the banks lose. They find their income from advances falling off, their payments for interest on deposits increasing, and the difference is made up by low-yielding investments. Such a state of things is unlikely to last ; the banks will reduce the interest both on deposits and advances, *unless* the central bank is enforcing a high rate. That it can do by restricting its own advances and discounts and selling securities, so

that it keeps the commercial banks short of cash. They will then try to reduce their deposits, and will become sellers of securities till deposits and advances are in due proportion. A wide disparity of rates may still persist.

The substitution of the raising of permanent capital for short-term borrowing is in any case likely to be so limited and gradual that the effect on the creation of credit would be small. But when the long-term rate of interest is high relatively to the short-term rate, the contrary substitution might be more considerable. It is easier to restrict or postpone the raising of capital than to enlarge or hasten it. Consequently there is likely to be an earlier and greater pressure on the money market. Here again, however, the central bank has the power to keep down the short-term rate.

The reaction of the long-term on the short-term rate is best understood as reinforcing the central bank's efforts to bring about either an expansion or a contraction of credit. There is very little reason for regarding the long-term rate as *setting a standard* for the short-term rate, to which on an average, after the elimination of fluctuations, the latter must conform.

CHAPTER VII

THE RATE OF INTEREST AND THE PRICE LEVEL

THE " REAL " RATE OF INTEREST

WE turn next to the experience of the post-war years. It was suggested above (p. 163–4) that the main influence affecting the price of Consols from the end of the war onwards was to be found in the prospects of the currency. Even during the war that may have been a contributory cause of the rising yield of Government securities, though the imperative need to collect all available resources for the war in any case required a yield that would look attractive in comparison with other openings for investment. At the time of the Armistice Consols rose to a price which made the yield only 4 per cent. But Consols still retained a special prestige conferring an artificially high price in comparison with other Government securities. The 5 per cent. War Loan did not rise to par.

The pound was at that time still pegged to the dollar at a rate of 4·76½, and the gold market was completely in abeyance. Under those conditions the only visible form inflation took·was a rise of commodity prices.

But at the end of March, 1919, the pound ceased to be pegged on the dollar, the rate of exchange became free to vary, and the export of gold was prohibited. Depreciation relative both to the dollar and to gold became possible and measurable.

We have seen how the prices of fixed-interest securities rise in times of depression and fall in times of activity. In times of activity expanding demand and rising prices of commodities offer more profitable opportunities for the widening of capital, and the competition of these opportunities withdraws money from fixed-interest securities and depresses their prices. In times of depression the opportunities for the widening of capital are diminished.

This tendency is by no means counteracted by the falling off of current savings at a time of depression (even if we leave out of account the appearance of the proceeds of liquidation of working capital seeking investment). For a shortage of savings only excludes from exploitation a portion of the openings, and those that are left are subject to the full influence of the depression.

And similarly at a time of activity the effect of expanding demand and rising prices is to make the whole range of investment projects more attractive. No possible increase in savings could counteract this effect, unless an actual glut of capital were in any case imminent.

Professor Irving Fisher, elaborating Marshall's doctrine, has expounded the relation which holds between the rate of interest and changing purchasing power of the monetary unit, or, in other words, a moving price level. If the change in purchasing power is not foreseen, and the market rate of interest consequently not affected by it, the true gain to the creditor, the " real " rate of interest, as Professor Fisher calls it, is compounded of the market rate and a coefficient representing the rate of change of the price level. If in a given interval of time the rate of interest is r per unit, (i.e. 100 r per cent.) and prices are rising by a fraction p per unit, the creditor receives $1 + r$ times his loan in money, but only $\dfrac{1 + r}{1 + p}$ in terms of goods. Or if prices fall at the rate of p per unit the creditor receives $\dfrac{1 + r}{1 - p}$ times his loan in terms of goods and gains more than his interest. The " real " rate of interest in the former case is $\dfrac{r - p}{1 + p}$ and in the latter $\dfrac{r + p}{1 - p}$.

If the change of purchasing power is foreseen, there will be a tendency to correct this divergence from the intended rate of interest, and to charge a rate of interest which will just compensate the change in prices. If, when prices are rising, the creditor is to receive $1 + r$ times his loan in terms of goods, the rate of interest would have to be

$(1 + r)(1 + p) - 1$ or $r + p + rp$. Similarly when prices are falling it would have to be $r - p - rp$.

PRICES AND FORWARD QUOTATIONS

Now it is quite impossible for the market to foresee a change in the price level even over a period of a few months with any approach to exactitude. But conditions do arise in which the expectation of such a change has a quite definite and even measurable effect on the market.

In the case of any one commodity an expectation of a change of price may be disclosed by quotations in a forward market. But in the case of a commodity of which a stock is held there is a limit to the divergence between the present or spot price and the forward price. For people will not sell on the spot at a price lower than the price for forward sales by more than the margin which would cover the cost of holding the goods in stock for the interval. If the cost of storing wheat is equivalent to 10 per cent. of its value per annum, and the short-term rate of interest is 5 per cent., the price three months forward cannot exceed the price for immediate delivery by more than 3¾ per cent. (15 per cent. for a quarter of a year). An expected fall of price is not so precisely limited. If for example big crops are anticipated and a consequent fall of the price of wheat, holders of the existing stocks will sell them off at the prevailing relatively favourable price. *If the stocks are sufficient*, these sales will depress the spot price, and may even bring it down below the low future price, because the sellers are escaping the cost of storage and interest. But the available supply may not be adequate to anticipate plenty to this extent, and, if so, the spot price may remain for a time substantially above the future price.

Wheat is a commodity which illustrates in a peculiar manner the relations between spot and forward prices; it is a seasonal product of which large stocks have to be held; its price is subject to large variations, depending on crop conditions which can be to some extent foreseen; and,

as it is very bulky in proportion to its value, the cost of storing it is high.

The behaviour of many other primary products is similar. But that of manufactured products is in some important respects different. A manufactured product is not seasonal, but is produced continuously, as the market may require. The conditions of supply being more or less fixed, the variations of price are mainly attributed to variations in demand. Manufactured goods are for the most part much less bulky in proportion to value than primary products, and are correspondingly less costly to store (though some are subject to the risk of changes of fashion or taste).

Variations in demand for finished products are difficult to foresee. Sometimes some new circumstance likely to affect demand for a product is definitely known beforehand. More often an anticipation of a rise or fall of price is due simply to the belief that an existing tendency for demand to increase or decrease will continue.

Apart from any anticipation of a rise of price, an existing expansion of demand brings about increased orders to producers. Not only are traders' stocks exhausted more quickly, so that the orders for their replenishment are hastened, but as greater sales require greater stocks, orders are given for greater quantities. Increased orders lead the producers to ask higher prices. If they have already been fully employed, the demand is more than they can supply ; if they have been under-employed, they have probably for that reason been content with prices and profits below normal. In either alternative increased business means a rise of price.

If, as is very probable, the purchasing traders are led by the growing activity of the producers to expect a rise of price, they will give *further* orders, in excess of those required by their stocks on the basis of actual current sales, in order to take advantage of the market while the price is still low. In effect the traders will be acquiring an additional stock by way of speculation. This will force up the

present or spot price, and will continue to do so till the speculative advantage has been eliminated. And that will occur when the difference between the spot price and the future price is no more than equal to the cost, for storage, interest, etc., of holding the speculative stocks for the interval of time that is expected to pass before the anticipated price is reached.

THE POST-WAR INFLATION, 1919–20

In the post-war inflation that set in in 1919 it was the demand not merely for one commodity but for all that was expanding. And traders were aware not only of the fact of expansion but of its cause. Owing to the strain of war finance paper currency and bank credit were being manufactured and were swelling the purchasing power of the public. In every trade people anticipated a further expansion of demand and a further rise of price. And traders proceeded accordingly to order additional supplies of goods with a view to adding to their stocks before the rise of price materialised.

To pay for these additional supplies of goods, they had to obtain bank advances. First the producers borrowed to pay the costs of production, then the purchasers borrowed to pay the price to the producers. Thus money in the form of bank credit was created, and additional demand was generated. The vicious circle of inflation revolved merrily. Prices were rising at the rate of 3 to 4 per cent. a month. The forward buyer or the trader who bought commodities with borrowed money made an extra profit at that rate. It appeared to be worth while to borrow at any rate of interest not exceeding the *expected* rate of the rise of prices.

Expectations were founded partly on a mere presumption that the near future would resemble the immediate past, partly on a reasoned calculation that the Government could not avoid creating more and more money. But such calculations had to be heavily discounted for the intervention of chance and for the efforts the Government would undoubtedly make to escape from its difficulties.

Bank rate was put up to 6 per cent. in November, 1919, and to 7 in April, 1920. The predominant rate for advances and overdrafts was perhaps 1 per cent. higher. Even 8 per cent. seems moderate in comparison with the rate at which prices had been rising. But in combination with unmistakable signs that the Government meant to emerge from its financial embarrassments, and that the Government and the Bank between them would insist on regaining control of the monetary situation, the rise of Bank rate sufficed to break the vicious circle That was because there was a change in expectations. Up to that moment the expected " real " rate of interest in Professor Irving Fisher's sense had probably been below zero, that is to say the anticipated rise of prices had been more than sufficient to offset the cost of interest at the market rate. But it is not to be assumed that the anticipated rate of rise of prices was equal at any stage to the actual rate, either to that which had been experienced in the immediate past or to that which was destined to follow in the near future. Any expectation had to be liberally discounted for the uncertainty of the situation.

Professor Fisher in his *Purchasing Power of Money* held that the fluctuations of the trade cycle were due to the adjustment of the market rate of interest to the real rate being incomplete. When prices were rising, the market rate rose, but not high enough to make the real rate normal ; when prices were falling, it fell, but not low enough. The book appeared in 1911, and the theory envisaged the trade cycle as it had been experienced up to that time. Nevertheless the difference between the conditions of 1919 and those of 1906 or 1899 was no more than one of degree, except that in 1919 the expectation of a continued rise of prices was reinforced by the palpable effects of an inflationary monetary policy.

Professor Fisher, perhaps, laid too much stress on the tendency to overlook the effect of rising or falling prices when determining the rate of interest. For Bank rate was settled by a method of trial and error, which allowed

automatically for all the factors at work. The delay in adjusting it, to which Professor Fisher quite rightly attributes the fluctuations, was really due to the practice of using the Bank of England's reserve as a criterion. The reserve responded very tardily to an expansive or contractive movement, so that there were long periods in which the Bank acquiesced in such movements without attempting to counteract them. But when it did resort to the rate of interest as a corrective, the Bank simply went on raising or lowering the rate till the desired effect followed. If in raising the rate it stopped short at 7 per cent. or 9 per cent., that was because the market responded.

When the forward price of a commodity falls below the spot price, that is because an increased supply is foreseen, and the existing stocks are not sufficient to permit of the increased supply being anticipated. When a currency is depreciating, an increased future supply is similarly foreseen, and traders seek to anticipate the future increase by borrowing from the banks. If the monetary authorities refuse to allow the banks to have sufficient cash reserves to enable them to satisfy the borrowers' demands, the effect is seen in a rise in the short-term rate of interest. The additional interest is really simply the difference between the spot and forward value of money in terms of commodities. If the additional interest were not charged, enough additional money would be created through bank advances to anticipate the future supply and the corresponding depreciation.

EFFECT OF CHANGING PRICE LEVEL ON THE LONG-TERM RATE OF INTEREST

The effect of a rising or falling price level on the short-term rate of interest is clear. The effect on the long-term rate, though in some respects more obscure, is still important.

We have already seen how an expansion of general demand, even if accompanied by no actual rise of prices, stimulates the widening and even also the deepening of capital, and how the long-term rate of interest will be raised

to maintain equilibrium in the investment market. It is almost certain that such an expansion of general demand will be accompanied by a rise of prices, which will accentuate the tendency by making projects for extending capacity and increasing output still more profitable.

The rise of prices may however be temporary. If consumption demand outstrips the capacity of the industries supplying it, the prices of consumable goods rise, and the pressure for the supply of plant to extend the capacity of the consumption industries at the same time causes a rise in the prices of the products of the instrumental industries. During this process, with a given level of wages, full employment requires a relatively higher price level, and, when the extension of capacity of the consumption industries is completed, the transfer of productive resources should be associated with a fall in the price level. For the increased output of consumable goods permits a replenishment of stocks and a reduction of prices to the consumer. And the instrumental industries revert to the level of activity corresponding to the supply of no more than normal growth and replacement of capital, and so there also the high prices subside.

In practice this process was complicated by monetary regulation. The original shortage of capacity in the consumption industries was ordinarily the result of underemployment in a period of depression. The expansion of demand was the sign of revival. In the early stages of revival there would still be surplus capacity in the consumption industries, but a stage would be reached at which the effects of the low level of capital outlay in the preceding years would be felt, and there would be pressure on the instrumental industries to overtake arrears. But even after full employment was attained, there would be no finality, so long as the monetary expansion continued. Even if wages remained unchanged, demand would go on expanding. Profits are a source of demand as well as wages ; they are a source of consumption demand as well as of savings. When a monetary expansion goes ahead

of wages, there are excess profits, and savings absorb a larger proportion than usual of the consumers' income. But under those conditions savings will not be held idle ; an active investment market will apply them rapidly to capital outlay. When arrears of widening are overtaken, not only will technological progress provide new openings for deepening, but new industries will be instituted and developed. Moreover rising prices and excess profits soon bring rising wages, tending to restore profits, savings and consumption to their normal proportions.

What brings the expansive process to an end is the *monetary* limit. In the century up to 1914 it was the state of the gold reserve. In 1919 the monetary system had been cut loose from the gold reserve. The result was that whereas in previous periods of activity the rise in the price level, the excess profits and the pressure of capital outlay were regarded as temporary, in 1919 people were contemplating the possibility of a permanent change in the price level. Those who bought or sold Consols were compelled to look forward to the price level not merely a few months but many years ahead. There might be a loss of real income which no change in the phases of industrial activity would rectify. It was that risk that brought Consols down to 44 and the 5 per cent. War Loan to 82 at the end of 1920.

In 1921 deflation of the currency brought recovery in securities. Yet the long-term rate of interest remained far above the pre-war level. The yield on Consols did not again fall to 4 per cent. till 1932 ; the yield on other Government securities oscillated about 4½ per cent.

That this should have been so despite the continuance of trade depression and unemployment is surprising. It is tempting to attribute it to the unprecedented association of trade depression with dear money for the greater part of the period. But at the outset in 1922–3, when money was cheap and the revival from a state of acute depression was beginning, Consols never rose above 60.

The explanation is, I think, that the enormous war borrowings of the Government had upset the balance in

the market between Government securities and all other forms of investment. It had been necessary to attract into Government securities the *main body* of savings. Up to 1914 Government securities had been sought mainly as a reserve investment, readily marketable and well adapted as collateral for bank advances. Once this essential reserve had been provided, the investor turned to securities of higher yield, relying on his own judgment or on expert advice to select them without any serious sacrifice of safety, though possibly at some sacrifice of marketability.

The exigencies of war led the Government to offer a yield which obliterated all these nice distinctions. Any one could obtain security, marketability and a high yield, combined, without any expert advice or exercise of judgment. And after the war, when securities with these characteristics amounted to thousands of millions of pounds, their scarcity value had been destroyed, and they still had to meet rival investments on more nearly equal terms in respect of yield.

Mr. Keynes has described the rate of interest as a " highly conventional phenomenon." He meant that lenders do not easily change their minds as to what is a reasonable or a " fairly safe " rate. That the rate is highly conventional is I think quite true, but the convention exists as much in the minds of borrowers as in those of lenders, As has been indicated above (p. 171), the sausage theory of capital, the idea of a clear-cut marginal yield of capital corresponding closely to the market long-term rate of interest, is a delusion. The relation of yield to the market rate of interest is vague and approximate. Industrialists accept the market rate of interest as an external fact to be reckoned with in their calculations of costs, but their expectation of profit is subject to so wide a margin of uncertainty that considerable variations in the rate of interest make very little impression upon it. The practical effect of a rise or fall in the prices of securities is felt in the hastening or postponement of enterprises, and promoters' judgment as to whether the investment market is favourable or unfavour-

able depends very much on whether the prevailing yield
of securities is below or above a rate which is for the time
being conventionally regarded as normal. So long as 4½
per cent. was regarded as a normal yield, a fractionally lower
yield was favourable to flotations. The revival of economic
activity which took place between 1921 and the re-establish-
ment of the gold standard in 1925 does not seem to have
been hampered at all by the continuance of a rate near this
level. House building, which is especially susceptible to
the long-term rate of interest, was, it is true, assisted during
this period by Government subsidies, and it is possible that,
without those subsidies, the deterrent effect of 4½ per cent.
might have been felt in a shrinkage of that form of capital
outlay. We cannot be sure that the other openings for
remunerative capital outlay would have been sufficient to
use up the available resources of the investment market.
If so, the pressure on the market would have brought about a
fall in the rate of interest notwithstanding any convention,
and we arrive at the paradoxical conclusion that the subsidy
kept the rate of interest up.

The aggravation of depression in 1930 brought cheap
money, and Government securities rose. But their yield
at its lowest still remained in the neighbourhood of 4½
per cent. Consols at 60½ in June, 1931, counted as high.

There then supervened the financial crisis. Consols fell
to 56½ at the beginning of September, 1931. The currency
had once more entered into people's calculations. The
suspension of the gold standard brought Consols down to
49½ and 5 per cent. War Loan to 90½. After some fluctuations Consols were still as low as 51 in December, 1931.

In 1932 on the other hand people awoke to the fact that
the currency was no longer being maintained at a pre-
cariously high level. The pound sterling was being valued
in a free market, and the pressure which had been threatening to depreciate it was no longer to be feared.

At the same time the devastating effect of the depression
on industrial investment was acutely felt. The outlets for
enterprise had never been so dead. A flood of investment

was turned towards Government securities and their yield fell. The skilful and courageous conversion of the 5 per cent. War Loan in the summer of 1932 anticipated an adjustment of the yield to 3½ per cent. The conversion itself helped to realise the expectation. And soon the yield fell lower still. In January, 1935, Consols actually touched 94, the highest price since the reduction of the interest to 2½ per cent. in 1903.

A contributory cause of this rise was the liquidation of working capital, resulting in an increase of bank deposits and a decrease of bank advances. The banks filled the gap by buying Government securities and the clearing banks' holding of investments rose from £296 millions in December, 1931, to £594 millions in December, 1934.

But another cause of the rise is to be found in the foreign money taking refuge from countries whose currency units were still being maintained at an impossible gold parity at the cost of intolerable efforts. Here again was the monetary cause at work.

At the same time it is worthy of note that the subsidies for house-building by private enterprise practically ceased after 1929. The transition to a very low long-term rate was accompanied by a great expansion in the volume of house building by private enterprise, without subsidy. The course of events was not inconsistent with the supposition that the subsidy had kept up the rate of interest.

A scrutiny of the prices of Government securities of different maturities in January, 1935, discloses the fact that the low yield was especially characteristic of those maturing in a period of a few years. Thus 4½ per cent. Conversion Stock which the Government had the option of repaying in 1940 stood at 113¾ and yielded less than 2 per cent.; 5 per cent. Conversion Stock which could be repaid in 1944 was at 124, and yielded less than 2¼ per cent. The 3 per cent. Conversion Stock which could not be repaid before 1948 was at 107½ and yielded nearly 2½ per cent.

At the same time the longer-dated stocks yielded 2¾ per cent. or more. The 3½ per cent. Conversion Stock,

which could be repaid in 1961, was at 112⅝ (or 111¾ *ex dividend*) and yielded 2·85 per cent.

If, taking the 5 per cent. Conversion Stock as a test, we assume the appropriate yield for a nine-year security to have been 2¼ per cent., then for that period a 3½ per cent. stock would yield surplus interest to the amount of 1¼ per cent. The present value of the surplus interest for nine years would very nearly account for the whole premium on the 3½ per cent. Conversion stock. That is to say, there was practically no more surplus interest to be allowed for after nine years, and the market quotations may be interpreted as implying that a 3½ per cent. security would be little above par at the end of that time. Such a calculation cannot be regarded as exactly reliable, but we need not hesitate to say that the high prices of Government securities were mainly based upon an assumed low yield for a moderate term of years, followed by a yield little if at all below 3½ per cent. thereafter. And that goes to confirm the view that the high prices were due to a demand for medium-term bonds, which were a suitable investment for banks, for surplus working capital or for refugee money. There were few medium-term gilt-edged bonds in the market at the time. But Treasury bills were being discounted at ½ per cent., and the 2½ per cent. Treasury bonds maturing in February, 1937, and therefore having about two years to run, were quoted at 104¼ and yielded less than ½ per cent.

In the contrary case where long-term securities are quoted at low prices, because there is fear of loss through depreciation of the currency, doubtless the effect is primarily felt on the first few years of a security's life. The fear of depreciation however may extend over a relatively long period. Professor Irving Fisher compares the relative yields of rupee loans and sterling loans of the Government of India in the period from 1865 to 1906 (*Theory of Interest*, pp. 403–7). The former were (till 1893) regarded as silver obligations and the latter as gold obligations, and people's views of the future value of silver in relation to gold might

well take into account a considerable period of years. Implicit in any such forecast is an opinion respecting the price level. If in 1890 people required a yield of 4 per cent. on an Indian Government rupee obligation when they were content with 3 per cent. on a sterling obligation of the same Government, one or other of these rates, if not both, must be regarded as allowing for the prospect of a change in the *relative* purchasing power of rupees and pounds.

Investors and traders, however, do not think in terms of price index numbers ; they cannot be supposed to introduce estimates of purchasing power in general into their calculations. By what process then did they arrive at the difference they made between rupee and sterling securities?

We may suppose that any one who sought an investment in India would compare the yield of rupee securities with the profits of trade and industry in India, whereas any one who sought an investment in England would compare the yield of sterling securities with the profits of trade and industry in England. The discrepancy arose because at the time trade and industry were relatively much less profitable in England than in India, and this difference was directly attributable to the depreciation of the rupee relative to the pound which gave the Indian producers the prospect of prices rising relatively to English prices.

This effect did not depend on the corresponding change in wages lagging behind the change in prices. Even if wages and prices both moved exactly with the rate of exchange, there was still the prospect of the profit of an Indian business reckoned in rupees rising relatively to the corresponding profit of an English business reckoned in pounds. The lag of wages would confer a further increase of profit on the Indian producer and inflict a diminution of profit on the English producer, and this effect might, in virtue of the trader's customary empiricism, accentuate the difference between rupee yields and sterling yields.

The "Natural" Rate of Interest

Writing in 1913, in my *Good and Bad Trade* (p. 66) I made a distinction between the "natural rate" of

interest, representing " the actual labour-saving value of capital at the level of capitalisation reached by industry," and the " profit rate," which " diverges from the natural rate according to the tendency of prices " and " represents the true profits of business prevailing for the time being." Though expressed on that occasion in terms of the sausage theory of capital, and without regard to the difference between profit and interest, the distinction is a real one. But it requires qualification in that there is no determinate " natural rate " of *short-term* interest.

Even in the case of the long-term rate the natural rate is largely governed by convention, and only loosely related to the wide range of yields among which the " margin " is distributed. But in the case of the stocks of commodities, which form the greater part and the readily variable part of working capital, the only " labour saving value " is in the gain of convenience in buying a suitable quantity at a time. That is not determined by " the level of capitalisation reached by industry," but can be varied within wide limits in a short time without any considerable change in the level of capitalisation generally. If the long-term rate of interest were steady at 4 per cent. and the short-term rate varied between 2 and 10, both might be in equilibrium with the natural rate. The steady long-term rate might represent (as nearly as may be) the labour-saving value of the capital actually in use, and the buying convenience of working capital might be rapidly adjusted to the variable short-term rate. But though there is no natural short-term rate of interest, it is still true that the short-term rate reflects any expectation of a rise or fall of the price level. And in estimating the effect of any given Bank rate, allowance must be made for the existence of any such expectation. At a time of rising prices an apparently high rate will count as low. Then, when the rate has been raised high enough, and the rise of prices has been stopped, as soon as the expectation has been dispelled and has given place to an expectation of falling prices, an apparently low Bank rate will count as high.

CHAPTER VIII

LATER REFERENCES TO THE TRADITION

BONAMY PRICE AND HENRY GIBBS

THE original adoption of Bank rate as an instrument of monetary regulation was founded on theoretical reasoning. But the practical application of it evolved in the nineteenth century was empirical. Starting from the postulate that a rise in the rate of discount must be a deterrent on the creation of credit, the Bank raised the rate whenever its reserve seemed insufficient, and went on raising it step by step till the desired effect was produced. When the reserve began to increase, the Bank lowered the rate step by step, and, if the reserve continued to rise, brought it down to the minimum of 2 per cent. and kept it there.

People did not ask why or how the effects of the discount rate were transmitted through the complex credit machine to the actual decisions of the traders, by which the amount of borrowing was determined. The explanations offered often implied an exaggerated idea of the effect of the charges for temporary borrowing on the trader's position. Witnesses at the Parliamentary inquiries of 1848 and 1858 were found to say that a 10 per cent. rate of discount made business impossible or would ruin the trader.

Professor Bonamy Price appended to his book, *Practical Political Economy*, a correspondence that had passed in 1877-8 between him and Henry Gibbs (a former Governor of the Bank of England, afterwards Lord Aldenham) on the subject of the Bank's policy and practice. " The grand formula," Price wrote, " is this : gold has gone away, up with the rate : gold has come in, down with it. I repudiate that formula absolutely ; and I think its consequences—not to the bankers who profit by it, but to the whole trading community—to be very mischievous " (p. 505).

Gibbs retorted : " What ruin can be produced by a rise in the rate of discount ? If you should think it could, you

would show that you mistook one of the effects for the cause. Calculate the debit entry to a man's Interest and Discount account on a loan of £50,000 for a month at 5 per cent. beyond what he had calculated on, and then bring me the man who has been ' ruined ' by a loss (if one may call it a loss) of £200 on a transaction of £50,000 " (p. 515).

Price stuck to his point, and quoted traders as saying " with even passion, that these rises are acutely felt, perplex traders, inflict severe losses by the largely increased sums paid for accommodation necessary and reckoned upon, and frequently turn legitimate enterprises into positive losses " (p. 526). Gibbs contended in reply that the trader who failed " fell a victim to the prevalent vice of over-trading—his goods were unsaleable, both those which he held on speculation and those he received on consignment " (p. 536). Price merely replied, " You scoff at loss," but added : " By the way, all admiration be given to you for that magnificent expression ' holding goods.' There you are in the very realities of banking."

Unfortunately they did not carry their discussion of this point further. Gibbs was undoubtedly right in maintaining that the direct loss inflicted on the trader was very slight. An unforeseen rise in the rate of discount might wipe out the profit on a particular transaction, for the margin of profit was sometimes very narrow. But that in itself could hardly be an embarrassment to the trader.

Why then did traders protest " with even passion " against dear money ? The key to the puzzle was to be found in " the magnificent expression ' holding goods '." If the banks raised their charges for " holding goods," traders became, as G. W. Norman said in 1840, less disposed to buy and more disposed to sell. It was not on the trader who paid the increased charges that the trouble fell, but on the trader from whom he would otherwise have bought goods.

BAGEHOT ON BANK RATE

Bagehot recognised the deflationary effect of a high Bank rate. " The rise in the rate of discount," he wrote, echoing

Horsley Palmer, " acts immediately on the trade of this country. Prices fall here ; in consequence imports are diminished, exports are increased, and therefore there is more likelihood of a balance in bullion coming to this country after the rise in the rate than there was before " (*Lombard Street*, p. 47). In his chapter on " Why Lombard Street is often very dull and sometimes extremely excited," he explained the operation of the vicious circle of depression or activity. He then proceeded to quote Macaulay on the South Sea Bubble, and to refer to the speculative manias of 1825 and 1866, but pointed out that, " so long as the savings remain in possession of their owners, these hazardous gamblings in speculative undertakings are almost the whole effect of an excess of accumulation over tested investment. Little effect is produced on the general trade of the country."

" But," he went on, " when these savings come to be lodged in the hands of bankers, a much wider result is produced. Bankers are close to mercantile life ; they are always ready to lend on good mercantile securities ; they wish to lend on such securities a large part of the money entrusted to them. When therefore the money so entrusted is unusually large and when it long continues so, the general trade of the country is, in the course of time, changed. Bankers are daily more and more ready to lend money to mercantile men ; more is lent to such men ; more bargains are made in consequence ; commodities are more sought after ; and in consequence prices rise more and more." So the vicious circle of inflation is joined.

" This is the meaning of the saying, ' John Bull can stand many things but he cannot stand 2 per cent '," for in England " the excess of savings over investments is deposited in banks ; here and here only is it made use of so as to affect trade at large ; here and here only are prices gravely affected. In these circumstances a low rate of interest, long protracted, is equivalent to a total depreciation of the precious metals " (pp. 132–4).

Bagehot's statement of the theory is open to criticism

in that he regards the bank deposits as being accumulated out of " savings," instead of being mainly created by the lending operations of the banks. But he appreciated clearly enough the fact that Bank rate worked through *mercantile* borrowing for the purchase of commodities.

Bagehot's book was much more concerned with the treatment of crises than with the operation of credit control through Bank rate under normal conditions. The bill of exchange system gave a special virulence to crises. When a trader obtains an advance from his banker to pay for goods, the payment is made in cash, and, so far as buyer and seller are concerned, the matter is settled ; the advance concerns no one but the banker and his customer. But when the seller of goods draws a bill on the buyer, the former remains responsible for the sum involved till the bill itself is paid off. During the life of the bill he sustains the liability of a guarantor. And any endorser who has received payment for the bill is in the same position.

The buyers of bills have to cultivate a knowledge of the names appearing on them. Such knowledge, unlike the banker's knowledge of his customers' affairs, is founded largely on hearsay and inference. The discount market of Bagehot's day had carried the discrimination of names to the pitch of a fine art, but still the market was often mistaken. Firms which had established a thoroughly good reputation on a sound foundation might yet at any time plunge into hazardous business unknown to their neighbours, and might keep going for years by exploiting the credit attaching to their names. The longer the imposture was kept up, the greater the crash when it came.

It is this linking up of one trader's credit with another's that Bagehot had in mind when he described the consequences of a panic :

" All men of experience try to ' strengthen themselves,' as it is called, in the early stage of a panic ; they borrow money while they can ; they come to their banker and offer bills for discount, which commonly they would not have offered for days or weeks to come " (pp. 49–50). In

those days a panic really did mean a race for liquidity. It was in such conditions that the lending power of the commercial banks would be exhausted, and the Bank of England would be called on to fulfil its duty as the lender of last resort, " the last lending-house " (p. 53). And Bagehot proceeded to formulate the appropriate treatment. " Periods of internal panic and external demand commonly occur together. The foreign drain empties the Bank till, and that emptiness and the resulting rise in the rate of discount tend to frighten the market." To treat " this compound disease," the Bank must raise the rate of interest as high as may be necessary to stop the foreign drain of gold, and at the rate of interest so raised it must lend freely (p. 56). By lending freely Bagehot meant lending " on all good banking securities," and not merely on the conventionally eligible bills and on Government securities (pp. 195-7). As we have seen, the Bank actually found it desirable to go further in dealing with the Baring crisis in 1890, and to participate in a guarantee where no specific acceptable security was forthcoming at all.

Bagehot's prescription for a panic is in reality just a re-statement of the policy of relying on a high Bank rate in place of a refusal to lend or a rationing of discounts. It takes for granted that the high Bank rate will have a sufficiently deterrent power.

Marshall and the Speculator

Marshall's evidence before the Gold and Silver Commission in 1887-8 marks the entry of the Bank rate tradition into academic economics. He had already, in *The Economics of Industry* (written in collaboration with Mrs. Marshall in 1879), outlined a theory of the trade cycle in terms of alternate expansions and contractions of *credit*. Like Bagehot, he regarded speculation as developing in the later stages of expansion, but in that work he had little to say as to the rate of interest, except that, when at last the turning point came, the cause was the misgivings of lenders whose reluctance took concrete form in a very high

rate of interest. He did not suggest that cheap money might itself be a stimulus to the speculators.

Questioned by the Chairman of the Gold and Silver Commission, Lord Herschell, as to the effect of an increase in the amount of gold in the country Marshall replied : " I should say it would act at once upon Lombard Street, and make people inclined to lend more ; it would swell deposits and book credits, and so enable people to increase their speculation with borrowed capital ; it would, therefore, increase the demand for commodities and so raise prices." (Question 9641.)

Lord Herschell objected that the discount rate had in the preceding years fallen as low as it could go, without stimulating speculation, and Marshall explained that he would not put the rate of discount in the first place, but would lay stress on the actual amount of money in the market to be loaned.   " If there is an extra supply of bullion, bankers and others are able to offer easy terms to people in business, including the bill brokers, and consequently there is more money on loan, and consequently people enter into the market as buyers of things, as starting new businesses, new factories, new railways, and so on." (Question 9676–7.)

At a later stage of his examination, four weeks afterwards, he put his explanation as follows (Question 9981 ; also *Money Credit and Commerce*, p. 75) :

" In my view the rate of discount is determined by the average profitableness of different business ; that is, determined partly by the amount of capital that is seeking investment as compared with the openings for new docks, new machinery, and so on ; and the extent of these openings is itself practically determined to a great extent by the belief that people have that prices will rise or fall, other things being equal, for people are unwilling to borrow if they think that prices will fall.   The supply of loans on the one hand and the desire of people to obtain loans on the other having fixed the rates of discount at anything, 8, 6, 5 or 2 per cent., then the influx of a little extra gold, going as it does into the hands of those who deal in credit, causes the

supply to rise relatively to the demand ; the rate of discount falls below its equilibrium level, however low that was, and therefore stimulates speculation."

Here he was attributing to the speculators a high degree of responsiveness to the rate of discount, and he added a qualification that may perhaps be read as indicating some doubts as to this responsiveness :

" There is, however," he proceeded, " a side issue which should not be overlooked and may be in some cases more important than the main issue. It is this : when the gold comes to the country, its arrival is known, and people expect that prices will rise. Now if a person doubting whether to borrow for speculative purposes has reason to believe that prices will rise, he is willing to take a loan at 3 per cent. which before he would not have taken at 2½ per cent., and consequently the influx of gold into the country, by making people believe that prices will rise, increases the demand for capital and raises therefore, in my opinion, the rate of discount."[1]

It was, I think, a mistake to try to explain the effect of Bank rate by its direct influence on " speculators." The term, taken in its widest sense, does, it is true, include not only the forward purchaser who intends either to resell or to prolong his contract without ever taking delivery of the goods, but any trader who borrows in order to buy more than usual of a commodity, whether for resale or for use in manufacture, in anticipation of a rise of price. But it excludes the trader who does *not* anticipate a rise of price, and also excludes the trader who, when he buys or produces, eliminates the chance of either a rise or a fall of price by a forward sale or " hedge."

Whatever the position or the anticipations of the trader may be, he ought to be amenable to the influence of the rate of interest. Even the pure speculator is not independent of it, for though the forward purchaser borrows no money, the possible premium of the forward price over the

---

[1] Reproduced with verbal alterations in *Money, Credit and Commerce*, p. 76.

spot price is limited by the cost of carrying a stock, and this cost includes interest. But where an expected rise of price is the primary consideration, the cost of interest is likely to be negligible. The margin of variation between high and low rates of interest may be put at about 4 per cent., only occasionally becoming as wide as, say, 6 per cent. But a speculator who is content to wait a month for a rise of price of $\frac{1}{2}$ per cent. is not a speculator at all. A trader who is inclined to allow for a moderate rise in the price of some commodity he has to buy may be deterred from hastening his purchases by a very small extra charge for interest, because though the rise of price he has in mind may be 5 or 10 per cent. he must abate this very liberally for the chance of no rise occurring or for such a reversal of conditions as may lead to an actual fall. He is hardly a " speculator." And in so far as his purchases have a speculative character, he is the less amenable to the rate of interest. It is the trader who has no expectation of a price movement at all who is most sensitive to it.

There is no evidence that considerations of this kind were in Marshall's mind. When he turned many years later to deal with the subject of speculation in commodities (*Industry and Trade*, pp. 250–68), he regarded the term " speculative " as " almost confined to dealing in things the future prices of which are eminently uncertain " (p. 252), to the exclusion of things of which the " supply can be varied by rapid and extensive changes in the rate of production ; so that their price is prevented from fluctuating rapidly and remains always close to normal cost of production." But he never examined the relation of speculation so defined to the short-term rate of interest.

When Marshall was giving evidence before the Gold and Silver Commission, the Chairman's questions repeatedly recurred to the topic of speculation, which Marshall himself had introduced at an early stage. But when Leonard Courtney put a question in more general terms, whether there was any evidence that a rise in the rate of discount does bring about forced sales of all commodities and so

bring down all prices, Marshall answered, " it brings about forced sales, or diminishes purchases." (Question 9970.)

THE AMERICAN MONETARY COMMISSION, 1908–12

The American National Monetary Commission, appointed in 1908 to consider " what changes are necessary or desirable in the monetary system of the United States or in the laws relating to banking and currency," issued their report in January, 1912. They expressed themselves to have been " struck by the paucity both in Europe and in America of material dealing with other phases of the subject than the history of the circulation privilege. It was practically impossible to find, at least in English, any satisfactory account of the operations of European banks other than note-issuing banks, any penetrating examination of the great credit institutions or of the organisation of credit in other countries. . . . It is a singular fact that most bankers, economists and legislators who had written upon banking had discussed banking questions in much the same language and from much the same point of view as English authorities who debated banking reform in England before the Act of 1844." (Report, pp. 4–5.)

Accordingly the commission " enlisted the services of the world's best experts in a fresh examination of banking in the leading countries as it is conducted to-day."

As a result of their investigations the Commission included in their recommendations a rediscounting system confined to " notes and bills of exchange arising out of commercial transactions ; that is, notes and bills of exchange issued or drawn for agricultural, industrial or commercial purposes, and not including notes or bills issued or drawn for the purpose of carrying stocks, bonds or other investment securities " (p. 60).

" We believe," they said, " that these provisions for creating new classes of investment obligations by establishing a standard of commercial bills to be used in moving and caring for the agricultural and other products of the

country, constitute very important features in our plan of reorganisation " (pp. 30–1).

This recommendation embodied the Bank rate tradition as it existed up to 1914. The foundation of that tradition was the influence of the short-term rate of interest upon the " moving and caring for " products. Short-term borrowing for carrying investment securities was regarded as outside the proper domain of rediscounting.

The Federal Reserve system as subsequently established did, it is true, depart from this ideal in that the rediscount of commercial paper secured by Government bonds was permitted. And of course the Bank of England had always made a practice both of holding Government securities and of making advances upon them. But the report of the Monetary Commission none the less affords clear evidence that, according to the Bank rate tradition at that time, the rediscounting system was based on short-term borrowing for acquiring and holding commodities.

THE CUNLIFFE AND MACMILLAN COMMITTEES

The Committee appointed in 1918, under the chairmanship of Lord Cunliffe, upon Currency and Foreign Exchanges after the War, was faithful to the Bank rate tradition. " Whenever before the war the Bank's reserves were being depleted," said the interim Report (par. 18), " the rate of discount was raised. This . . . by reacting upon the rates for money generally, acted as a check which operated in two ways. O₁ the one hand, raised money rates tended directly to attract gold to this country or to keep gold here that might have left. On the other hand, by lessening demands for loans for business purposes, they tended to check expenditure and so to lower prices in this country, with the result that imports were discouraged and exports encouraged, and the exchanges thereby turned in our favour." This was a very fair summary of the views of the Fathers and Prophets of a hundred years ago. In an earlier passage the Report pointed out how precarious was the relief given to the foreign exchange position by the

attraction of foreign money. " It would have resulted in the creation of a volume of short-dated indebtedness to foreign countries which would have been in the end disastrous to our credit " (par. 5). Thus all the weight was attached to the other effect of a high Bank rate—deflation. But very little stress was laid upon " the consequent slackening of employment."

The Committee on Finance and Industry, presided over by Lord Macmillan, which was appointed in 1929 and reported in 1931, was much more pre-occupied with this last aspect of the matter.   They failed, however, to extract any definite admission of the tendency of a high Bank rate to cause unemployment from the representatives of the Bank of England.[1]

The examination of the Governor, Mr. Montagu Norman, on the subject of Bank rate was started with the following questions and answers :

" If that instrument [Bank rate] is used for the purpose of preserving the stock of gold, is it effective for that purpose ?—It is effective.

" How far is the instrument with which you are equipped effective for the purpose ?—It is effective.

" For that purpose ?—It is effective in my opinion." (Questions 3324–6.)

No doubt, it was well to make sure.

Questioned next in regard to the effect of Bank rate on the internal business of the country as distinguished from the external or foreign exchange position, Mr. Norman said : " I should think its internal effect was as a rule greatly exaggerated—that its actual ill effects were greatly exaggerated and that they are much more psychological than real." (Question 3328.)

" But even if it has psychological consequences, they may be depressing consequences and may be serious ?— Yes, but not so serious as they are usually made out to be.

" . . . I think that the disadvantages to the internal

---

[1] But see Mr. Norman's remarks about " the struggle for gold," quoted above (p. 142).

position are relatively small compared with the advantages to the external position." (Questions 3331–2.)

Asked whether financial policy had not something to do with the phenomenal fall in price levels that had occurred, Mr. Norman replied : " I believe practically nothing, in so far as the most recent and heavy falls are concerned."

Mr. Keynes, who was a member of the Committee, put a series of detailed questions leading up to an exposition of the traditional doctrine of the working of Bank rate : " The method of its operation on the internal situation is that the higher Bank rate would mean curtailment of credit, that the curtailment of credit would diminish enterprise and cause unemployment, and that that unemployment would tend to bring down wages and cost of production generally. . . . The virtue of Bank Rate is that, while it would have a quick effect on the international situation, it would also have a slow and perhaps more important effect on the internal position, by setting up tendencies to bring about a new level of money costs of production so as to enable us to have more nearly that level of exports which the international situation requires of us. If the effect of Bank rate on the internal situation were of a negligible character, all that would not happen. Am I right," he ended, " in thinking that you would agree with that, what I call, perhaps wrongly, orthodox theory of Bank rate ? " Mr. Norman responded with a grudging and unconvinced assent : " I should imagine that, as you have stated it, that is the orthodox theory, taking a long view, and as such I should subscribe to it—I could not dispute it with you."

" If that is so," Mr. Keynes went on, " half the point of Bank rate is that it should have an effect on the internal situation ? "

" Well," was the reply, " I do not think so necessarily apart from the short money position." (Questions 3390–1.)

Presently Lord Macmillan intervened (Questions 3431–3): " when the international position requires, in your view, a raising of the Bank rate, that in turn is made effective by restriction of credit, is it not ?—May be.

" And may it not therefore have . . . a consequent deterrent effect on enterprise in this country ? In your view, I take it, that is inevitable and possibly salutary ?—I think it may be inevitable.

" And again, speaking in the broadest terms, is it your view that the consequences of that internal restriction of credit, unfortunate as they may appear to be, are outweighed by the advantages of the maintenance of the international position ?—Yes, there is very large benefit."

There were two points which were not adequately brought out in this examination : first, that the depressing effect of a high Bank rate on industry is not merely incidental to the process of making the foreign exchanges favourable, but is the very substance and foundation of that process ; secondly, that the depressing effect is not dependent on the " restriction of credit," but is wrought by the high charges for advances of all kinds, loans, overdrafts and bills, throughout the credit system. The restriction of credit, in the special sense of a reduction by the Bank of England of its holding of bills and securities, was merely a device for making Bank rate effective in the discount market. It would seem that Mr. Norman's doubts as to the importance of the internal influence of Bank rate were due to the narrowness of the scope of the discount market in which he supposed that influence to operate. The Committee did not raise this point. Nor did they refer to the essential unsoundness of a reliance on the attraction of foreign money to redress the exchange position.

Later in the inquiry the Deputy-Governor of the Bank, Sir Ernest Harvey, gave a more formal exposition of the attitude of the Bank to Bank rate in the following terms :

" If I were asked to state in a few words what the Bank's policy has been, I should say that it has been to maintain a credit position which will afford reasonable assurance of the convertibility of the currency into gold in all circumstances, and, within the limits imposed by that objective, to adjust the price and volume of credit to the

requirements of industry and trade. I should say at this
stage that we regard the Bank rate as our principal weapon
for carrying that policy into effect. . . . Now what are the
guides which prompt the Bank to make use of the weapon
of the Bank rate ? I should say that they were the state of
the Bank's reserves, the condition of the money market,
both as regards rates and also as regards the volume and
character of the funds, domestic and foreign in the market,
and, thirdly, the position and trend of the foreign exchanges.
I may be asked, I have been asked, do we not pay attention
to the condition of trade ? I say that if the machine is
functioning properly the condition of trade should be
reflected in the factors to which I have referred. " (Question
7512.)

Presently Mr. Keynes took up the question of deflation :
" Everybody admits the efficiency of Bank rate in its effect
on the exchanges, but it is argued that against that you
have the possible detrimental effect on the home situation ?
—Certainly if industry is relying to too great an extent
upon accommodation from the bankers.

" If it is only relying to a normal extent, the results
would be the same, would they not ?—In kind but not in
degree.

" If you curtail the basis of credit you would, it seems
to me, partly get a further favourable effect on foreign
exchanges in that some part of the credit which you have
destroyed might have been employed in purchasing foreign
securities.   But if you rule out that part, the rest, assuming
that people are keeping about the same amount of their
resources in the form of fixed deposits with the banks,
would sooner or later have to come off the weekly wages
bill, would it not ? Credit is partly employed for foreign
purposes.   As regards home purposes it is partly employed
for financial transactions and partly for making the wheels
of business go round.   Undoubtedly part of the curtailment
would affect that part of the credit which is used for trade
purposes, and you would expect some part to come off
what is used to make the wheels of industry go round ?—

" Some part would, I imagine. As to the importance of the part, I think it is possibly magnified at the present time by reason of the fact that . . . industry has probably borrowed more heavily from the bankers than is desirable, in other words has obtained too large a proportion of its credit in the form of bankers' credit instead of in the form of investment credit." (Questions 7555–7.)

Thus Sir Ernest Harvey took refuge in the doctrine of what used to be called " overtrading " ; Bank rate had to be raised to reduce the volume of credit when it had been imprudently extended. That would have been an appropriate defence for dear money from time to time in the nineteenth century or in 1920, though even then it would have been pertinent to ask why dear money could not be applied at an earlier stage when a very mild dose would prevent the over-trading from developing.

But in 1930, when dear money had recently been applied, at a time of depression, unemployment and shrunken profits, to preserve a gold parity that was becoming intolerable, the plea was quite out of place.

The Report of the Committee stated the traditional doctrine :

" The nineteenth-century philosophy of the gold standard was based on the assumptions that (a) an increase or decrease of gold in the vaults of Central Banks would imply respectively a ' cheap ' or a ' dear ' money policy, and (b) that a ' cheap ' or a ' dear ' money policy would affect the entire price structure and the level of money-incomes in the country concerned."

When they added that " in the modern-post-war world neither of these assumptions is invariably valid," they did not mean that Bank rate no longer worked as efficaciously as in the nineteenth century, but that, on the one hand, central banks, nowadays, are apt to withhold the treatment formerly judged appropriate and to offset gains or losses of gold by sales or purchases of securities instead of trying to correct them ; and that, on the other hand, when a change in Bank rate is resorted to, there may

result an adjustment of wholesale prices without any corresponding adjustment of costs.[1]

" Bank rate policy," pursues the Report at a later stage (par. 221), " is quite a proper instrument, not only for the correction of temporary disequilibrium in the international loan market, but also for regulating the pace of expansion and enterprise at home, and for putting pressure on costs to accommodate themselves to changes in our relative situation or in the international price level. But it is only adequate by itself for such purposes within certain limits. When substantial changes in the level of our industrial costs are necessary to correspond to substantial changes in the value of money, changes in bank rate alone cannot hope to achieve all that is necessary. . . .

" For consider how bank rate policy works out in such a case. Its efficacy depends in the first instance on reducing the profits of business men. When, in the effort to minimise this result, output and employment are contracted, it depends on decreasing the amount of business profits and increasing unemployment up to whatever figure is necessary to cause business men either to decrease their costs by additional economies or to insist on, and their workers to accept, a reduction of wages." Once more it is of James Morris being questioned by Cayley that we are reminded : " and it will lead to a disemployment of labour ?— Probably for a time it may lead to a disemployment of labour " (above p. 29).

The Macmillan Committee were impressed by the dangers of a " rigid " economic structure and by the impracticability and undesirability of reductions of wages. But rigid wages were no new thing. We have seen how between 1857 and 1914 there were periods of prolonged and substantial rises of wages, but the reductions were relatively slight and fleeting. In the time of gold scarcity from 1874 to 1886 the reduction of wages was small, and, if unemployment was severe, that was just because wages resisted reduction. (The reductions that actually occurred

[1] Report, paragraphs 43-4.

were mainly due to the sliding scales in the coal and iron industries.) The gold standard worked smoothly because the supply of currency under it was ample enough to allow wages to rise from 100 in 1850 to 198 in 1914. Even so the recurrent spells of deflation were a source of trouble and distress, because wages resisted reduction and unemployment resulted.

But that was not a weakness in the Bank rate policy. The weakness was in the monetary policy which required deflation. If the Bank rate policy was a contributory cause that was only because it was not applied judiciously. Inflation was allowed to go too far before it was stopped, and then stopping it was not enough ; it had to be reversed.

CHAPTER IX

PAST AND FUTURE

FUNCTIONING OF CHANGES IN BANK RATE

SINCE Bank rate worked by deterring traders from holding goods, it would be a *rise* in the rate rather than a high rate that would be felt, and similarly it would be a *fall* in the rate rather than a low rate that would encourage traders to add to their stocks and so would stimulate business. For so long as the rate, whether high or low, remained unchanged, traders would adapt the size of their stocks to it, and, the adaptation once completed, no further effect was to be expected. But though the direct effect of the rise or fall of the rate on stocks of goods would be exhausted, the tendency once started, might be prolonged and amplified by the vicious circle of contraction or expansion. Thus it was a matter of chance whether the effect was anything more than transitory.

We have seen how there was apt to be a superficial response to a rise in Bank rate, an attraction of foreign money, a liquidation of merchants' stocks abroad, a reflux of currency from banks at home. The restoration of the reserve would lead to a reduction of the rate before the underlying tendency to expansion had been really checked, and the reduction of the rate would then undo the restrictive effect of the rise. That might occur several times, even half-a-dozen times as in the years 1871–4, before a rise in the rate was found to have established a definite contractive tendency. That, when it did occur, meant that the vicious circle of contraction was joined.

These tentative oscillations of Bank rate gradually became less noticeable, and eventually in the years of activity 1911–13 were entirely absent.

A state of activity could not be stopped instantaneously by a rise of Bank rate. The adaptation of traders' stocks would take a minimum period of some months. Theo-

retically it would not be absolutely completed till every trader had turned over his stock once, but in practice it would be sufficient for the main body of traders to have done so. But the process would be prolonged, and possibly very greatly prolonged, by the execution of existing contracts. So long as producers are fully employed carrying out orders previously received, industry goes on generating incomes, and therefore demand, in undiminished volume.

Another circumstance which tends to delay the recession of activity is the lag of retail prices. So long as retail prices are low relatively to consumption demand, the volume of sales exceeds output, and there is a growing shortage of stocks. Only when the pressure on producers is already being felt in a rise of wholesale prices and a delay in deliveries are retail prices raised, and by that time there is a shortage of retailers' stocks which causes the pressure to continue. The rise in Bank rate, in order to achieve its object, must be sufficient to counteract the tendency to continued activity due to this shortage of stocks.

We must not imagine a continuing conflict of motives in the mind of each retailer. The question what stocks of any commodity he should hold only arises for any one retailer at intervals. The shortage of stocks causes pressure on producers in that orders for replenishment come at shorter intervals. The high short-term rate of interest counteracts this because the retailers give smaller orders for a given volume of sales.

At a time when demand is high and stocks are short, traders are likely to give increased forward orders in anticipation of a rise of prices. But increased orders do not necessarily mean increased stocks of goods. What determines the stocks to be held and therefore the short-term borrowing, is not the amount ordered but the amount delivered. A trader buying six months' requirements of a commodity may take delivery of the whole amount on the spot, or may stipulate for delivery at intervals of two months, one month or even a week.

In 1919–21 Bank rate was at 6 to 7 per cent. for over twenty months, of which twelve months were at 7 without a break. The policy of maintaining a high rate continuously without intermission had become established. There must be no vacillation. The pressure on the larynx must be maintained till all trace of inflation has been suppressed. Desdemona must not be able to make remarks several minutes after the act of strangulation.

That was quite in accordance with the evolution that had been in progress up to 1914. What was a new departure was the continuance of the high rate, not merely long after the reaction in industry had become indubitably and securely established, but after depression had been so aggravated as to become a grave social problem. The deepening depression was not so much due to the directly deterrent effect of dear money on the holding of stocks, as to the vicious circle of deflation. A reduction of the rate before the end of 1920 or in January, 1921, especially a reduction by three or four points in a few weeks, might have broken the vicious circle and restored industry to normal activity with no more than a slight and transitory depression. As it was, the reduction of the rate did not begin till April, 1921, and it proceeded by steps of ½ per cent. at a time at long intervals so that the reduction from 7 per cent. to 3 took 14½ months.

The departure from the gold standard was undoubtedly a new fact of far-reaching importance. If the United States had persisted in deflation in the grand style, it might have been impossible to stabilise the pound above $3.50 or thereabouts. But it is quite conceivable that the Federal Reserve Banks might have modelled their discount policy on that of the Bank of England, and saved American industry from the acute depression of 1921. If so, little or no depreciation of the pound might have eventuated.

When it came to the actual return to the gold standard in 1925, the application of a 4½ to 5 per cent. Bank rate (except for one short spell at 4 per cent.) for four years of severe unemployment was a still greater breach with the

traditional Bank rate policy. We have seen that at the time of gold scarcity from 1875 to 1886 there were repeated advances of Bank rate to 5 per cent. in times of depression (and in 1878 to 6). Each such advance delayed revival, but the subsequent reduction of the rate gave a renewed stimulus, so that revival was resumed, and activity was ultimately reached in 1881 or 1889 only after a somewhat longer depression than usual.

In 1925 revival was interrupted by the 5 per cent. Bank rate, but up to 1929 there was no evidence of reversion to the vicious circle of deflation. Rather there was a state of uneasy equilibrium with an unemployment rate of about 10 or 11 per cent. Traders' stocks and short-term borrowing must have been adjusted to the high Bank rate in the first few months, so that thereafter there was little or no positive deflationary effect. There were even some signs in 1927–8 of a renewed improvement, which may be attributed in part to the measures of credit expansion in the United States, and in part to French purchases of bills in London and New York and the consequent reduction of Bank rate to 4½ per cent. in April, 1927.

These favourable influences abroad were terminated before revival had become anything but a mere flicker by the adoption of dear money in New York in July, 1928, and by the reduction of the foreign exchange holding of the Bank of France and the resulting absorption of gold by France at the beginning of 1929. Thus it came about that Bank rate was put up to 5½ and 6½ per cent. in 1929 while depression still prevailed. That the vicious circle of deflation would be rapidly and decisively joined was inevitable. And it was at that juncture that occurred the long delay in the transition from dear to cheap money, which was spread over six months.

STEPS UP AND DOWN

Those who followed the financial newspapers at the time may recollect that appeal was frequently made to a rule which the Bank of England was believed to follow, that,

whereas when Bank rate was raised it was by steps of a whole point at a time, when the rate was lowered it was by steps of a half per cent. only. It may not be without interest to trace the origin of this tradition. Walter Bagehot in *Lombard Street* (p. 173) quoted a passage from Goschen's *Foreign Exchange*, calling attention to the relatively wide difference in rates of interest requisite to attract money from one centre to another in view of the exchange risk. " Accordingly," wrote Bagehot, " Mr. Goschen recommended that the Bank of England should as a rule, raise their rate by steps of 1 per cent. at a time when the object was to affect the foreign exchanges. And the Bank of England, from 1860 onward, have acted upon that principle."

In 1899 Mr. Edward Johnstone, the Editor of the *Economist*, who was entrusted with the preparation of the eleventh edition of Bagehot's book, added a footnote saying : " occasionally the Bank now moves by steps of ½ per cent. ; but the rule that may be said to be broadly observed is that while in lowering the rate it may be expedient to move by steps of ½ per cent., in raising it the advance should be by steps of 1 per cent."

In reality there was very little foundation for any such statement. Reductions from 4½ per cent. or lower were usually made by steps of ½ per cent., but so were advances within that limit, though the jump from 3 to 4 was quite common. Advances above 4 per cent. were nearly always by 1 per cent. at a time, but then so were reductions from 5 per cent. or above. In the period from 1899 to 1914 it became usual to reduce from 5 to 4½ instead of to 4, as if the Bank had thought that they ought to take a step towards conforming to Mr. Johnstone's rule, but they still reduced by a whole point from 7 to 6 and 6 to 5.

In January, 1917, for the first time since 1870, Bank rate was reduced from 6 per cent. to 5½ and not to 5, and thereafter Mr. Johnstone's rule appears to have been applied with the utmost rigour till 1931.

In the days when the ideals of chivalry still survived in

war it used to be said that the artillery might advance at
a trot or a gallop, but retreated only at a foot's pace, a rule
quite reminiscent of Mr. Johnstone's. Yet obviously the
rule could not be without exceptions. One of the most
brilliant passages in Napier's *Peninsular War* describes what
happened when Captain Norman Ramsay's battery was cut
off by the French cavalry at Fuentes Onoro. " Suddenly the
multitude became violently agitated, an English shout
pealed high and clear, the mass was rent asunder, and
Norman burst forth at the head of his battery, his horses,
breathing fire, stretched like greyhounds along the plain,
the guns bounded behind them like things of no weight, and
the mounted gunners followed in close career." From 6
per cent. to 5 and 5 to 4 then to 3½ and 3, the transition from
dear to cheap money in February and March, 1932, was
effected in nine weeks.

This was a reversion to pre-Johnstone practice. But
when it occurred the opportunity had already been lost.
The battle was over, and the brilliant manœuvre was an
empty demonstration, signifying no more than the great
rhinocereeros what leaps from crag to crag and 'owls 'orrid.

Moreover, there was very little to be said for Goschen's
original recommendation. If it was desired to attract
foreign money by a rise in Bank rate, what was wanted
was not a rise by any specified amount but the creation of
a sufficient difference between the market rate in London
and in the other centres concerned to offset the exchange
risk. If gold was being exported to one of these other
centres, and the exchange upon it was at the export gold
point, there was no exchange risk, and a small gain of
interest might suffice. Or if gold was being imported from
one of the centres, so that the exchange risk was at its
maximum, a relatively large gain might be required. But
even then the existing difference in interest rates might
be so considerable that a small additional difference would
be enough. And Goschen never suggested that reductions
of Bank rate ought to be by smaller steps than increases.

But Goschen's recommendation was in any case only

applicable to the case where " the object was to affect the foreign exchanges," and he meant where the object was to attract foreign money. The attraction of foreign money is merely one of those superficial results which really interfere with the smooth working of Bank rate, and like the others has the disadvantage of being reversed as soon as Bank rate is reduced. In view of the notoriously disturbing effects of movements of funds seeking temporary investment from one country to another in recent years, it is hardly necessary to labour the point. There may be reasons for moving Bank rate either by big steps or by small, but, whatever they are, the attraction of foreign funds ought not to be among them.

Bank Rate and the Trade Cycle

Bank rate has been revealed in the foregoing pages as an instrument for effecting precisely those fluctuations which constitute the trade cycle. The primary purpose of manipulations of Bank rate is to increase or decrease transactions, to raise or depress the price level, to enlarge or compress the consumers' income, to stimulate or restrain the employment of labour. If we want to know how the scenery gets shifted, here we see the scene-shifters actually handling it.

I do not mean to suggest that that of itself is enough to dispose of all controversy on the subject. Indeed, one of the aspects of Bank rate which call for explanation is the tardy and uncertain response of economic activity to its operation. We get periods of several years in which dear money fails to check activity, alternating with equally long periods in which cheap money only stimulates it very gradually. It would not be inconsistent with the course of events to suppose that there is a struggle against some extraneous non-monetary force, and that the turning point only comes when that force has spent itself. The contribution of Bank rate might be quite secondary.

I have explained the alternating persistence of an excess

or deficiency of activity as due to the vicious circle of expansion or contraction. I think it is no exaggeration to say that that principle, with its power of amplifying indefinitely any departure from monetary equilibrium, even if initially slight, is essential to all the present-day theories of the trade cycle. For example, the whole group of theories which trace the cycle to some kind of disequilibrium in the investment market must at some stage invoke repercussions or a multiplier to account for a disturbance in the capital goods industries infecting the whole economic system, of which they form quite a small part. The same applies to theories of over-production, or of over-extension of important industries.

There is no difficulty in supposing that a similar amplifying power exists in the case of Bank rate, though what has to be amplified is not a tendency to activity or depression arising in a restricted part of the economic system but a slight pressure extending over almost the whole.

A state of growing activity, however started, means an interior demand for currency. Under nineteenth-century conditions it would invariably be international in character, so that most countries, if not all, would be experiencing an increasing interior demand. Evidently that could not go on for ever ; the cumulative tendency would be bound eventually to outstrip the output of gold. When a world-wide shortage of gold occurred, what was to happen ? Reliance was placed on the rate of discount as a means of checking the expansion. In the early stages of revival there would be plenty of gold, and Bank rate would be kept low ; presently local shortages of gold would appear, and some countries would put up their rates. At first every rise in discount rates would readily attract gold both from interior circulation and from abroad, and the rates would soon be put down again. But, as activity increased, it would become more and more difficult to replenish gold reserves by this quick and ready method. If the Bank of England tried to attract gold from abroad, foreign central banks would offer resistance by raising their discount rates.

Bank rate was adjusted by a method of trial and error. If a rise failed to restore the reserve, a further rise was resorted to. When there was a general shortage of gold, there was no limit to the rise of Bank rate ; it could be advanced to whatever level was found necessary.

Now the history of the period from 1857 to 1914 shows quite definitely that somehow or other the demand for currency was adjusted to the supply of gold, and the demand for currency followed closely the fluctuations in economic activity. The conclusion that Bank rate, on which the Bank of England invariably relied to regulate the demand for currency through economic activity, was an effective instrument for the purpose seems unassailable. When there was a shortage of gold, the reserve was saved not through chance, but because Bank rate was raised high enough to be effectively deterrent. Even if non-monetary causes were at work to affect economic activity, that conclusion still holds. Those causes could be allowed free play so long as the supply of gold was sufficient. But, once the supply of gold fell short, the Bank of England could not afford to remain inactive ; it was compelled to intervene with its one effective weapon. All the Bank's other expedients were auxiliaries to Bank rate.

It may be argued, perhaps, that in reality excessive expansion was often ended not by dear money but by the outbreak of a financial crisis either in London, as in 1847, 1857 and 1866, or somewhere else. Indeed, every trade recession was accompanied by something that might be called a crisis in some part of the world. But the crisis did not *start* the recession. Some reaction from activity had begun before the crisis broke out. That was so even in 1857 and 1907, though in those years the interval was very short. Something had already adversely affected the demand for commodities, and it was the consequent fall of prices and embarrassment of traders who held goods with borrowed money, or had bought them forward, that became the cause of the crisis. The embarrassments invariably followed a time of dear money, which was expressly de-

signed to cause them, and which, if the result intended had not followed, would have been intensified.[1]

PSYCHOLOGICAL REACTIONS

The pressure applied to traders by a moderate rise in the short-term rate of interest, say, 1 per cent., is undeniably very slight. Yet apparently the Bank of England always counted on a rise of 1 per cent. or even of ½ per cent. having a noticeable effect. The explanation is, I think, twofold. In the first place, when the use of Bank rate to restrict credit became an established practice, traders, being aware of the intentions of the Bank, were inclined to anticipate them. When Bank rate went up from 3 to 4 per cent., a trader would reason that this was intended to have a restrictive effect on markets, and that, if the effect was not brought about, the rate would simply go higher and higher till it was (see above, pp. 61, 202 and 212-3). Those who took that view would restrict their purchases and demand would fall off, and so the 4 per cent. rate might be found potent enough, even though, if unsupported by traders' anticipations, a 6 or 7 per cent. rate might have been necessary.

Secondly a rise in Bank rate was a signal to the banks, as well as to the traders. Part of the Bank of England's programme would be a contraction in the amount of credit granted by banks to traders. A banker would anticipate a condition of monetary stringency by putting pressure on his customers to borrow less. Every banker reserves to himself an absolute discretion to refuse to lend. In practice no one bank can afford to exercise this pressure when its competitors are not doing so. But when the Bank of England puts its rate up, all the banks are likely to start cutting down their lending together. In 1920, before the final rise of Bank rate to 7 per cent. in April, an attempt was made to ration credit through the concerted action of the joint-stock banks. But it broke down, and such a

---

[1] There were one or two occasions on which crises broke out before the state of trade had reached the turning point, for example the German and American crises of 1873, and the French *Union Générale* crisis of January, 1882. But in these cases activity continued for some time *after* the crises.

procedure is really impracticable, for it is impossible to arrive at a workable specification of the kind of transactions to be restricted and the extent of the restriction to be applied to them. On the other hand a rise of Bank rate, as soon as the banks believe the restrictive intention of the Bank of England is to be taken seriously, probably leads to a spontaneous limitation of their lending. And when this becomes general no one bank can afford to lag behind the rest, or its liberality will quickly be felt in a persistently adverse balance at the clearing.

If the efficacy of Bank rate depended on these psychological reactions it would be precarious ; for, if people ceased to believe in it, the reactions would no longer occur. But the psychological reactions are in reality no more than a reinforcement of a tendency which in any case exists. Were they absent, that would only mean that Bank rate would have to be raised higher.

Cheap Money and the Credit Deadlock

Bank rate can always be used to contract credit if only it be raised high enough. But there is a limit to the power of stimulating an expansion of credit by lowering Bank rate. Two per cent. is the customary minimum below which Bank rate has never been reduced, but the market rate of discount has frequently been below 1 per cent. Once the rate is so low as to have practically no deterrent effect on the borrowing of money for the purchase of goods, traders will have adjusted their stocks of goods purely to suit their convenience, and cannot be induced to add to them by reducing the rate further. All that can be effected by the instrumentality of Bank rate is to reduce it to the minimum and leave it there, in the hope that the naturally expansive tendency of credit will eventually prevail in the absence of any deterrent influence. We find prolonged periods of cheap money starting in conditions of depression and gradually merging into revival, for example from 1858 to 1860, from 1867 to 1871, from 1879 to 1881, from 1893 to 1896, and from 1908 to 1909. Theoretically depression

may get business into a state of deadlock, traders being so unwilling to borrow that even very cheap money would fail to start revival. But on all these occasions signs of revival appeared early in the period of cheap money. In the depressions from 1875 to 1879 and from 1883 to 1887 the beginning of revival was long deferred. But these were the times of gold scarcity, when the spells of cheap money were interrupted by repeated advances of Bank rate to 5 per cent. (and in 1878 to 6).

It is only in recent years that the theoretical possibility of a depression too deep and persistent to be cured by cheap money has become a painful reality. The return to cheap money starting in February, 1932, failed to overcome the deadlock. Once Bank rate had been reduced to 2 per cent., it had shot its bolt. Revival might have been hastened either by lavish open market purchases by the Bank of England or by a further depreciation of the pound. Some further depreciation did occur. Having recovered from 70 per cent. of gold parity in December, 1931, to 77 per cent. in April, 1932, it fell after some fluctuations to 62 per cent. in the spring of 1934, and 60 in the latter part of that year. But this depreciation did little more than compensate the continuing rise in the purchasing power of gold. The progress of revival was terribly slow. Since June, 1935, there has been no considerable further depreciation of the pound sterling relative to the United States dollar and the price of gold has not departed far from 140s. a fine ounce. The recovery of business since then has been dependent on a fall in the purchasing power of gold. The index of prices in terms of gold, calculated by the League of Nations from the indexes of volume of the foreign trade of certain countries in comparison with its value, having fallen from 100 in 1929 to 41½ in 1935 rose to 48 in the third quarter of 1937. A renewed appreciation of gold, revealed in a slight fall of the index, has since been accompanied by an interruption of recovery, and in America by a serious reversal of it.

In so far as the credit deadlock had been due to the

intensity of the depression, it had been resolved probably by 1934. But the revival from then till the middle of 1937 never gained such impetus as to justify a rise of Bank rate. Consequently, when the setback came, Bank rate was already so low that the traditional remedy of reducing it was not available.

In fact, as I have already pointed out, it is the *changes* in Bank rate that are effective in bringing about the desired results of compressing or enlarging the consumers' income. If a state of activity exists at a time of dear money, and traders' stocks have already been fully adjusted to the short-term rate of interest, the mere continuance of the same level of dear money will have no further deterrent effect. And similarly the mere continuance of cheap money, when traders' stocks are full, will not cure depression. That possibility has always been inherent in the credit system.

In a wisely managed credit system any tendency to depression or to undue activity will be discerned at an early stage, and checked by a reduction or advance of Bank rate before the vicious circle has been joined. If action is taken before the incipient contraction or expansion of demand has gone far enough to influence the attitude of the majority of traders towards their stocks of goods or their expectations of future prices, a change in the cost of short-term borrowing will have a clear field in which to work its effect, and will not have to meet the competition of rival forces.

In an imperfect world the ideal of prompt and early action cannot always be attained. A situation will arise from time to time in which the vicious circle of expansion or contraction is joined, and it is a state of excessive activity or depression that demands treatment. Excessive activity, evidenced by rising prices and excess profits under conditions of full employment, calls for a rapid advance of Bank rate by perhaps two or three points, even if there is an ample reserve. Depression, evidenced by falling prices, vanishing profits and growing unemployment, calls for a

rapid reduction of Bank rate, even in face of a low reserve. Under nineteenth-century conditions there was no recognition at all of the desirability of using Bank rate as a corrective of fluctuations of activity in their early stages. The vicious circle was always allowed to take hold, and consequently these relatively drastic measures were invariably called for at some stage. The state of the reserve was misleading, not only because the flow of currency into active circulation among the public lagged behind the growth of activity, but also because the reserve was too easily replenished by transitory movements such as the attraction of liquid funds from abroad and the transfer of currency from the country banks to London. The apparent strength of the reserve led to a premature relaxation of credit, and these proceedings would be repeated till at last neither foreign countries nor country banks had any surplus gold, and relaxation became impossible till the corner was turned.

When the corner was turned and the danger of excessive activity had been successfully overcome, the invariable practice up to 1914 was to reduce Bank rate by rapid steps. After the crisis of 1847 the rate was reduced from 8 per cent. to 4 in nine weeks and three days. After that of 1857 it was reduced from 10 per cent. to 3 in seven weeks, and after that of 1866 from 10 per cent. to 4 in twelve weeks. A similar practice was pursued till 1914 whenever Bank rate had been raised to 6 per cent. or more, and the tendency to excessive activity had been successfully reversed.[1]

That is why the danger of a credit deadlock, a failure of cheap money to induce an expansion of credit, never materialised in those days. Even when dear money was imposed in the midst of a depression, as in the 'seventies and 'eighties, its relaxation was rapid enough to set revival going again after its interruption.

THE GOLD STANDARD AND INTERNATIONAL CO-OPERATION

The practice of basing Bank rate policy on the reserve was an inevitable corollary of the gold standard. But even

[1] See my *Art of Central Banking*, pp. 234-5.

within the limits of the gold standard as practised in the nineteenth century a more far-sighted procedure would have been possible. The power of London as a financial centre was such that an advance of Bank rate at an early stage of a world-wide expansion might have kept the activity within bounds. The cyclical fluctuations might thereby have been reduced within relatively narrow limits.

That would sometimes have meant acquiescing in considerable departures of the reserve from normal, disregarding a deficiency if a latent tendency towards diminished activity could be relied on to replenish it in time, and disregarding a surplus if a latent tendency towards increased activity would use it up.

But a credit policy so adjusted could only have smoothed out short-period fluctuations. It could not counteract big changes in the supply of gold or in the monetary demand for it. The increased output of gold from 1850, and again the further increase from 1890 could not have been prevented from causing monetary expansion. Heroic measures for the sterilisation of gold were not thought of. Nor could the demands arising from the spread of the gold standard from 1871 onwards have been met otherwise than by imposing such a monetary contraction as would release the gold required.

The demands for gold were themselves the results of decisions taken by the countries concerned, and those decisions were sometimes deliberately modified in order to relieve the strain on the London money market. Here we have the beginnings of international co-operation in monetary policy. But it was only the introduction of a new monetary system, the transition to gold, which afforded the opportunity in each case.

From about 1890 gold reserves began to be raised to much more substantial amounts, and monetary measures were no longer dictated so exclusively by the needs of active circulation. Paris more than once relieved London either by a direct loan of gold from the Bank of France to the Bank of England, as in 1890, or by purchases of sterling

bills which supported the exchange, as in 1906 and 1907. But it is only since the war that the monetary demand for gold has become an affair of reserves alone, and the active circulation of gold coin has ceased to form part of it. The reserve, which was formerly a working balance to absorb the fluctuations in the stock of gold in so far as the fluctuations in the monetary circulation did not correspond with them, has become the main body of monetary gold. Bank rate is still, as it was intended to be a hundred years ago, an instrument for regulating the foreign exchanges. But whereas at that time this function was itself a means of adjusting the flow of currency into circulation to the available supply of gold, the gold standard has now become exclusively an affair of the foreign exchanges. The demand for gold as a material of industry uses up no more than a small fraction of the current output of gold, and gold reserves may be regarded as destined solely to meet the demand for export.

This change has brought the regulation of the purchasing power of gold within the control of the monetary authorities, provided they are in a position to vary their gold holdings upwards and downwards to any required extent. It makes an international gold standard possible, free from those fluctuations in the purchasing power of gold which have caused the breakdown of such a standard in recent years. The purchasing power of gold can be adjusted to the purchasing power of the currency units that are fixed in terms of gold.

Open Market Operations of the Central Bank

That presupposes some method of regulating the purchasing power of the currency unit itself. And in the last resort no other method than the use of Bank rate is available. Even issues of paper money by the Government are under present-day conditions no more than the equivalent of open market purchases of securities by the central bank. The Government pays out paper money to its employees and its creditors, but they are not willing to

hold any greater amount of paper money than before. So much as is in excess of what they need as pocket money they deposit in the banks, and the banks deposit it in the central bank. The result is thus to increase not the currency in circulation but the deposits in the central bank to the credit of the other banks. The inflationary effect depends entirely on the action taken by the banks to extend their lending on the strength of these increased deposits. The enlargement of the reserves of the banks leads to cheap money.

The actual reduction in the short-term rate of interest does not tell the whole story. Bankers always claim a certain discretion in lending, and may put pressure on customers to reduce or postpone their borrowing, or may even refuse to lend in certain cases altogether. When they find their cash reserves embarrassingly large, they become the more willing to lend, and customers (who are at least as much guided sometimes by the smiles or frowns of the banker as by the rate of interest that he charges) are likely to borrow more freely. A credit deadlock which is impervious to cheap money may thus yield to treatment through open market purchases of securities.

In the period 1922-8, when the policy of the Federal Reserve Banks of the United States was greatly influenced by the wise guidance of the late Benjamin Strong, the Governor of the New York Federal Reserve Bank, frequent and judicious use was made of open market operations. To regard this as an innovation in central bank practice would be a mistake. Open market operations preceded the use of Bank rate. Up to 1833, the Bank of England had to rely entirely upon them, and it was their inadequacy that led the Bank to turn to Bank rate to complete its control over the currency. For the half-century up to 1890 open market operations were confined to an occasional " borrowing on Consols " to make Bank rate effective. But subsequently more systematic borrowing from the discount market or from the joint-stock banks was resorted to, and the purchase of securities in the cheap

money period from 1894 to 1896 contributed to the revival of business.

In one respect, however, the open-market operations of the Federal Reserve Banks were more efficacious. The member banks of the Federal Reserve system were reluctant to have recourse to the rediscounting facilities made available to them. When therefore the Federal Reserve Banks reduced the supply of cash by selling securities in the market, the member banks tried to avoid sending bills to be rediscounted, and resorted to measures of credit contraction. The shortage of cash thus exerted a deterrent influence even when it was not supported by a high rediscount rate.

A similar though less forcible deterrent effect can be traced in the London discount market. The banks do not themselves get bills rediscounted, but when they find it necessary to replenish their cash, whether because the Bank of England has been selling securities or for any other reason, they do so either by buying fewer bills or by calling in loans from the discount houses. It is the discount houses that have to come to the Bank of England. That does not lead the discount houses to refuse to take bills; they will always buy good bills at a price. But the knowledge that the discount market is " in the Bank " does influence the outlook of the banks.

Bank Rate and Treasury Bills

There has, however, been a change in the conditions of the money market since the war, which has deprived open market sales of securities of any but an ephemeral effect on credit. That change is the enormous expansion of the floating debt of the Government. Treasury bills to an amount of something like £40,000,000 have to be issued every week to replace bills falling due. They are put up to competitive tender, and are acquired partly by the discount houses, partly by banks, partly by other agencies which need short-term sterling securities. If the discount houses are in debt to the Bank of England, they can simply refrain

from tendering for Treasury bills. If, as is likely, the result is an insufficiency of applications for the bills, the Government has to borrow from the Bank of England, and in effect the reduction made in the Bank's assets by its sales of securities is filled by its loans to the Government.

In the nineteenth century, when the Bank of England's reserve was diminished to any considerable extent by a loss of gold or an increase in the note circulation, there resulted a stringency in the money market and Bank rate became effective. But in recent years that has not been so.

In November, 1925, and again in September, 1929, big losses of gold caused no corresponding stringency in the money market because there were insufficient tenders for Treasury bills, and the Bank had to take them to fill the gap.

It should not be forgotten that in recent years the American Treasury has likewise run up a huge floating debt, and if, while the debt still exists, the Federal Reserve Banks have occasion to repeat the expedient of contracting credit through open market operations, they may find that they can no longer do so.

The device recently adopted of varying the statutory reserve proportions of the member banks of the Federal Reserve system has the same weak point. The Federal Reserve Act required every member bank to hold a reserve not less than a prescribed proportion of its deposit liabilities (7, 10 or 13 per cent. according to the district). The power given to the Federal Reserve Board under recent amending legislation to increase these proportions has been used, and in 1937 they were raised to double the former percentage. In 1938 they have been lowered again to 1¾ times.

The raising of the reserve proportions works just like open market sales by the Federal Reserve Banks. It diminishes the surplus reserves of the member banks, and may compel them to borrow from the Federal Reserve Banks. In 1936-7 the raising of the proportions was intended to counteract the effect of an excessive growth in

the stock of gold which had swollen the surplus reserves to an unprecedented level.   But if at some future time the same procedure is employed for the purpose of starting a contraction of credit, the member banks can up to a point maintain their reserves by abstaining from taking Treasury bills.   To get the bills taken it will be necessary to offer them on more attractive terms and that will be equivalent for practical purposes to a rise of the rediscount rate.   For no trader can expect to get short-term accommodation on more favourable terms than the Government, and the market will be adjusted accordingly.

Either the sale of securities by the central bank or the increase of statutory reserve proportions for the commercial banks is to be regarded as a device for making Bank rate effective.   And if it does so, banks and discount houses will be willing to buy Treasury bills at a rate corresponding to Bank rate.   There should be no deficiency of tenders.

In the nineteenth century a rise in Bank rate came into vogue as a milder alternative to the absolute refusal to lend, to which the Bank of England had formerly had recourse.   The enlargement of the Government's floating debt has had the effect of making a refusal to lend impracticable.   For the banks and discount houses would counter such a refusal by simply abstaining from taking Treasury bills, and the Government would be driven to borrow from the Bank and so create cash.

Thus the growth of the Government's floating debt has made Bank rate more indispensable in the regulation of credit than before.

Bank Rate without the Gold Standard

It is sometimes argued that the suspension of the gold standard has stultified the use of Bank rate.   The purpose of Bank rate always used to be to regulate the amount of the gold reserve, and, when it is no longer necessary to attract gold, the Bank rate's occupation, it is said, is gone. Since 1932 it has been possible to maintain the spell of

cheap money unbroken. Is not that because the gold standard has been in abeyance ?

That is a superficial view. The gold reserve was used as an indicator of the monetary situation, and monetary contraction or monetary expansion was applied according as the reserve was below or above the prudent level. When the gold standard is suspended or abandoned, that does not mean that monetary contraction or expansion need no longer be applied. The alternative dangers of inflation and deflation remain, and if the gold reserve is not employed as an indicator, other symptoms must be observed, such as the state of employment, the level of profits or a rise or fall of the price level. And when the threat of inflation or deflation is detected, it is in Bank rate that the essential corrective is to be found.

The absence of any metallic or international monetary standard actually facilitates the use of Bank rate as a corrective. For if the currency unit is fixed in terms of foreign units, any rise or fall of Bank rate is apt to be accompanied by an inflow or outflow of funds seeking temporary investment, resulting in a delusive and pre- carious restoration of the monetary position. If the central bank has to allow for the effects of such an inflow or outflow of funds, the extent of which is difficult to measure with exactitude, particularly over short periods, its task is made more difficult. When the currency unit is free to vary relatively to foreign units, a disparity of short-term interest rates is reflected in a premium or discount on forward exchange rates, which should counteract the tendency of foreign balances to seek temporary investment in the centre where rates are high.

The point was clearly put by Mr. Keynes in 1923 in his *Tract on Monetary Reform* (p. 137) :

" Dear money—that is to say, high interest rates for short-period loans—has two effects. The one is indirect and gradual—namely in diminishing the volume of credit quoted by the banks. The effect is much the same now as it always was. It is desirable to produce it when prices

are rising and business is trying to expand faster than the
supply of real capital and effective demand can permit in the
long run.   It is undesirable when prices are falling and
trade is depressed.

" The other effect of dear money, or rather of dearer
money in one centre than in another, used to be to draw
gold from the cheaper centre for temporary employment
in the dearer.   But nowadays the only immediate effect
is to cause a new adjustment of the difference between the
spot and forward rates of exchange between the two
centres."

In recent years the migration of balances from country
to country has, it is true, caused more trouble than ever
before.   But that is attributable not to disparities of
interest rates but to distrust of currencies.   When the
French franc was being maintained at so high a value in
terms of American dollars and English pounds that a
depreciation of the franc was anticipated, refugee money
from France was constantly being placed in London and
New York.   The short-term rate of interest was far higher
in Paris than in London or New York, but the difference
was more than compensated by the enormous discount on
forward francs.

If at some future time the world reverts to an international monetary standard, a condition of its smooth
working will be that the relative values of the several
currency units be so far consistent with internal equilibrium
in each country that there will be no general expectation
of a change in the parity of any one of them becoming
necessary.

Diminished Use of Bank Advances

For some years there has been a noticeable tendency for
some traders to dispense with bank advances, and to meet
their maximum requirements of working capital from their
own resources.   They think it worth while to incur the
not very   heavy loss of interest involved in periodically
accumulating an idle cash balance, in order to escape from

a position of dependence on the banker. If this tendency goes further, may it not impair the efficacy of Bank rate ?

If the temporary borrowing by traders were to shrink within narrow limits, the banking system would be profoundly modified. Neither advances for carrying securities nor advances to consumers would be so sensitive to restrictive measures. Nevertheless Bank rate would probably still be found the most reliable instrument for regulating credit, even if higher rates became necessary than in the past to evoke a given response.

And it must not be supposed that the trader who abjures temporary borrowing is wholly impervious to the influence of Bank rate. For, when his working capital is at a low level, he will place his idle cash on deposit, and the deposit rate (with unimportant exceptions) follows Bank rate. If the deposit rate is a constant amount below Bank rate, while the rate for bank advances is a constant amount above Bank rate, a given rise or fall in Bank rate will make as much difference to the former as to the latter. There is usually, it is true, a maximum imposed on the deposit rate, but if the maximum is 5 per cent. and the deposit rate is 1½ per cent. below Bank rate, the maximum is not operative unless Bank rate rises to 7 per cent.   If Bank rate rises from 3 to 6½ per cent., and the rates for advances and deposits rise from 4 and 1½ per cent. respectively to 7½ and 5, the inducement to delay purchases of goods is precisely the same whether the purchase involves temporary borrowing or withdrawing a deposit. The difference (and no doubt in practice an important one) is that in the case of an advance the banker can add the force of persuasion or of a refusal to lend to the directly deterrent effect of the higher rate.

But anything like a general abandonment of the practice of relying on temporary advances to finance working capital is not at all likely to occur.   To avoid the need of such advances by issuing a larger amount of share capital is to divide up the profit of the business among a larger number of participants.   To the established concern mak-

ing a public issue that may not matter, but to a concern that is being started by a limited syndicate of promoters, an extension of the circle is a palpable disadvantage. Nor is a debenture debt, where practicable, likely in all cases to be more attractive than intermittent bank advances. And for any expanding business the raising of new capital can hardly be made always to anticipate needs, and there will be intervals when recourse must be had to bank advances.

Sometimes the whole system of credit regulation through Bank rate is assailed as being burdensome to industry. Such attacks have their source, I think, in a confusion of thought. As we have seen, the direct burden of short-term interest on the trader who borrows is small. As Henry Gibbs said, " bring me the man who has been ruined by a loss of £200 on a transaction of £50,000." What is detrimental to industry is not the direct addition to costs but the deflationary effect, the discouragement of the purchase of goods. But deflation is implicit in any monetary system which allows inflation to occur. Its consequences are equally painful by whatever method it may be brought about. A system of bank advances free of interest could be evolved if an adequate method of controlling the amount and purpose of the advances could be devised, and if some source other than interest could be provided for meeting the cost of banking services. But the relief thereby granted to industry would be insignificant, unless some means were found of preventing deflation from occurring, either as a necessary corrective of an undesirable inflation or as itself an undesirable departure from stable conditions.

GOVERNMENT EXPENDITURE AS A MEANS OF CREDIT REGULATION

As a result of a deplorably prevalent tendency to disparage, distrust or ignore the Bank rate tradition, various proposals have been put forward to do the work of credit control by other means. All or nearly all these proposals

are directed to attaining this object by regulating the disbursements of the Government and public authorities.

It is necessary to distinguish the proposals that are merely intended to afford relief during a depression by giving employment from those which are designed to dispel the depression itself by reacting on the monetary situation. Even the proposals of the former kind, however, cannot be dissociated from their monetary effects. If for example we suppose that the monetary policy followed is such as to keep the quantity of money fixed, and that the consumers' income is rigidly related to the quantity of money, no amount of Government expenditure will give any additional employment at all. So long as the consumers' income cannot be enlarged, any employment given by the Government is offset by an equal diminution of employment given by private enterprise.[1]

Undoubtedly the condition that the consumers' income is rigidly related to the quantity of money is certain not to be fulfilled. The ratio between the two, the " income velocity " of money, is susceptible of wide variations. At a time of depression income velocity is likely to be low, and quite possibly the Government expenditure might increase it. In fact it is upon this possibility that the whole proposal, whether for relief expenditure or for dispelling the depression, is really based. In either case an enlargement of the consumers' income is essential, and the difference between them is only one of degree.

But variable though income velocity may be, we cannot take for granted that additional Government expenditure will increase it. If it does not, then to ensure the enlargement of the consumers' income there must be an increase in the quantity of money. And on that assumption, it is the increase in the quantity of money that is the effective cause, and the Government expenditure is superfluous.

It is only when the Government expenditure *does* increase the income velocity of money that it plays an

---

[1] Not necessarily an exactly equal diminution ; the same amount of income may give either more or less employment when passing through Government hands.

active part in the expansion.   In what circumstances then
will this occur ?

The essential condition is that there are idle balances
somewhere that will be drawn upon.   Two cases may be
distinguished.   The idle balances may already exist, or
the action of the banks in expanding credit may bring them
into existence.

We have seen (above, pp. 250–3) how, at a time of depression, a low short-term rate of interest may fail to induce
traders to borrow, and the banks, seeking to expand credit,
may have recourse to the investment market and buy securities. The long-term rate of interest will then be forced down,
but there may be a lag of a long interval between the fall
in the long-term rate and the stimulus to capital outlay.

It is under such conditions that Government expenditure is called in to perform the function which has come to
be called in America " priming the pump." The Government by borrowing intervenes to collect the idle funds from
the investment market and to pay them away to those
whom, directly or indirectly, it employs.

To collect the idle funds, it must offer more favourable
terms to the holders than the existing investment market ;
in other words, the long-term rate of interest must rise.
The market will become less favourable to other borrowers,
and it may be that flotations and promotions are actually
postponed, especially if the unfavourable state of the market
is judged to be temporary.   But that need not necessarily
defeat the purpose of the expenditure, for the Government
may increase its undertakings to a sufficient extent to
compensate any falling off of private enterprise and to
provide the requisite stimulus to activity in addition.

If the treatment is successful, the consumers' income
will be enlarged, and, that process once begun, the principle
of the vicious circle should come into play to continue it
and accelerate it.   That is the significance of " priming
the pump " ; the phrase implies a process similar to the
surmounting of a dead centre.

The idle funds to be drawn upon by the Government

are not confined to those of dealers in the investment market itself. They include the idle working capital in the hands of traders, which can be tempted into securities. They would also include idle balances in the hands of consumers, representing savings withheld from the purchase of securities, if, as Mr. Keynes holds, such balances are considerable enough to be taken into account.

The Government induces a release of cash, and, if its operations are of sufficient magnitude the release of cash will counteract the absorption of cash which is the underlying cause of the trade depression. If this condition is fulfilled, the dead centre ought to be surmounted in quite a short time. As soon as consumption demand begins to increase, the vicious circle of expansion does the rest ; the widening of capital is resumed, and the further intervention of the Government in the investment market becomes unnecessary.

But expenditure *of sufficient magnitude* is the essential condition. Anything short of that will merely delay the progress of depression without stopping it, and the menace of the vicious circle of deflation will remain. This device of starting revival by means of Government expenditure is usually embodied in a programme of public works. The Government is to incur debt, and, if the money raised is applied to public works, there will be something to show for it. That is on the assumption that the works are of some real utility ; they need not be income-yielding, but to rank as an asset they must be useful or must add to the amenities of the community. Unfortunately works of this character that can be entered upon at any given moment are limited in amount. They involve much planning and preparation, and the execution of any one work usually occupies a considerable period of time, extending to many months or several years. It is often suggested that the necessary planning and preparation should be carried out in anticipation of future needs, so that at any time there will be a programme of works ready to be put into operation at short notice. But needs cannot usually be foreseen very

long before they are actually felt and, even if they are, the plans devised in advance to meet them are only too apt to need modification after a short interval. It is in fact quite impracticable to organise a sudden burst of expenditure on public works at the moment at which a monetary expansion is found to be desirable.

Moreover public works require specialised productive resources, which are limited in amount. A programme which suffices to employ these resources to the full may yet be insufficient to break the vicious circle of deflation. The specialised productive power may be expanded, but that takes time, and it sows the seeds of new dislocations to materialise when the emergency is over.

These limitations attach to a programme of public works. But the policy of stimulating activity through a deficit is not necessarily associated with public works. They are only introduced to make the deficit respectable. " It is not the Government expenditure that gives employment, but the Government borrowing. The borrowing would have the same effect if it were to meet a deficit due to a remission of taxation."[1] For a simple deficit there is nothing to show in the future. But public works, if not wanted, are worse than nothing at all, for they require expenditure on maintenance. The white elephant has to be fed.

There has recently been a noticeable tendency for economists to make the transition from an advocacy of public works to an advocacy of deficits, as may be seen for example in recent works by Messrs. Durbin,[2] Harrod[3] and Meade.[4] Mr. Meade would apply the deficit to subsidising consumers. Mr. Keynes concedes (in a review of Mr. Meade's work, *Economic Journal*, March, 1938, p. 71) that " consumers' subsidies can be introduced without preparation and on an easily adjustable scale, on occasions when, for one reason or another, an adequate increase in

---

[1] See my *Trade and Credit*, pp. 112–3.
[2] *The Problems of Credit Policy*, pp. 204–5 and 230–6.
[3] *The Trade Cycle*, pp. 200–6 and 213–25.
[4] *Consumers' Credits and Unemployment*.

investment is impracticable." The same principle is to be detected in the Alberta Social Credit Act, 1937, passed under the lead of Mr. Aberhart's Government, which provides on the one hand for subsidies in the forms of a " retail discount " on retail sales and (if funds remain available) of a consumers' dividend ; but on the other hand, should inflation and rising prices supervene, for a *negative* retail discount, or in other words a sales tax, to be applied to redeeming the credit instruments which supply the medium in which the subsidies are to be paid. The Act was repealed in 1938 and a new Act setting up a Board to introduce Social Credit was passed in place of it. Whether the repeal implies a reconsideration of this particular feature I do not know.

Nevertheless even modifications of taxation or subsidies to consumers, though more manageable than a programme of public works, could hardly be applied with the same delicacy of adjustment as Bank rate. Indeed they are not really intended to do the work of Bank rate ; they are offered as a palliative in cases where a severe depression already exists. They are not defended as an improvement on Bank rate, but their advocates simply assume as axiomatic that Bank rate does not work.

As we have seen, conjunctures do occur at which Bank rate does not work. A depression may be so severe that the reduction of Bank rate to a minimum fails to start revival. And if through any concatenation of circumstances depression prevails at a time when Bank rate is already at a minimum, nothing further can be done through Bank rate. In that event a policy of public works or deficits *may* be a remedy. But there is no certainty that it will, at any rate within the limits to which Governments and Legislatures will be willing to proceed. In the past eight years the national debt of the United States has been doubled, and the greater part of the increase has been deliberately incurred for the purpose of stimulating the revival of activity. But the stage of " priming the pump " has never been reached at all (except possibly in

the months April to July, 1933, immediately following the suspension of the gold standard, and for a fleeting interval in November, 1933, *before* the public works policy was initiated). The lavish expenditure of the Government must of course have contributed something to the revival that took place up to 1937, but at no time did revival gain a firm hold.

And the device of adjusting Government expenditure and taxation does not offer even a plausible prospect of dealing with an undue *expansion* of credit. The contrary of a deficit is a surplus. But no surplus is ever likely to check a state of undue activity. For at a time of high demand any funds applied to the redemption of debt will be immediately employed through the investment market in capital outlay. The surplus might, it is true, be applied to extinguishing floating debt. But the reduction of floating debt is quite a distinct measure from the budget surplus itself ; it might for example be effected without any surplus at all by a funding operation. Moreover the reduction of floating debt, unless accompanied by a reduction of the cash reserves of the banking system, is likely to be followed by an increase in advances to traders, which at a time of trade activity will promptly fill the gap.

In fact a budget surplus is completely ineffective as an expedient for checking inflation, unless it is supported by the whole deflationary apparatus, including an appropriately high Bank rate, and, if it is effective with that support, that is because the deflationary apparatus would be effective without the budget surplus.

Of course in the case where inflation is due to a deficit being met by the creation of credit, it may be essential to cover the deficit by a balanced budget, and, where there are debt maturities that cannot be covered by genuine loans, a surplus may be necessary to prevent them from being a source of further inflation. That is because inflationary borrowing by the Government is not amenable to the same motives as inflationary borrowing by traders, and requires special treatment. It is, I think, the prominence

of inflation attributable to Government borrowing in many countries after the war, and the wild excesses reached in some of them, that have led many people to look for the means of regulating credit in the budget. But any plan for the regulation of credit must be applicable to the case where inflation arises from causes in the banking system, as well as to the case of inflationary Government finance.

The plan based on budget deficits is in reality only applicable to the case where a depression is already so severe that there is an accumulation of idle balances ready to be mobilised by Government borrowing, and its efficacy even in that case is by no means certain.

In any depression, even if quite mild, there will probably be *some* accumulation of idle funds, for there will be balances accumulated by traders out of the proceeds of liquidation of working capital. But so long as the investment market is functioning normally, and can find openings in capital outlay for all the resources it receives, these balances will not materially affect the situation. It is only when there is an excessive lag in the response of capital outlay, and the long-term rate of interest is forced down to what is regarded as an artificial level, that the flow of idle balances into the investment market is held up.

This pressure on the investment market is due not only to the accumulation of idle funds by traders, but also to the repayment of bank advances and the need of the banks for investments to fill the gap made thereby in their earning assets. If the banks could induce short-term borrowers to come forward, so as to increase their advances, the trouble would solve itself, not only because the demand for investment securities would be less, but because there would be a revival of general demand. It is only when the vicious circle of deflation has gained such a hold as to cause a credit deadlock, that the banks find themselves unable to expand credit.

That state of things is exceptional—so exceptional that it probably *never* occurred before 1930. Even in the protracted spells of cheap money that did occasionally occur

in the nineteenth century there is evidence that the corner was turned towards revival at an early stage, and that, though progress was slow, there was never a complete deadlock. The vogue gained among economists in recent years by public works or budget deficits as a means of stimulating activity may be explained by the fact that a deadlock has actually occurred. Supporters of the policy do not seem to have been in the least degree discouraged by its failure even under the exceptional conditions in which theoretically it might be expected to be of some use.

At the same time the international aspect of the question must not be left out of consideration. The private enterprise displaced by Government borrowing may be an export of capital. A very substantial relief may be secured at a time of depression by a capital-exporting country in this way, in so far, at any rate, as the Government expenditure is directed at home and neither to the acquisition of imported products nor to the diversion of goods from export (conditions which are not in general fulfilled, it may be pointed out, by an armament programme). There is a favourable effect upon the balance of payments, which, with a given foreign exchange value of the currency unit, permits of an enlargement of the consumers' income.[1]

That shows that Government expenditure may really contribute to the relief of unemployment, but it affords only a very equivocal recommendation for such a measure as a means of regulating credit. For at a time of depression, owing to the diminution of savings, the export of capital from the wealthy financial centres falls off. Thereby the depression is intensified in the countries which have previously been importing capital. If the capital exporting countries take measures to reduce still further the amount of capital they export, the depression in the latter countries is still further aggravated.

In the nineteenth century the London discount market regulated credit for the whole world. There have been times since the war when its pre-eminence has not been so

[1] See my *Art of Central Banking*, pp. 435–8.

evident and New York has taken an equally prominent part. It is possible that in the future the credit system of the world will be controlled from two or more centres. But even so those centres will be in great creditor countries, which are normally or potentially exporters of capital. If they set out to deal with a depression by diverting their own stream of savings to meet Government expenditure at home, so as to gain the advantages of a favourable balance of payments, they would be increasing the strain on the new countries and primary producers, which are in any case the weakest part of the system. The result to the world as a whole would be not credit regulation but chaos.

MANAGED MONEY

Relief by deficit is, as we have seen, only appropriate at all, even with all its drawbacks, when a depression already exists. Now we have also seen that it is the actual purpose of credit regulation in certain conditions to cause a depression. That is so whenever a monetary expansion has gone further than the system adopted, whatever it may be, will allow, and has to be corrected. Before starting to devise palliatives for a depression, it will be better first to see whether the monetary authorities can avoid actually causing it. That that can be done has been indicated above (pp. 252–5). Prompt action to check an undue expansion at the outset followed by equally prompt action to relieve the pressure when it has become effective, would do what is required. But that procedure will not be a complete remedy if the monetary system itself is such as to involve deflation.

The gold standard has often been criticised on the ground that it links up the monetary unit with the hazards of gold discoveries and of the technical conditions of gold production. These hazards do undoubtedly constitute a serious defect in the gold standard. But they have not been the cause of the most disastrous fluctuations in the value of gold that have occurred in the past hundred years.

Cyclical fluctuations apart, those have been due to big changes in the monetary systems of individual countries. The excessive rise of prices and wages in the period from 1850 to 1873 was not attributable exclusively to the enlarged output of gold. It was contributed to by the suspension of specie payments in the United States, France, Austria-Hungary, Russia and Italy. The gold scarcity that followed was due to the adoption of the gold standard by Germany and other countries, and its restoration in France and the United States.

The precipitous drop in the purchasing power of gold between 1914 and 1920 was due to the general abandonment of the gold standard by European countries and the concentration of redundant gold in the United States. The rise in the purchasing power of gold associated with the depression that began in 1930 was started by the sudden absorption of gold by France in 1929.

If severe depressions are to be avoided, it will be necessary not only to institute a system of credit regulation guided by a sensitive discernment of incipient movements and directed to prompt corrective action, but also to avoid those big discontinuities in monetary systems and practices which have caused such disastrous disturbances in the past. Such a system is often disparaged as a " managed " standard, with the implication that management is a task beyond human capacity. But the problem is quite as much that of avoiding mismanagement.

Once the monetary authorities of the world can bring themselves to refrain from *causing* depressions, their task will become relatively easy.

At the same time it is important to appreciate what an extremely sensitive and delicate instrument Bank rate is. Its successful use depends on unceasing attention to the tendencies of economic activity, and to all the various symptoms by which monetary policy and credit policy have to be guided. As has been pointed out above, it is a change in Bank rate, rather than the continuance either of a high rate or of a low rate unchanged, which produces

an effect. But the effect produced may be either strictly limited, a temporary retardation or modification of whatever movement is in progress at the time, or it may be the starting point of a big new movement amplified by the inherent instability of credit, the vicious circle of expansion or contraction. Whether the effect is to be large or small depends often on a psychological response. The rise or fall of Bank rate is required to counteract expectations. Whenever any change is at work, there may be expectations either of further changes in the same direction or of a reversal of the changes already made. Expectations are not measurable, and the extent of the rise or fall required can only be discovered by trying.

The empiricism of Bank rate policy in the nineteenth century was crude, because it did not take account of these refinements. But in the nature of things the policy must remain empirical ; the requirements could never be confined within a formula, however elaborate.

The power of Bank rate is in a sense negative. A rise of Bank rate acts like a brake applied to check an expansive movement. A reduction frees the system from the action of the brake, and opens the way to an expansive movement. But, as we saw above (pp. 250–3), the mere release of the system may not suffice to start an expansion and there may be a deadlock. Bank rate may be compared to the damper of a kitchen stove. To open the damper and increase the draught of air will stimulate combustion, provided the fuel is still alight. But if the last spark has been extinguished, no amount of air will make any difference. The spread of a conflagration is a familiar example of a vicious circle. Any stove, grate or furnace is simply a contrivance for a " managed conflagration."

The source of activity in the economic system, the motive power, is profit. The outstanding importance of monetary policy in the dynamics of the system is due to the dependence of profit on the flow of money. So long as there is a normal flow, sufficient to provide a normal margin of profit over wages in conditions of full employ-

ment, activity is sustained. This state of things once secured, Bank rate can be held at a moderate level, corresponding to the prevailing long-term rate of interest, and any lapse towards depression can be quickly corrected by lowering the rate. So long as that is possible, the regulation of credit is effective both ways; for an incipient expansion can always be checked by a rise in Bank rate. If the adjustments of Bank rate are wisely and promptly applied, quite small changes will suffice. That is well illustrated by American experience during the late Benjamin Strong's Governorship of the New York Federal Reserve Bank. From 1922 to 1928 very slight variations of the rediscount rate, supported by judicious open market operations, sufficed to keep approximately stable conditions of activity. The vagaries of the Stock Market (due, as I think, to the adjustment of share values to a fall of the purchasing power of the dollar by one half since 1914[1]) did not detract from the soundness of the state of activity prevailing in industry. The experience of the period of revival and activity in Great Britain from 1909 to 1914 teaches the same lesson.

The adequacy of these small changes of Bank rate, however, depends upon psychological reactions. The vicious circle of expansion or contraction is itself partly, but not exclusively, a psychological phenomenon. It is the expectation of expanding demand that leads to a creation of credit and so causes demand to expand ; and it is the expectation of flagging demand that deters borrowers and so causes demand to flag. But these expectations are not purely psychological ; they are partly based on material facts, such as the state of stocks of commodities. The vicious circle may in either case have any degree of persistence and force within wide limits ; it may be so mild as to be easily counteracted, or it may be so violent as to require heroic measures.

Even when activity has been successfully stabilised, and

[1]The purchasing power of the dollar is best estimated from the rise in the index of wages, and from the rise in the national income. The commodity price level is affected by the cheapening of production.

the credit system has proved amenable to slight variations of Bank rate, some disturbance may arise, either economic or political, which profoundly influences expectations. Prompt and drastic treatment may be needed to maintain or to restore stability.

Or a mere miscalculation may allow a considerable departure from stable activity to arise, and a relatively big change in Bank rate may be necessary to correct it. On those occasions the necessary change ought to be brought into operation in a short space of time. That particularly applies to a reduction of Bank rate when there is a danger of depression.

The foregoing principles apply to any monetary system. In the particular case of a gold standard the task of the monetary authorities is complicated by their obligation to maintain stability of the rates of exchange on other gold standard countries. If a state of inflation or deflation develops in the gold-using world as a whole, each country has to conform to it and to suffer the consequences. In one respect the task of the monetary authorities is facilitated ; the state of the gold reserve and of the foreign exchanges supplies them with a definite indicator of the position. But the indicator is not in all respects reliable. The response of the country's credit system to a rise or fall of Bank rate may be obscured by imports or exports of gold representing movements of funds seeking temporary investment at the highest available rate of interest.

Even a country which has suspended or abandoned the gold standard cannot avoid being guided to some extent by the state of the foreign exchanges, at any rate over short periods. Rates of exchange are very sensitive to speculative movements, and such movements are not confined to speculation in the technical sense, but extend to the operations of all those traders who acquire assets or assume liabilities in more than one currency. Any such trader can hasten or retard his operations in any currency, and in doing so may be influenced by the same motives as the speculator.

Now speculation in foreign exchange, if left to a free market, may materially raise or lower rates of exchange, and any variation in the foreign exchange value of a currency has immediate reactions on the prices of commodities. The whole range of foreign trade products (that is to say, of importable or exportable products susceptible to competition in international markets) is affected, and is likely to be thrown out of relation to the prices of home-trade products and wages.

Therefore the monetary authorities of a country which has been cut loose from any metallic or international standard find themselves compelled in some degree to regulate the foreign exchanges, either by buying and selling foreign currencies or gold, or (deplorable alternative) by applying exchange control. Thus at any moment the problem of monetary policy presents itself as a choice between a modification of the rate of exchange and an adjustment of the credit system through Bank rate. And if the modification of the rate of exchange is such as to favour stable activity, the need for a change in Bank rate may be all the less. When a credit deadlock has thrown Bank rate out of action, modifications of rates of exchange may be found to be the most valuable and effective instrument of monetary policy.[1]

In Mr. Bernard Shaw's play, *The Doctor's Dilemma*, the genuinely scientific doctor, Sir Colenso Ridgeon, has invented a cure for tuberculosis, of which the essence is that the injection which is to stimulate the phagocytes (the white blood corpuscles) to eat up the disease germs must be made in the appropriate phase of the patient's system. " Everything depends on your inoculating at the right moment. Inoculate when the patient is in the negative phase and you kill ; inoculate when the patient is in the positive phase and you cure."

The number of patients for which the infinitely delicate tests of the phase can be made at Ridgeon's clinic is strictly limited and the choice has to be made between two patients

[1] See my *Trade Depression and the Way Out*, pp. 153–8 and 171–2.

who need the treatment. The rejected patient is handed over to the eminent and fashionable physician, Sir Ralph Bloomfield Bonington, who, without a glimmer of comprehension of the niceties of the treatment, announces that he is going to stimulate the phagocytes. " Having made a promise to your wife," he tells his victim, " to stimulate those phagocytes, I *will* stimulate them. And I take no further responsibility." The patient dies. And Ridgeon's comment is : " it is not an indictable offence to call in B.B. Perhaps it ought to be ; but it isn't."

The adaptation of the injection to the phase in the case of money is an equally delicate and even more intricate operation. The behaviour of traders and bankers is less predictable and more wayward than that of phagocytes. The system has an indefinite number of degrees of freedom, and its inherent instability is incessantly threatening to get out of control.

" There can be no doubt in our judgment," said the Macmillan Committee, " that ' bank rate policy ' is an absolute necessity for the sound management of a monetary system, and that it is a most delicate and beautiful instrument for the purpose " (par. 218).

Bank rate is used, as we have seen, to induce an absorption or release of cash by dealers in commodities. A dealer holds a working balance of money and a working balance of the commodities he deals in. It is characteristic of a working balance that it is constantly *varying* ; it exists to bridge over the disparities between inflow and outflow, whether of money or of commodities. Provided neither the balance of money nor the balance of commodities ever falls dangerously low, the precise amount of either is a matter of very little consequence to the holder. Either may vary in a very casual and arbitrary manner, and a very slight inducement may cause these variations to be modified. Bank rate has to work through this very volatile material.

But the same material remains to be dealt with under *any* monetary system. In a completely collectivist community which uses money, traders' balances become a

mere matter of book-keeping. There being no independent traders, but only Government agents engaged in managing economic enterprises, money practically ceases to be in circulation as soon as it passes out of the control of consumers. But consumers' balances remain subject to fortuitous variations.

A collectivist community need not rely on the short-term rate of interest to enlarge or compress the consumers' income. The particular incomes which compose the consumers' income are paid by the State, and the State can alter them by an executive decision in any desired proportion. And it can use this power simply to leave them unaltered, so that the flow of purchasing power is stable. But it will still be possible for people to accumulate balances or to spend out of balances, causing demand to fall short of the consumers' income or to exceed it. If in the collectivist system there is no provision for the investment of savings at interest, there may be a large accumulation of savings in the form of cash balances constituting a potential demand which it might be difficult to meet. Unless the practice of using money as a store of value is to be prevented (for example, by introducing some kind of perishable money embodying a negative rate of interest) the danger of a flight from the currency would be a real one.

These possibilities are outside the scope of a work on Bank rate, but they illustrate the far-reaching character of the monetary problems which in one kind of economic system Bank rate is used to solve.

APPENDIX I

Bank Rate		Number of weeks at: 2	2½	3	3½	4	4½	5	5½	6	6½	7	8	9	10	Price of Consols	Reserve	£'000
1844—																		
5 Sept.	2½	..	58	..	..	..	..	..	..	..	..	..	..	..	..	99 11/16	31 Aug.	8867
1845—																		
16 Oct.	3	..	..	3	..	..	..	..	..	..	..	..	..	..	..	98	11 Oct.	7549
6 Nov.	3½	..	..	..	42	..	..	..	..	..	..	..	..	..	..	95¾	1 Nov.	5838
1846—																		
27 Aug.	3	..	..	20	..	..	..	..	..	..	..	..	..	..	..	95⅝	22 Aug.	10029
1847—																		
14 Jan.	3½	..	..	..	1	..	..	..	..	..	..	..	..	..	..	93⅛	9 Jan.	7471
21 Jan.	4	..	..	..	..	11	..	..	..	..	..	..	..	..	..	91¾	16 Jan.	7269
8 April	5	..	..	..	..	..	..	17	..	..	..	..	..	..	..	87⅝	3 April	4391
5 Aug.	5½	..	..	..	..	..	..	..	11 4/7	..	..	..	..	..	..	88	31 July	4439
25 Oct.	8	..	..	..	..	..	..	..	..	..	..	..	4	..	..	79⅞	23 Oct.	1994
																	30 Oct.	1606
22 Nov.	7	..	..	..	..	..	..	..	..	..	..	1 3/7	..	..	..	84⅛	20 Nov.	4719
2 Dec.	6	..	..	..	..	..	..	..	..	3	..	..	..	..	..	85⅝	27 Nov.	5563
23 Dec.	5	..	..	..	..	..	..	5	..	..	..	..	..	..	..	85¾	18 Dec.	8233
1848—																		
27 Jan.	4	..	..	..	..	20	..	..	..	..	..	..	..	..	..	89	22 Jan.	8065
15 June	3½	..	..	..	20	..	..	..	..	..	..	..	..	..	..	84⅛	10 June	10213
2 Nov.	3	..	..	55	..	..	..	..	..	..	..	..	..	..	..	86	28 Oct.	8683
1849—																		
22 Nov.	2½	..	57	..	..	..	..	..	..	..	..	..	..	..	..	94⅛	17 Nov.	11856
1850—																		
26 Dec.	3	..	..	53	..	..	..	..	..	..	..	..	..	..	..	97¾	21 Dec.	10863
1852—																		
1 Jan.	2½	..	16	..	..	..	..	..	..	..	..	..	..	..	..	97¼	27 Dec. '51	12600
22 April	2	37	..	..	..	..	..	..	..	..	..	..	..	..	..	99⅜	17 April '52	11504
1853—																		
6 Jan.	2½	..	2	..	..	..	..	..	..	..	..	..	..	..	..	100⅛	1 Jan.	11474
20 Jan.	3	..	..	19	..	..	..	..	..	..	..	..	..	..	..	99⅜	15 Jan.	9487
2 June	3½	..	..	..	13	..	..	..	..	..	..	..	..	..	..	99⅝	28 May	9363
1 Sept.	4	..	..	..	..	2	..	..	..	..	..	..	..	..	..	97¾	27 Aug.	8187
15 Sept.	4½	..	..	..	..	..	2	..	..	..	..	..	..	..	..	95⅝	10 Sept.	8004
29 Sept.	5	..	..	..	..	..	..	32	..	..	..	..	..	..	..	92⅜	24 Sept.	7745
1854—																		
11 May	5½	..	..	..	..	..	..	..	12	..	..	..	..	..	..	88¼	6 May	4634
3 Aug.	5	..	..	..	..	..	..	35	..	..	..	..	..	..	..	92⅝	29 July	6970
1855—																		
5 April	4½	..	..	..	..	..	4	..	..	..	..	..	..	..	..	92¾	31 March	9717
3 May	4	..	..	..	..	6	..	..	..	..	..	..	..	..	..	88⅝	28 April	9140
14 June	3½	..	..	..	12	..	..	..	..	..	..	..	..	..	..	92	9 June	12313
6 Sept.	4	..	..	..	..	1	..	..	..	..	..	..	..	..	..	90⅜	1 Sept.	8834
13 Sept.	4½	..	..	..	..	..	2	..	..	..	..	..	..	..	..	90⅝	8 Sept.	8075
27 Sept.	5	..	..	..	..	..	..	1	..	..	..	..	..	..	..	89	22 Sept.	7860
4 Oct.	5½	..	..	..	..	..	..	..	2	..	..	..	..	..	..	88	29 Sept.	6766
18 Oct.	6	..	..	..	..	..	..	..	..	32	..	..	..	..	..	87¼	13 Oct.	5104
1856—																		
29 May	5	..	..	..	..	..	..	4	..	..	..	..	..	..	..	95⅛	24 May	5702
26 June	4½	..	..	..	..	..	13 6/7	..	..	..	..	..	..	..	..	94¾	21 June	7570
1 Oct.	5	..	..	..	..	..	..	5/7	..	..	..	..	..	..	..	92	27 Sept.	6020
6 Oct.	6	..	..	..	..	..	..	..	..	5 3/7	..	..	..	..	..	92⅛	4 Oct.	4333
13 Nov.	7	..	..	..	..	..	..	..	..	..	..	3	..	..	..	92¼	8 Nov.	3766
4 Dec.	6½	..	..	..	..	..	..	..	..	..	2	..	..	..	..	94¼	29 Nov.	5402
18 Dec.	6	..	..	..	..	..	..	..	..	15	..	..	..	..	..	93⅞	13 Dec.	6465
1857—																		
2 April	6½	..	..	..	..	..	..	..	..	..	11	..	..	..	..	93⅜	28 March	5406
18 June	6	..	..	..	..	..	..	..	..	4	..	..	..	..	..	93⅞	13 June	6612
16 July	5½	..	..	..	..	..	..	..	12	..	..	..	..	..	..	91½	11 July	6105
8 Oct.	6	..	..	..	..	..	..	..	..	4/7	..	..	..	..	..	90	3 Oct.	5190
12 Oct.	7	..	..	..	..	..	..	..	..	..	..	1	..	..	..	89¼	10 Oct.	4595
19 Oct.	8	..	..	..	..	..	..	..	..	..	..	..	2 3/7	..	..	89⅝	17 Oct.	3816
5 Nov.	9	..	..	..	..	..	..	..	..	..	..	..	..	4/7	..	89	4 Nov.	2706
9 Nov.	10	..	..	..	..	..	..	..	..	..	..	..	..	..	6 3/7	88⅞	11 Nov.	1462
																	12 Nov	581

APPENDIX I (*continued*)

Bank Rate		2	2½	3	3½	4	4½	5	5½	6	6½	7	8	9	*Price of Consols*	*Reserve*		*Increase in Reserve*	*Net Imports of Gold*	*Interior Demand*
																	£'000	£'000	£'000	£'000
1857—																18 Nov.	1553	6418	3747	—2671
24 Dec.	8	..	..	..	..	..	..	..	..	..	..	..	2	..	93⅛	23 Dec.	7971	—352	1686	38‡
1858—																				
7 Jan.	6	..	..	..	..	..	..	..	..	1	..	..	..	..	94⅜	6 Jan.	7619	541	386	—155
14 Jan.	5	..	..	..	..	..	..	2	..	..	..	..	..	..	94⅝	13 Jan.	8160	2049	1296	—753
28 Jan.	4	..	..	..	..	1	..	..	..	..	..	..	..	..	94⅜	27 Jan.	10209	—15	430	445
4 Feb.	3½	..	..	..	1	..	..	..	..	..	..	..	..	..	95½	3 Feb.	10194	1252	665	—587
11 Feb.	3	..	..	43	..	..	..	..	..	..	..	..	..	..	96	10 Feb.	11446	1911	6092	4181
9 Dec.	2½	..	20	..	..	..	..	..	..	..	..	..	..	..	98	8 Dec.	13357	633	1143	510
1859—																9 March	13990	—3813	—156	3657
28 April	3½	..	..	..	1	..	..	..	..	..	..	..	..	..	92⅛	27 April	10177	—752	—361	391
5 May	4½	..	..	..	..	..	4	..	..	..	..	..	..	..	90¾	4 May	9425	1722	435	—1287
2 June	3½	..	..	..	1	..	..	..	..	..	..	..	..	..	93⅝	1 June	11147	152	237	85
9 June	3	..	..	5	..	..	..	..	..	..	..	..	..	..	93⅛	8 June	11299	—595	1128	1723
14 July	2½	..	27	..	..	..	..	..	..	..	..	..	..	..	95¾	13 July	10704	—2398	1815	4213
1860—																				
19 Jan.	3	..	..	1⁵⁄₇	..	..	..	..	..	..	..	..	..	..	95⅜	18 Jan.	8306	101	149	48
31 Jan.	4	..	..	..	..	8²⁄₇	..	..	..	..	..	..	..	..	94	25 Jan.	8407	—896	—780	116
																1 Feb.	7511	1255	—48	—1303
29 March	4½	..	..	..	..	..	2	..	..	..	..	..	..	..	94¼	28 March	8766	—3121	104	3225
12 April	5	..	..	..	..	..	..	4	..	..	..	..	..	..	94½	11 April	5645	2322	736	—1586
10 May	4½	..	..	..	..	..	2	..	..	..	..	..	..	..	95⅜	9 May	7967	1129	326	—803
24 May	4	..	..	..	..	24	..	..	..	..	..	..	..	..	95	23 May	9096	901	1202	301
																19 Sept.	9997	—2831	—1548	1283
8 Nov.	4½	..	..	..	..	..	⁵⁄₇	..	..	..	..	..	..	..	93⅛	7 Nov.	7166	—35	—154	—119
13 Nov.	5	..	..	..	..	..	..	²⁄₇	..	..	..	..	..	..	93⅜					
15 Nov.	6	..	..	..	..	..	..	..	..	2	..	..	..	..	92⅞	14 Nov.	7131	1304	—340	—1307
29 Nov.	5	..	..	..	..	..	..	4⁴⁄₇	..	..	..	..	..	..	93⅜	28 Nov.	8435*	—806	—2264	—341
31 Dec.	6	..	..	..	..	..	..	..	..	1	..	..	..	..	92½	26 Dec.	7629*	—1013	142	1345
1861—																				
7 Jan.	7	..	..	..	..	..	..	..	..	..	..	5³⁄₇	..	..	92½	2 Jan.	6616*	—419	—726	—324
																9 Jan.	6197*	159	—712	—1650
14 Feb.	8	..	..	..	..	..	..	..	..	..	..	..	5	..	92⅛	13 Feb.	6356*	1969	—230	—2199
21 March	7	..	..	..	..	..	..	..	..	..	..	2	..	..	91⅞	20 March	8325*	—674	503	1177
4 April	6	..	..	..	..	..	..	..	..	1	..	..	..	..	91⅜	3 April	7651*	—212	77	289
11 April	5	..	..	..	..	..	..	5	..	..	..	..	..	..	91⅝	10 April	7439*	—625	—144	296
16 May	6	..	..	..	..	..	..	..	..	11	..	..	..	..	91¾	15 May	6814*	—1034	—2086	—1540†
																17 July	5780	769	652	—117
1 Aug.	5	..	..	..	..	..	..	2	..	..	..	..	..	..	90⅛	31 July	6549	645	349	—296

‡Fiduciary Issue temporarily increased by £2,000,000, 13 Nov. to 24 Dec. 1857
* Including the following amounts of silver bullion :

28 Nov. 1860	£337,000		9 Jan.	£1,627,000
26 Dec.	£1,454,000		13 Feb. to 10 April	£848,000
2 Jan. 1861	£1,644,000		15 May	£663,000

†Fiduciary Issue increased by £175,000 on 10th July, 1861.

APPENDIX I (*continued*)

Bank Rate		*Number of weeks at:* 2	2½	3	3½	4	4½	5	5½	6	6½	7	8	9	*Price of Consols*	*Reserve*		*Increase in Reserve*	*Net Imports of Gold*	*Interior Demand*
1861—																	£'000	£'000	£'000	£'000
15 Aug.	4½	..	..	..	..	..	2	..	..	..	..	..	..	..	90½	14 Aug.	7194	806	154	—652
29 Aug.	4	..	..	..	..	3	..	..	..	..	..	..	..	..	92½	28 Aug.	8000	814	848	34
19 Sept.	3½	..	..	..	7	..	..	..	..	..	..	..	..	..	93¾	18 Sept.	8814	—727	1021	1748
7 Nov.	3	..	..	9	..	..	..	..	..	..	..	..	..	..	93	6 Nov.	8087	2255	958	—1297
1862—																				
9 Jan.	2½	..	19	..	..	..	..	..	..	..	..	..	..	..	92	8 Jan.	10342	525	2601	2076
																7 May	10867	—752	—949	—197
22 May	3		..	7	..	..	..	..	..	..	..	..	..	..	93½	21 May	10115	—675	—1542	—865
																18 June	9440	450	1549	1099
10 July	2½	..	2	..	..	..	..	..	..	..	..	..	..	..	92¼	9 July	9890	618	989	371
24 July	2	14	..	..	..	..	..	..	..	..	..	..	..	..	92⅞	23 July	10508	—1356	881	2237
30 Oct.	3	..	..	11	..	..	..	..	..	..	..	..	..	..	93⅝	29 Oct.	9152	—687	—625	62
1863—																				
15 Jan.	4	..	..	..	..	1 6/7	..	..	..	..	..	..	..	..	92¾	14 Jan.	8465	—304	—45	259
28 Jan.	5	..	..	..	..	..	..	3 1/7	..	..	..	..	..	..	92⅛	28 Jan.	8161	1768	734	—1034
19 Feb.	4	..	..	..	..	9	..	..	..	..	..	..	..	..	92⅝	18 Feb.	9929	—692	1035	1727
23 April	3½	..	..	..	1	..	..	..	..	..	..	..	..	..	93⅛	22 April	9237	—107	309	416
30 April	3	..	..	2 2/7	..	..	..	..	..	..	..	..	..	..	93⅛	29 April	9130	—464	—501	—37
16 May	3½	..	..	..	5/7	..	..	..	..	..	..	..	..	..	93¼	13 May	8666	—170	—123	47
21 May	4	..	..	..	..	23 4/7	..	..	..	..	..	..	..	..	93⅝	20 May	8496	—1280	3442	4722
2 Nov.	5	..	..	..	..	..	..	3/7	..	..	..	..	..	..	93	28 Oct.	7216	—808	9	817
5 Nov.	6	..	..	..	..	..	..	..	..	3 6/7	..	..	..	..	92¼	4 Nov.	6408	1105	—794	—1899
2 Dec.	7	..	..	..	..	..	..	..	..	..	..	1/7	..	..	90⅛	25 Nov.	7513	—837	—222	615
3 Dec.	8	..	..	..	..	..	..	..	..	..	..	..	3	..	90⅛	2 Dec.	6676	790	—279	—1069
																9 Dec.	7466	1744	329	—1415
24 Dec.	7	..	..	..	..	..	..	..	..	..	..	3 6/7	..	..	91¼	23 Dec.	9210	—1615	751	2366
1864—																				
20 Jan.	8	..	..	..	..	..	..	..	..	..	..	..	3 1/7	..	90⅛	13 Jan.	7595	—798	—254	544
																20 Jan.	6797	1163	111	—1052
11 Feb.	7	..	..	..	..	..	..	..	..	..	..	2	..	..	90⅝	10 Feb.	7960	834	79	—755
25 Feb.	6	..	..	..	..	..	..	..	..	7 2/7	..	..	..	..	91⅝	24 Feb.	8794	—2320	427	2747
16 April	7	..	..	..	..	..	..	..	..	..	..	2 3/7	..	..	91⅛	13 April	6474	—222	—411	—189
																20 April	6252	10	—345	—355
2 May	8	..	..	..	..	..	..	..	..	..	..	..	3/7	..	91¼	27 April	6262	—642	77	719
5 May	9	..	..	..	..	..	..	..	..	..	..	..	..	2	90¾	4 May	5620	1478	600	—878
19 May	8	..	..	..	..	..	..	..	..	..	..	..	1	..	91¾	18 May	7098	849	344	—505
26 May	7	..	..	..	..	..	..	..	..	..	..	3	..	..	91⅞	25 May	7947	879	570	—309
16 June	6	..	..	..	..	..	..	..	..	5 4/7	..	..	..	..	90	15 June	8826	—2700	—123	2577
25 July	7	..	..	..	..	..	..	..	..	..	..	1 3/7	..	..	90⅛	20 July	6126	—115	—62	53
		..	..	..	..	..	..	..	..	..	..	..	..	..		27 July	6011	—413	51	464

APPENDIX I (*continued*)

Bank Rate		*Number of weeks at:* 2	2¼	2½	3	3½	4	4½	5	5½	6	7	8	9	10	*Price of Consols*	*Reserve*		*Increase in Reserve*	*Net Imports of Gold*	*Interior Demand*
1864—																		£'000	£'000	£'000	£'000
4 Aug.	8	..	..	..	..	..	..	..	..	..	..	..	5	..	..	89⅞	3 Aug.	5598	1213	754	—459
8 Sept.	9	..	..	..	..	..	..	..	..	..	..	..	..	9	..	87½	7 Sept.	6811	1096	1571	475
10 Nov.	8	..	..	..	..	..	..	..	..	..	..	..	2	..	..	90⅜	9 Nov.	7907	1309	574	—735
24 Nov.	7	..	..	..	..	..	..	..	..	..	..	3	..	..	..	91¼	23 Nov.	9216	378	—54	—432
15 Dec.	6	..	..	..	..	..	..	..	..	..	4	..	..	..	..	89⅝	14 Dec.	9594	—1329	64	1393
1865—																					
12 Jan.	5½	..	..	..	..	..	..	..	..	2	..	..	..	..	..	90¼	11 Jan.	8265	556	—122	—678
26 Jan.	5	..	..	..	..	..	..	..	5	..	..	..	..	..	..	89⅞	25 Jan.	8821	697	479	—218
2 March	4½	..	..	..	..	..	..	4	..	..	..	..	..	..	..	88¾	1 March	9518	540	336	—204
30 March	4	..	..	..	..	..	5	..	..	..	..	..	..	..	..	89⅛	29 March	10058	—2331	598	2929
4 May	4½	..	..	..	..	..	..	3	..	..	..	..	..	..	..	90⅝	3 May	7727	1360	287	—1073
25 May	4	..	..	..	..	..	1	..	..	..	..	..	..	..	..	90⅞	24 May	9087	491	687	196
1 June	3½	..	..	..	..	2	..	..	..	..	..	..	..	..	..	91¼	31 May	9578	388	38	—350
15 June	3	..	..	..	6	..	..	..	..	..	..	..	..	..	..	90⅛	14 June	9966	—2884	716	3600
27 July	3½	..	..	..	..	1	..	..	..	..	..	..	..	..	..	90	26 July	7082	—621	173	794
3 Aug.	4	..	..	..	..	..	8	..	..	..	..	..	..	..	..	90⅛	2 Aug.	6461	647	534	—113
28 Sept.	4½	..	..	..	..	..	..	4/7	..	..	..	..	..	..	..	89⅜	27 Sept.	7108	—2002	81	2083
2 Oct.	5	..	..	..	..	..	..	..	3/7	..	..	..	..	..	..	89¼					
5 Oct.	6	..	..	..	..	..	..	..	..	..	2/7	..	..	..	..	89¼	4 Oct.	5106	—32	344	376
7 Oct.	7	..	..	..	..	..	..	..	..	..	..	6 5/7	..	..	..	88⅜	11 Oct.	5074	3457	2078	—1379
23 Nov.	6	..	..	..	..	..	..	..	..	..	5	..	..	..	..	89⅛	22 Nov.	8531	—940	—620	320
28 Dec.	7	..	..	..	..	..	..	..	..	..	..	1	..	..	..	87¼	27 Dec.	7591	—1611	—65	1546
1866—																					
4 Jan.	8	..	..	..	..	..	..	..	..	..	..	..	7	..	..	87¼	3 Jan.	5980	2280	180	—1750*
22 Feb.	7	..	..	..	..	..	..	..	..	..	..	3	..	..	..	87⅜	21 Feb.	8260	544	259	—285
15 March	6	..	..	..	..	..	..	..	..	..	7	..	..	..	..	87	14 March	8804	—3168	890	4058
3 May	7	..	..	..	..	..	..	..	..	..	..	5/7	..	..	..	86⅝	2 May	5636	176	—57	—233
8 May	8	..	..	..	..	..	..	..	..	..	..	..	3/7	..	..	86⅜	9 May	5812	—4609	196	4805
11 May	9	..	..	..	..	..	..	..	..	..	..	..	..	1/7	..	85¼					
12 May	10	..	..	..	..	..	..	..	..	..	..	..	..	..	13 5/7	85⅛	16 May	1203	—343	43	386
																	30 May	860	3751	4185	434
16 Aug.	8	..	..	..	..	..	..	..	..	..	..	..	1	..	..	87⅞	15 Aug.	4611	979	333	—646
23 Aug.	7	..	..	..	..	..	..	..	..	..	..	1	..	..	..	88½	22 Aug.	5590	1344	1058	—286
30 Aug.	6	..	..	..	..	..	..	..	..	..	1	..	..	..	..	89⅛	29 Aug.	6934	40	223	183
6 Sept.	5	..	..	..	..	..	..	..	3	..	..	..	..	..	..	89⅛	5 Sept.	6974	1706	503	—1203
27 Sept.	4½	..	..	..	..	..	..	6	..	..	..	..	..	..	..	89⅝	26 Sept.	8680	—350	1331	1681
8 Nov.	4	..	..	..	..	..	6	..	..	..	..	..	..	..	..	89⅜	7 Nov.	8330	3385	1011	—2374
20 Dec.	3½	..	..	..	..	7	..	..	..	..	..	..	..	..	..	89⅜	19 Dec.	11715	—715	856	1571

* Fiduciary Issue increase by £350,000 21st February, 1866.

APPENDIX I (*continued*)

Bank Rate		2	2¼	2½	3	3½	4	4½	5	5½	6	7	8	9	10	*Price of Consols*	*Reserve*		*Increase in Reserve*	*Net Imports of Gold*	*Interior Demand*
1867—																		£'000	£'000	£'000	£'000
7 Feb.	3	..	..	..	16	..	..	..	..	..	..	..	..	..	..	90⅞	6 Feb.	11000	1488	1590	102
30 May	2½	..	..	8	..	..	..	..	..	..	..	..	..	..	..	94	29 May	12488	1281	2160	879
25 July	2	69	..	..	..	..	..	..	..	..	..	..	..	..	..	94⅜	24 July	13769	—3100	9685	12785
1868—																					
																	28 Oct.	10669	—801	—1293	—492
19 Nov.	2½	..	..	2	..	..	..	..	..	..	..	..	..	..	..	94⅛	18 Nov.	9868	—291	63	354
3 Dec.	3	..	..	..	17	..	..	..	..	..	..	..	..	..	..	92¾	2 Dec.	9577	—616	—56	560
1869—																					
1 April	4	..	..	..	..	..	5	..	..	..	..	..	..	..	..	93	31 March	8961	—1384	—155	1229
6 May	4½	..	..	..	..	..	..	5	..	..	..	..	..	..	..	93¼	5 May	7577	3211	982	—2229
10 June	4	..	..	..	..	..	2	..	..	..	..	..	..	..	..	92⅝	9 June	10788	1128	597	—531
24 June	3½	..	..	..	..	3	..	..	..	..	..	..	..	..	..	92⅞	23 June	11916	—1059	849	1908
15 July	3	..	..	..	5	..	..	..	..	..	..	..	..	..	..	93¼	14 July	10857	1413	1844	431
19 Aug.	2½	..	..	11	..	..	..	..	..	..	..	..	..	..	..	93	18 Aug.	12270	—2739	369	3108
4 Nov.	3	..	..	..	37	..	..	..	..	..	..	..	..	..	..	93¼	3 Nov.	9531	2569	3310	741
1870—																					
																	13 July	12100	—924	243	1167
21 July	3½	..	..	..	..	3/7	..	..	..	..	..	..	..	..	..	89⅜	20 July	11176	—1101	—652	449
23 July	4	..	..	..	..	..	5/7	..	..	..	..	..	..	..	..	90⅜					
28 July	5	..	..	..	..	..	..	..	1	..	..	..	..	..	..	89⅝	27 July	10075	—744	365	1109
4 Aug.	6	..	..	..	..	..	..	..	..	..	1	..	..	..	..	89	3 Aug.	9331	969	854	—115
11 Aug.	5½	..	..	..	..	..	..	..	..	1	..	..	..	..	..	91⅛	10 Aug.	10300	950	1163	213
18 Aug.	4½	..	..	..	..	..	..	1	..	..	..	..	..	..	..	91⅛	17 Aug.	11250	497	352	—145
25 Aug.	4	..	..	..	..	..	1	..	..	..	..	..	..	..	..	91½	24 Aug.	11747	533	993	460
1 Sept.	3½	..	..	..	..	2	..	..	..	..	..	..	..	..	..	91⅞	31 Aug.	12280	1203	1941	738
15 Sept.	3	..	..	..	2	..	..	..	..	..	..	..	..	..	..	92⅛	14 Sept.	13483	600	797	197
29 Sept.	2½	..	..	22	..	..	..	..	..	..	..	..	..	..	..	91⅞	28 Sept.	14083	—773	514	1287
1871—																					
2 March	3	..	..	..	6	..	..	..	..	..	..	..	..	..	..	91⅝	1 March	13310	—287	1443	1730
13 April	2½	..	..	9	..	..	..	..	..	..	..	..	..	..	..	92⅝	12 April	13023	4185	2802	—1383
15 June	2¼	..	4	..	..	..	..	..	..	..	..	..	..	..	..	91⅞	14 June	17208	—562	1850	2412
13 July	2	10	..	..	..	..	..	..	..	..	..	..	..	..	..	93⅝	12 July	16646	764	1343	579
																	26 July	17410	—3699	—2333	1366
21 Sept.	3	..	..	..	1	..	..	..	..	..	..	..	..	..	..	93⅛	20 Sept.	13711	—2634	—828	1806
28 Sept.	4	..	..	..	..	..	1 3/7	..	..	..	..	..	..	..	..	92¾	27 Sept.	11077	—2157	—1635	522
7 Oct.	5	..	..	..	..	..	..	..	5 5/7	..	..	..	..	..	..	92¼	4 Oct.	8920	—855	—178	677
																	11 Oct.	8065	6061	—1270	—7331
16 Nov.	4	..	..	..	..	..	2	..	..	..	..	..	..	..	..	93⅛	15 Nov.	14126	1053	—56	—1109
30 Nov.	3½	..	..	..	..	2	..	..	..	..	..	..	..	..	..	93⅝	29 Nov.	15179	470	142	—328
14 Dec.	3	..	..	..	16	..	..	..	..	..	..	..	..	..	..	92⅜	13 Dec.	15649	—4313	—3294	1019

APPENDIX I (*continued*)

Bank Rate		*Number of weeks at:* 2	2½	3	3½	4	4½	5	6	7	8	9	*Price of Consols*	*Reserve*		*Increase in Reserve*	*Net Imports of Gold*	*Interior Demand*
1872—															£'000	£'000	£'000	£'000
4 April	3½	..	..	..	1	..	..	..	..	..	..	..	93	3 April	11336	—847	—273	574
11 April	4	..	..	..	..	4	..	..	..	..	..	..	92⅞	10 April	10489	—560	—8	552
9 May	5	..	..	..	..	..	..	3	..	..	..	..	92⅝	8 May	9929	34	—373	—407
											..	..		15 May	9963	1510	847	—663
30 May	4	..	..	..	..	2	..	..	..	..			93⅛	29 May	11473	1490	437	— 1053
13 June	3½	..	..	..	1	..	..	..	..	..	..	..	92⅞	12 June	12963	630	519	—111
20 June	3	..	..	4	..	..	..	..	..	..	..	..	92¼	19 June	13593	—2095	1228	3323
18 July	3½	..	..	..	8 6/7	..	..	..	..	..	..	..	92⅛	17 July	11498	480	—996	—1476
					..							..		24 July	11978	—627	496	1123
18 Sept.	4	..	..	..	..	1 1/7	..	..	..	..	..		92⅜	18 Sept.	11351	—329	—193	136
26 Sept.	4½	..	..	..	..	..	1	..	..	..	..	..	92⅞	25 Sept.	11022	—2100	—310	1790
3 Oct.	5	..	..	..	..	..	..	1	..	..	..	..	92⅛	2 Oct.	8922	—190	—173	17
10 Oct.	6	..	..	..	..	..	..	..	4 2/7	..	..	..	92⅛	9 Oct.	8732	317	—470	—787
9 Nov.	7	..	..	..	..	..	..	..	..	2 5/7	..	..	92¼	6 Nov.	9049	195	74	—121
												..		13 Nov.	9244	3819	266	—3553
28 Nov.	6	..	..	..	..	..	..	..	2	..	..		92⅞	27 Nov.	13063	770	—86	—856
12 Dec.	5	..	..	..	..	..	..	4	..	..	..	..	91⅝	11 Dec.	13833	—795	990	1785
1873—												..						
9 Jan.	4½	..	..	..	..	..	2	..	..	..	..		92¼	8 Jan.	13038	1508	—521	—2029
23 Jan.	4	..	..	..	..	1	..	..	..	..	..	..	92⅞	22 Jan.	14546	579	72	—507
30 Jan.	3½	..	..	..	7 6/7	..	..	..	..	..	..	..	92	29 Jan.	15125	93	—1303	—1396
26 March	4	..	..	..	..	6	..	..	..	..	..	..	92¾	19 March	15218	—1523	—791	732
												..		26 March	13695	—2701	8	2709
7 May	4½	..	..	..	..	..	3/7	..	..	..	..		93⅜	30 April	10994	—716	—414	302
10 May	5	..	..	..	..	..	..	1	..	..	..	..	93⅜	7 May	10278	—94	—907	—813
17 May	6	..	..	..	..	..	..	..	2 4/7	..	..	..	93¼	14 May	10184	—103	—268	—165
												..		21 May	10081	441	321	—120
4 June	7	..	..	..	..	..	..	..	..	1 1/7	..		94	28 May	10522	—708	159	867
											..	..		4 June	9814	1221	100	—1121
12 June	6	..	..	..	..	..	..	..	4	..	..	..	92½	11 June	11035	142	40	—102
10 July	5	..	..	..	..	..	..	1	..	..	..	..	92⅝	9 July	11177	133	393	260
17 July	4½	..	..	..	..	..	1	..	..	..	..	..	92⅞	16 July	11310	1038	714	—324
24 July	4	..	..	..	..	1	..	..	..	..	..	..	92¾	23 July	12348	75	868	793
31 July	3½	..	..	..	3	..	..	..	..	..	..	..	92⅝	30 July	12423	864	1235	371
21 Aug.	3	..	..	5	..	..	..	..	..	..	..	..	92⅝	20 Aug.	13287	—109	796	905
														10 Sept.	13178	61	—550	—611
25 Sept.	4	..	..	..	..	4/7	..	..	..	..	..	..	92⅝	24 Sept.	13239	—3285	—484	2801
29 Sept.	5	..	..	..	..	..	..	2 1/7	..	..	..	..	92¼	1 Oct.	9954	—839	84	923

APPENDIX I (*continued*)

Bank Rate		Number of weeks at: 2	2½	3	3½	4	4½	5	6	7	8	9	Price of Consols	Reserve		Increase in Reserve	Net Imports of Gold	Interior Demand
1873—															£'000	£'000	£'000	£'000
14 Oct.	6	..	..	..	..	..	..	..	$\frac{4}{7}$	..	..	..	92½	8 Oct.	9115	—1254	—709	545
18 Oct.	7	..	..	..	..	..	..	..	..	2	..	..	92⅛	15 Oct.	7861	251	—629	—880
														22 Oct.	8112	343	—416	—759
1 Nov.	8	..	..	..	..	..	..	..	..	..	$\frac{6}{7}$	..	92⅝	29 Oct.	8455	—384	484	868
7 Nov.	9	..	..	..	..	..	..	..	..	..	..	$1\frac{6}{7}$	92⅜	5 Nov.	8071	1631	—79	—1710
20 Nov.	8	..	..	..	..	..	..	..	..	..	1	..	92¾	19 Nov.	9702	1547	599	—948
27 Nov.	6	..	..	..	..	..	..	..	1	..	..	..	93⅛	26 Nov.	11249	200	856	656
4 Dec.	5	..	..	..	..	..	..	1	..	..	..	..	91⅞	3 Dec.	11449	1013	79	—934
11 Dec.	4½	..	..	..	..	..	4	..	..	..	..	..	91⅞	10 Dec.	12462	—616	660	1276
1874—																		
8 Jan.	4	..	..	..	..	1	..	..	..	..	..	..	92¼	7 Jan.	11846	103	—109	—212
15 Jan.	3½	..	..	..	15	..	..	..	..	..	..	..	92	14 Jan.	11949	—1555	—233	1322
30 April	4	..	..	..	..	4	..	..	..	..	..	..	92¾	29 April	10394	595	931	336
28 May	3½	..	..	..	1	..	..	..	..	..	..	..	93⅜	27 May	10989	360	677	317
4 June	3	..	..	2	..	..	..	..	..	..	..	..	92½	3 June	11349	1647	996	—651
18 June	2½	..	6	..	..	..	..	..	..	..	..	..	92⅜	17 June	12996	—2223	—424	1799
30 July	3	..	..	1	..	..	..	..	..	..	..	..	92⅛	29 July	10773	—1565	—515	1050
6 Aug.	4	..	..	..	..	2	..	..	..	..	..	..	92¼	5 Aug.	9208	1844	1421	—423
20 Aug.	3½	..	..	..	1	..	..	..	..	..	..	..	92¼	19 Aug.	11052	693	207	—486
27 Aug.	3	..	..	7	..	..	..	..	..	..	..	..	92⅝	26 Aug.	11745	—2339	2031	4370
15 Oct.	4	..	..	..	..	$4\frac{4}{7}$	..	..	..	..	..	..	92⅞	14 Oct.	9406	—368	—466	—98
														11 Nov.	9038	—220	—102	118
16 Nov.	5	..	..	..	..	..	..	2	..	..	..	..	93⅜	18 Nov.	8818	473	—60	—533
30 Nov.	6	..	..	..	..	..	..	..	$5\frac{3}{7}$	..	..	..	93¼	25 Nov.	9291	—651	136	787
														2 Dec.	8640	1825	2353	528
1875—																		
7 Jan	5	..	..	..	..	..	..	1	..	..	..	..	92	6 Jan.	10465	479	182	—297
14 Jan.	4	..	..	..	..	2	..	..	..	..	..	..	92⅜	13 Jan.	10944	986	1133	147
28 Jan.	3	..	..	3	..	..	..	..	..	..	..	..	92⅝	27 Jan.	11930	—1730	—1399	331
18 Feb.	3½	..	..	..	20	..	..	..	..	..	..	..	92⅞	17 Feb.	10200	3009	6205	3196
8 July	3	..	..	3	..	..	..	..	..	..	..	..	93⅞	7 July	13209	2175	2373	198
29 July	2½	..	2	..	..	..	..	..	..	..	..	..	94⅛	28 July	15384	31	241	210
12 Aug.	2	8	..	..	..	..	..	..	..	..	..	..	94⅜	11 Aug.	15415	—1827	871	2698
														29 Sept.	13588	—1216	—211	1005
7 Oct.	2½	..	1	..	..	..	..	..	..	..	..	..	$94\frac{1}{16}$	6 Oct.	12372	—1583	—1092	491
14 Oct.	3½	..	..	..	1	..	..	..	..	..	..	..	93⅞	13 Oct.	10789	—530	—504	26
21 Oct.	4	..	..	..	..	4	..	..	..	..	..	..	$94\frac{1}{16}$	20 Oct.	10259	316	—522	—838
18 Nov.	3	..	..	6	..	..	..	..	..	..	..	..	94⅞	17 Nov.	10575	—1396	—1883	—487
30 Dec.	4	..	..	..	..	1	..	..	..	..	..	..	94	29 Dec.	9179	—1047	—688	359

APPENDIX I (*continued*)

Bank Rate		*Number of weeks at:* 2	2½	3	3½	4	4½	5	6	*Price of Consols*	*Reserve*		*Increase in Reserve*	*Net Imports of Gold*	*Interior Demand*
1876—												£'000	£'000	£'000	£'000
6 Jan.	5	..	..	..	..	..	..	3	..	93¾	5 Jan.	8132	2348	207	—2141
27 Jan.	4	..	..	..	..	8	..	..	..	94½	26 Jan.	10480	3007	726	—2281
23 March	3½	..	..	..	2	..	..	..	..	94 5/16	22 March	13487	—507	686	1193
6 April	3	..	..	2	..	..	..	..	..	94 11/16	5 April	12980	412	916	504
20 April	2	54	..	..	..	..	..	..	..	94⅞	19 April	13392	8852	10200	1348
											20 Sept.	22244	—11317	—9611	1706
1877—															
3 May	3	..	..	9	..	..	..	..	..	94 1/16	2 May	10927	364	—717	—1081
											9 May	11291	1883	1516	—367
5 July	2½	..	1	..	..	..	..	..	..	94 5/16	4 July	13174	737	1391	654
12 July	2	6 5/7	..	..	..	..	..	..	..	94⅝	11 July	13911	—1791	—1864	—73
28 Aug.	3	..	..	5 2/7	..	..	..	..	..	95⅛	22 Aug.	12120	9	—564	—573
											29 Aug.	12129	—2408	—148	2260
4 Oct.	4	..	..	..	..	1	..	..	..	95 13/16	3 Oct.	9721	—290	—641	—351
11 Oct.	5	..	..	..	..	..	..	7	..	95 3/16	10 Oct.	9431	2116	418	—1698
29 Nov.	4	..	..	..	..	6	..	..	..	96⅞	28 Nov.	11547	355	5	—350
1878—															
10 Jan.	3	..	..	3	..	..	..	..	..	95¼	9 Jan.	11902	1080	—585	—1665
31 Jan.	2	8	..	..	..	..	..	..	..	95 3/16	30 Jan.	12982	—1066	—1673	—607
28 March	3	..	..	9	..	..	..	..	..	95¼	27 March	11916	—1685	—520	1165
											10 April	10231	1107	1748	641
30 May	2½	..	4	..	..	..	..	..	..	97 5/16	29 May	11338	—92	410	502
											12 June	11246	—388	—498	—110
27 June	3	..	..	1	..	..	..	..	..	95 3/16	26 June	10858	—1776	—1200	576
4 July	3½	..	..	..	4	..	..	..	..	95 13/16	3 July	9082	—179	—256	—77
1 Aug.	4	..	..	..	..	1 4/7	..	..	..	94 13/16	31 July	8903	—300	223	523
12 Aug.	5	..	..	..	..	..	..	9	..	94⅛	7 Aug.	8603	310	—96	—406
											14 Aug.	8913	1302	2897	1595
14 Oct.	6	..	..	..	..	..	..	..	5 3/7	94 7/16	9 Oct.	10215	—1698	971	2669
											16 Oct.	8517	3794	2444	—1350
21 Nov.	5	..	..	..	..	..	..	8	..	95 11/16	20 Nov.	12311	—794	3214	4008
										2½ per cent. Annuities					
1879—															
16 Jan.	4	..	..	..	..	2	..	..	..	78	15 Jan.	11517	1333	541	—792
30 Jan.	3	..	..	6	..	..	..	..	..	78	29 Jan.	12850	6452	699	—5753
13 March	2½	..	4	..	..	..	..	..	..	78⅛	12 March	19302	—640	910	1550
10 April	2	30	..	..	..	..	..	..	..	78½	9 April	18662	2710	1699	—1011
											30 July	21372	—4709	—5125	—416
6 Nov.	3	..	..	32	..	..	..	..	..	79⅛	5 Nov.	16663	—102	—5228	—5126

APPENDIX I (continued)

Bank Rate, Number of weeks at each rate, and Price of 2½ per cent. Annuities

Date	Bank Rate	2	2½	3	3½	4	4½	5	6	Price of 2½ per cent. Annuities
1880—										
17 June	2½		25							80
9 Dec.	3			5						81¼
1881—										
13 Jan.	3½				5					81¾
17 Feb.	3			10						82¾
28 April	2½		16							84¾
18 Aug.	3			1						87¾
25 Aug.	4					6				87¾
6 Oct.	5							16¾		86
1882—										
30 Jan.	6								3¾	86
23 Feb.	5							2		85½
9 March	4					2				85½
23 March	3			21						86
17 Aug.	4					4				83½
14 Sept.	5							19		83½
1883—										
25 Jan.	4					3				86½
15 Feb.	3½				2					87¼
1 March	3			10						87¼
10 May	4					18				88½
13 Sept.	3½				2					87½
27 Sept.	3			19						88
1884—										
7 Feb.	3½				5					90½
13 March	3			3						90⅞
3 April	2½		11							90⅞
19 June	2	16								91¼
9 Oct.	3			3						92¼
30 Oct.	4					1				92½
6 Nov.	5							12		91¼

Reserve returns (£'000)

Date	Reserve	Increase in Reserve	Net Imports of Gold	Interior Demand
1880—				
3 March	16561	833	646	−187
16 June	17394	−2285	1114	3399
3 Nov.	15109	−1126	−1606	−480
8 Dec.	13983	−1406	−1851	−446
1881—				
12 Jan.	12578	336	−493	−899
19 Jan.	12914	3666	1148	−2518
16 Feb.	16580	250	189	−31
2 March	16830	−2311	−2042	269
13 April	14519	1378	122	−506*
27 April	15897	−2568	839	3407
3 Aug.	13329	−44	−695	−651
17 Aug.	13285	−360	−221	139
24 Aug.	12925	−2603	−2112	491
5 Oct.	10322	654	−2328	−2982
1882—				
25 Jan.	10976	−1801	−1608	193
1 Feb.	9175	761	−468	−1229
8 Feb.	9936	2482	1363	−1119
22 Feb.	12418	800	876	76
8 March	13218	1895	883	−1012
22 March	15113	4422	1383	5805
16 Aug.	10691	466	−221	−687
13 Sept.	11157	1220	703	−517
1883—				
24 Jan.	12377	911	231	−680
14 Feb.	13288	769	10	−759
28 Feb.	14057	−3750	−1205	2545
9 May	10307	4174	2458	−1716
12 Sept.	14481	−355	307	−48
26 Sept.	14636	−2623	−3040	417
1884—				
6 Feb.	12213	2896	835	−2061
12 March	15109	439	1877	1438
2 April	15548	819	1236	917
18 June	15867	−5394	−2501	2893
8 Oct.	10473	−411	−356	55
29 Oct.	10062	−545	−229	316
5 Nov.	9517	4421	−230	−4651

* Fiduciary Issue increased by £750,000, 27 April 1881.

APPENDIX I (*continued*)

Bank Rate		*Number of weeks at:* 2	2½	3	3½	4	4½	5	6	*Price of 2½ per cent. Annuities*	*Reserve*		*Increase in Reserve*	*Net Imports of Gold*	*Interior Demand*
1885—												£'000	£'000	£'000	£'000
29 Jan.	4	..	..	..	..	7	..	..	..	91⅜	28 Jan.	13938	4332	1229	—3103
19 March	3½	..	..	..	7	..	..	..	..	87	18 March	18270	—484	658	1142
7 May	3	..	..	1	..	..	..	..	..	87⅛	6 May	17786	—237	157	394
14 May	2½	..	2	..	..	..	..	..	..	88	13 May	17549	820	478	—342
28 May	2	24	..	..	..	..	..	..	..	88	27 May	18369	—852	1017	1869
											22 July	17517	—5744	—2547	3197
12 Nov.	3	..	..	5	..	..	..	..	..	88¼	11 Nov.	11773	525	—205	—730
17 Dec.	4	..	..	..	..	5	..	..	..	88	16 Dec.	12298	102	—613	—715
1886—															
21 Jan.	3	..	..	4	..	..	..	..	..	88½	20 Jan.	12400	2504	1073	—1431
18 Feb.	2	11	..	..	..	..	..	..	..	89¾	17 Feb.	14904	—3165	409	3574
6 May	3	..	..	5	..	..	..	..	..	88¾	5 May	11739	—340	—619	—279
10 June	2½	..	11	..	..	..	..	..	..	88½	9 June	11399	823	1266	443
26 Aug.	3½	..	..	..	8	..	..	..	..	89⅛	25 Aug.	12222	—1430	—256	1174
21 Oct.	4	..	..	..	..	8	..	..	..	88¾	20 Oct.	10792	852	—642	—1494
16 Dec.	5	..	..	..	..	..	..	7	..	89	15 Dec.	11644	—761	—1271	—510
1887—															
											12 Jan.	10883	2352	664	—1688
3 Feb.	4	..	..	..	..	5	..	..	..	88½	2 Feb.	13235	2696	578	—2118
10 March	3½	..	..	..	2	..	..	..	..	88¼	9 March	15931	1125	394	—731
24 March	3	..	..	3	..	..	..	..	..	89	23 March	17056	—1669	505	2174
14 April	2½	..	2	..	..	..	..	..	..	90¾	13 April	15387	484	64	—420
28 April	2	14	..	..	..	..	..	..	..	91	27 April	15871	—4750	—1182	3568
4 Aug.	3	..	..	4	..	..	..	..	..	93	3 Aug.	11121	562	—942	—1504
1 Sept.	4	..	..	..	..	19	..	..	..	93¼	31 Aug.	11683	643	667	474*
1888—															
12 Jan.	3½	..	..	..	1	..	..	..	..	95¾	11 Jan.	12326	724	4	—720
19 Jan.	3	..	..	4	..	..	..	..	..	95¾	18 Jan.	13050	2134	340	—1794
16 Feb.	2½	..	4	..	..	..	..	..	..	95¾	15 Feb.	15184	1323	716	—607
15 March	2	8	..	..	..	..	..	..	..	97¼	14 March	16507	—5296	—1229	4067
10 May	3	..	..	4	..	..	..	..	..	95¾	9 May	11211	1436	1064	—372
7 June	2½	..	9	..	..	..	..	..	..	95¼	6 June	12647	—1689	535	2224
9 Aug.	3	..	..	5	..	..	..	..	..	96	8 Aug.	10958	1738	25	—1713
13 Sept.	4	..	..	..	..	3	..	..	..	94¼	12 Sept.	12696	—2394	—171	2223
4 Oct.	5	..	..	..	..	..	..	14	..	94¼	3 Oct.	10302	350	—1615	—1965
											5 Dec.	10652	435	1692	1257
1889—										*Consols*					
											2 Jan.	11087	1404	125	—1279
10 Jan.	4	..	..	..	..	2	..	..	..	99⅛	9 Jan.	12491	1501	183	—1318
24 Jan.	3½	..	..	..	1	..	..	..	..	99	23 Jan.	13992	554	—184	—738
31 Jan.	3	..	..	11	..	..	..	..	..	98⅞	30 Jan.	14546	—561	1380	1941

* Fiduciary Issue increased by £450,000, 5th October, 1887.

APPENDIX I (*continued*)

Bank Rate		*Number of weeks at:* 2	2½	3	3½	4	4½	5	6	*Price of Consols*	*Reserve*		*Increase in Reserve*	*Net Imports of Gold*	*Interior Demand*
												£'000	£'000	£'000	£'000
18 April	2½	..	16	..	..	..	..	..	..	98⅝	17 April	13985	—2407	2202	4609
8 Aug.	3	..	..	3	..	..	..	..	..	98¼	7 Aug.	11578	723	84	—639
29 Aug.	4	..	..	..	..	4	..	..	..	97⅞	28 Aug.	12301	91	—242	—333
26 Sept.	5	..	..	..	..	..	..	13 4/7	..	97	25 Sept.	12392	—2802	—894	1908
30 Dec.	6	..	..	..	..	..	..	..	7 3/7	97	24 Dec.	9590	—281	—55	226
1890—															
											1 Jan.	9309	6868	1940	—4678*
20 Feb.	5	..	..	..	..	..	..	2	..	97⅜	19 Feb.	16177	190	449	259
6 March	4½	..	..	..	..	..	1	..	..	97 5/16	5 March	16367	538	118	—420
13 March	4	..	..	..	..	4	..	..	..	97 5/16	12 March	16905	—1798	1199	2997
10 April	3½	..	..	..	1	..	..	..	..	98	9 April	15107	536	156	—380
17 April	3	..	..	10	..	..	..	..	..	98¼	16 April	15643	—2476	—654	1822
26 June	4	..	..	..	..	5	..	..	..	96⅝	25 June	13167	—1132	—58	1074
31 July	5	..	..	..	..	..	..	3	..	96	30 July	12035	2252	2442	190
21 Aug.	4	..	..	..	..	5	..	..	..	96⅜	20 Aug.	14287	—68	340	408
											3 Sept.	14219	—1056	—1027	29
25 Sept.	5	..	..	..	..	..	..	6 1/7	..	94⅞	24 Sept.	13163	—2572	—1099	1473
											8 Oct.	10591	616	249	—367
7 Nov.	6	..	..	..	..	..	..	..	3 6/7	94 3/16	5 Nov.	11207	—102	—175	—73
											12 Nov.	11105	3447	3177	—270
											19 Nov.	14552	2121	2152	31
4 Dec.	5	..	..	..	..	..	..	5	..	96	3 Dec.	16673	—1141	316	1457
1891—															
8 Jan.	4	..	..	..	..	2	..	..	..	96	7 Jan.	15532	1522	—166	—1688
22 Jan.	3½	..	..	..	1	..	..	..	..	97¼	21 Jan.	17054	545	—78	—623
29 Jan.	3	..	..	11	..	..	..	..	..	97⅛	28 Jan.	17599	—4602	—2875	1727
16 April	3½	..	..	..	3	..	..	..	..	96	15 April	12997	—786	719	1505
7 May	4	..	..	..	..	1	..	..	..	95	6 May	12211	234	380	146
14 May	5	..	..	..	..	..	..	3	..	95¼	13 May	12445	5216	4764	—452
4 June	4	..	..	..	..	2	..	..	..	94⅞	3 June	17661	1775	2000	225
18 June	3	..	..	2	..	..	..	..	..	95	17 June	19436	—1191	2468	3659
2 July	2½	..	12	..	..	..	..	..	..	95 5/16	1 July	18245	—1139	1090	2229
											12 Aug.	17106	—347	—1458	—1111
24 Sept.	3	..	..	5	..	..	..	..	..	94⅛	23 Sept.	16759	—3512	—2211	1301
29 Oct.	4	..	..	..	..	6	..	..	..	95	28 Oct.	13247	—647	—290	357
											4 Nov.	12600	2569	1525	—1044
10 Dec.	3½	..	..	..	6	..	..	..	..	95 5/16	9 Dec.	15169	—380	—695	—315
1892—															
21 Jan.	3	..	..	11	..	..	..	..	..	95¾	20 Jan.	14789	660	643	—17
7 April	2½	..	3	..	..	..	..	..	..	96⅛	6 April	15449	—165	336	501
28 April	2	25	..	..	..	..	..	..	..	96⅜	27 April	15284	2600	5540	2940

* Fiduciary Issue increased by £250,000, 19 Feb., 1890.

APPENDIX I (*continued*)

Bank Rate		*Number of weeks at :* 2	2½	3	3½	4	4½	5	6	*Price of Consols*	*Reserve*		*Increase in Reserve*	*Net Imports of Gold*	*Interior Demand*
												£'000	£'000	£'000	£'000
											21 Sept.	17884	—2779	685	3464
20 Oct.	3	..	..	14	..	..	..	..	..	96⅞	19 Oct.	15105	2259	—162	—2421
1893—															
26 Jan.	2½	..	14	..	..	..	..	..	..	98¼	25 Jan.	17364	—2353	1395	3748
4 May	3	..	..	1	..	..	..	..	..	98⅞	3 May	15011	—896	—703	193
11 May	3½	..	..	..	1	..	..	..	..	98¼	10 May	14115	—792	—150	642
18 May	4	..	..	..	..	3	..	..	..	97¾	17 May	13323	4076	3499	—577
8 June	3	..	..	1	..	..	..	..	..	99⅛	7 June	17399	2198	1674	—524
15 June	2½	..	7	..	..	..	..	..	..	99	14 June	19597	—2784	1371	4155
3 Aug.	3	..	..	1	..	..	..	..	..	98½	2 Aug.	16813	—2197	—670	1527
10 Aug.	4	..	..	..	..	2	..	..	..	98⅛	9 Aug.	14616	400	—1842	—2242
24 Aug.	5	..	..	..	..	..	..	3	..	97⅝	23 Aug.	15016	2569	475	—2094
14 Sept.	4	..	..	..	..	1	..	..	..	98⅛	13 Sept.	17585	746	777	31
21 Sept.	3½	..	..	..	2	..	..	..	..	97⅞	20 Sept.	18331	—1677	216	1893
5 Oct.	3	..	..	17	..	..	..	..	..	98⅛	4 Oct.	16654	3085	—551	—3636
1894—															
1 Feb.	2½	..	3	..	..	..	..	..	..	98¾	31 Jan.	19739	2863	917	—1596*
22 Feb.	2	133	..	..	..	..	..	..	..	99½	21 Feb.	22602	8292	14536	6244
											5 Sept.	30894	—6057	—3921	2136
											19 Dec.	24837	16160	16406	246
1895—															
1896—															
											26 Feb.	40997	—4875	4349	9224
											5 Aug.	36122	—3742	—3780	—38
10 Sept.	2½	..	2	..	..	..	..	..	..	112½	9 Sept.	32380	—1087	—1765	—678
24 Sept.	3	..	..	4	..	..	..	..	..	109⅛	23 Sept.	31293	—5373	—3137	2236
22 Oct.	4	..	..	..	..	13	..	..	..	108⅛	21 Oct.	25920	—1625	—2714	—1089
											30 Dec.	24295	3155	251	—2904
1897—															
21 Jan.	3½	..	..	..	2	..	..	..	..	112½	20 Jan.	27450	794	304	—490
4 Feb.	3	..	..	9	..	..	..	..	..	113⅛	3 Feb.	28244	—663	1117	1780
8 April	2½	..	5	..	..	..	..	..	..	112¼	7 April	27581	—1970	416	2386
13 May	2	19	..	..	..	..	..	..	..	113½	12 May	25611	—1042	1640	2682
											1 Sept.	24569	—219	—1358	—1139
23 Sept.	2½	..	3	..	..	..	..	..	..	111⅜	22 Sept.	24350	—3426	—1333	2093
14 Oct.	3	..	..	25	..	..	..	..	..	111⅝	13 Oct.	20924	1829	—2297	—4126
1898—															
											26 Jan.	22753	—4402	1261	5663
7 April	4	..	..	..	..	7	..	..	..	111⅛	6 April	18351	8194	6524	—1670
26 May	3½	..	..	..	1	..	..	..	..	111⅛	25 May	26545	—499	1633	2132
2 June	3	..	..	4	..	..	..	..	..	112	1 June	26046	1025	407	—618
30 June	2½	..	12	..	..	..	..	..	..	111⅜	29 June	27071	—3576	—1778	1798
22 Sept.	3	..	..	3	..	..	..	..	..	109⅞	21 Sept.	23495	—3204	186	3390
13 Oct.	4	..	..	..	..	14	..	..	..	109⅜	12 Oct.	20291	1812	460	—1352

* Fiduciary Issue increased by £350,000, 21 February, 1894.

APPENDIX I (*continued*)

Bank Rate		*Number of weeks at:* 2	2½	3	3½	4	4½	5	6	*Price of Consols*	*Reserve*		*Increase in Reserve*	*Net Imports of Gold*	*Gold Set Aside*	*Interior Demand*
1899—												£'000	£'000	£'000	£'000	£'000
19 Jan.	3½	..	..	..	2	..	..	..	..	111⅜	18 Jan.	22103	867	402	—	—465
2 Feb.	3	..	..	23	..	..	..	..	..	111	1 Feb.	22970	—2939	5179	—	8118
13 July	3½	..	..	..	11 5/7	..	..	..	..	106¼	12 July	20031	3393	5449	—	2056
3 Oct.	4½	..	..	..	..	..	2/7	..	..	102¾	27 Sept.	23424	—2773	—381	—	2392
5 Oct.	5	..	..	..	..	..	..	8	..	102¾	4 Oct.	20651	—1315	—545	750	20
30 Nov.	6	..	..	..	..	..	..	..	6	102⅛	29 Nov.	19336	—1328	—611	—	717
											13 Dec.	18008	3824	3568	350	—606
1900—																
11 Jan.	5	..	..	..	..	..	..	1	..	98¾	10 Jan.	21832	1281	1623	400	—58
18 Jan.	4½	..	..	..	..	..	1	..	..	100½	17 Jan.	23113	809	—343	—	—1152
25 Jan.	4	..	..	..	..	17	..	..	..	101⅛	24 Jan.	23922	—1798	1907	—500	5180*
24 May	3½	..	..	..	3	..	..	..	..	101	23 May	22124	—1121	—166	—	955
14 June	3	..	..	5	..	..	..	..	..	101⅜	13 June	21003	—2092	—297	—500	2295
19 July	4	..	..	..	..	24	..	..	..	98¼	18 July	18911	6142	5855	—500	213
											19 Sept.	25053	—8841	—2910	100	5831
1901—																
3 Jan.	5	..	..	..	..	..	..	5	..	97⅜	2 Jan.	16212	1672	—371	—100	—1943
											9 Jan.	17884	3630	210	—	—3420
7 Feb.	4½	..	..	..	..	..	2	..	..	96¾	6 Feb.	21514	2953	1164	—	—1789
21 Feb.	4	..	..	..	..	15	..	..	..	97⅝	20 Feb.	24467	220	5717	—	5497
6 June	3½	..	..	..	1	..	..	..	..	93⅝	5 June	24687	916	—167	—	—1083
13 June	3	..	..	20	..	..	..	..	..	93⅛	12 June	25603	1454	3662	—	2208
											21 Aug.	27057	—3175	—2019	—	1156
31 Oct.	4	..	..	..	..	12	..	..	..	92¼	30 Oct.	23882	—3772	—1725	—	2047
1902—																
											1 Jan.	20110	4589	300	—	—4289
23 Jan.	3½	..	..	..	2	..	..	..	..	94	22 Jan.	24699	485	11	—	—474
6 Feb.	3	..	..	34	..	..	..	..	..	94⅜	5 Feb.	25184	629	8083	—	7854†
											3 Sept.	25813	—2197	—1269	—	928
2 Oct.	4	..	..	..	..	33	..	..	..	93⅛	1 Oct.	23616	—2609	—1789	—	820
											10 Dec.	21007	4174	5385	—	1211
1903—																
21 May	3½	..	..	..	4	..	..	..	..	91⅝	20 May	25181	1642	1291	—	—351
18 June	3	..	..	11	..	..	..	..	..	91⅛	17 June	26823	—2417	660	—	3077
											29 July	24406	36	—249	—	—10‡
3 Sept.	4	..	..	..	..	32	..	..	..	90⅛	2 Sept.	24442	—6773	—5350	—	1423
1904—											23 Dec.	17669	6474	1329	—	—5145
14 April	3½	..	..	..	1	..	..	..	..	88¼	13 April	24143	718	—162	—	—880
21 April	3	..	..	46	..	..	..	..	..	88⅛	20 April	24861	4144	5758	—	1614
											21 Sept.	29005	—9264	—6892	—	2372
											21 Dec.	19741	11115	5041	—	—6074

* Fiduciary Issue increased by £975,000, 21 March, 1900.
† Fiduciary Issue increased by £400,000, 20 August, 1902.
‡ Fiduciary Issue increased by £275,000, 26 August, 1903.

APPENDIX I (*continued*)

Bank Rate		*Number of weeks at:* 2	2½	3	3½	4	4½	5	5½	6	7	8	10	*Price of Consols*	*Reserve*		*Increase in Reserve*	*Net Imports of Gold*	*Gold Set Aside*	*Interior Demand*
1905—																£'000	£'000	£'000	£'000	£'000
9 March	2½	..	26	..	..	..	..	..	..	..	..	..	..	91	8 March	30856	—5595	5419	1000	10014
															2 Aug.	25261	—566	—1090	400	—924
7 Sept.	3	..	..	3	..	..	..	..	..	..	..	..	..	90¼	6 Sept.	24695	—887	—866	600	—579
28 Sept.	4	..	..	..	..	27	..	..	..	..	..	..	..	89 11/16	27 Sept.	23808	—2135	—1065	1000	70
															18 Oct.	21673	1496	2910	2000	—586
															6 Dec.	23169	—555	—2244	500	—2189
1906—															24 Jan.	22614	3833	7424	1445	2146
5 April	3½	..	..	..	4	..	..	..	..	..	..	..	..	90⅞	4 April	26447	—4555	—1934	—	2621
3 May	4	..	..	..	..	7	..	..	..	..	..	..	..	89¾	2 May	21892	1295	—2286	—1500	—2081
															23 May	23187	3481	1954	—945	—582
21 June	3½	..	..	..	12	..	..	..	..	..	..	..	..	88¾	20 June	26668	—1906	6038	—250	8194
13 Sept.	4	..	..	..	..	4	..	..	..	..	..	..	..	86⅛	12 Sept.	24762	—6472	—8224	—	—1752
11 Oct.	5	..	..	..	..	..	..	1 1/7	..	..	..	..	..	86⅜	10 Oct.	18290	572	—1129	—	—1701
19 Oct.	6	..	..	..	..	..	..	..	..	12 6/7	..	..	..	86¼	17 Oct.	18862	—674	—1482	—	—808
															24 Oct.	18188	4405	3862	1000	—1543
1907—																				
17 Jan.	5	..	..	..	..	..	..	12	..	..	..	..	..	87⅛	16 Jan.	22593	2542	4521	2300	—321
11 April	4½	..	..	..	..	..	2	..	..	..	..	..	..	86¼	10 April	25135	770	1237	475	—8
25 April	4	..	..	..	..	16	..	..	..	..	..	..	..	85¾	24 April	25905	—946	2389	—1820	5155
15 Aug.	4½	..	..	..	..	..	11	..	..	..	..	..	..	81¾	14 Aug.	24959	3798	1807	—	—1991
															18 Sept.	28757	—7923	—2784	—	5139
31 Oct.	5½	..	..	..	..	..	..	..	4/7	..	..	..	..	82	30 Oct.	20834	—3139	—6265	—	—3126
4 Nov.	6	..	..	..	..	..	..	..	..	3/7	..	..	..	82						
7 Nov.	7	..	..	..	..	..	..	..	..	..	8	..	..	82	6 Nov.	17695	3778	4823	—2500	3545
1908—																				
2 Jan.	6	..	..	..	..	..	..	..	..	2	..	..	..	83¾	1 Jan.	21473	4394	—743	—	—5137
16 Jan.	5	..	..	..	..	..	..	1	..	..	..	..	..	83¾	15 Jan.	25867	1656	346	—	—1310
23 Jan.	4	..	..	..	..	6	..	..	..	..	..	..	..	84⅛	22 Jan.	27523	1995	2233	—	238
5 March	3½	..	..	..	2	..	..	..	..	..	..	..	..	87½	4 March	29518	1761	1321	—	—440
19 March	3	..	..	10	..	..	..	..	..	..	..	..	..	87⅜	18 March	31279	—4084	2318	—	6402
															6 May	27195	467	—254	—	—721
28 May	2½	..	33	..	..	..	..	..	..	..	..	..	..	87½	27 May	27662	—6649	—10314	—2205	—1460
1909—																				
14 Jan.	3	..	..	11	..	..	..	..	..	..	..	..	..	83⅛	13 Jan.	21013	3037	—894	—	—3931
															27 Jan.	24050	6704	8118	—	1414
1 April	2½	..	27	..	..	..	..	..	..	..	..	..	..	84¾	31 March	30754	—1826	4754	—	6580
															1 Sept.	28928	—5292	—4750	—	542
7 Oct.	3	..	..	1	..	..	..	..	..	..	..	..	..	83 1/16	6 Oct.	23636	—686	—1203	—	—517
14 Oct.	4	..	..	..	..	1	..	..	..	..	..	..	..	82⅜	13 Oct.	22950	—627	—1405	—	—778
21 Oct.	5	..	..	..	..	..	..	7	..	..	..	..	..	82⅛	20 Oct.	22323	—349	—513	—	—164
															27 Oct.	21974	4032	4104	—	72
9 Dec.	4½	..	..	..	..	..	4	..	..	..	..	..	..	82¾	8 Dec.	26006	—2718	1068	—	3786

APPENDIX I (*continued*)

Bank Rate		*Number of weeks at:* 2	2½	3	3½	4	4½	5	5½	6	7	8	10	*Price of Consols*		*Reserve*	*Increase in Reserve*	*Net Imports of Gold*	*Gold Set Aside*	*Interior Demand*
1910—																£'000	£'000	£'000	£'000	£'000
6 Jan.	4					2								82⅝	5 Jan.	23288	3623	—604	—	—4227
20 Jan.	3½				3									82½	19 Jan.	26911	316	—232	—	—548
10 Feb.	3			5										82	9 Feb.	27227	— 2284	—2020	750	—486
17 March	4					11								81⅛	16 March	24943	5574	10921	1915	3432
2 June	3½				1									82½	1 June	30517	1424	616	80	—888
9 June	3			16										82⅛	8 June	31941—	—2768	2121	—	4889
															10 Aug.	29173	—1334	—3459	—	—2125
29 Sept.	4					3								80⅞	28 Sept.	27839	—5037	—4594	—	443
20 Oct.	5							6						80	19 Oct.	22802	—784	—1410	—	—626
															26 Oct.	22018	3668	4739	—	1071
1 Dec.	4½						8							79⅝	30 Nov.	25686	1491	—975	—	—2466
1911—																				
26 Jan.	4					3								79½	25 Jan.	27177	1844	1268	500	—1076
16 Feb.	3½				3									80¼	15 Feb.	29021	826	1266	300	140
9 March	3			28										81	8 March	29847	2726	11660	—	8934
21 Sept.	4					20								76¾	20 Sept.	32573	—7712	—5607	—	2105
															8 Nov.	24861	4542	887	—	—3655
1912—																				
8 Feb.	3½				13									78	7 Feb.	29403	—191	3716	655	3252
9 May	3			16										78¼	8 May	29212	1782	5493	—	3711
29 Aug.	4					7								75½	28 Aug.	30994	—3606	—4817	—	—1211
17 Oct.	5							26						73	16 Oct.	27388	541	4638	2020	2077
1913—																				
17 April	4½						24							75	16 April	27929	4808	13799	220	9271
															3 Sept.	32237	—5825	—4122	—	1703
2 Oct.	5							14						73⅜	1 Oct.	26412	—820	—3785	—	—2965
															15 Oct.	25592	925	5562	1105	3532
1914—																				
8 Jan.	4½						2							71⅝	7 Jan.	26517	5609	1616	700	—4693
22 Jan.	4					1								73⅞	21 Jan.	32126	1758	1203	100	—655
29 Jan.	3			26										74⅞	28 Jan.	33884	—4587	6020	675	9932
														75½	22 July	29297	—2422	529	280	2671
30 July	4					1/7								71	29 July	26875	—16908			
31 July	8											1/7		70						
1 Aug.	10												6/7	—	1 Aug.	9967	5563		—	
7 Aug.	6									1/7										
8 Aug.	5							100 5/7												
														—	12 Aug.	15530				

Bank Rate		*Number of weeks at:* 2	2½	3	3½	4	4½	5	5½	6	6½	7	*Price of Consols*		*Gold in Bank* £'000	*Note Issue** £'000
1916—																
13 July	6	..	..	..	..	..	..	..	..	27	..	..	60½	12 July	85,806	160,670
1917—																
18 Jan.	5½	..	..	..	..	..	..	..	11	..	..	..	53⅝	17 Jan.	82,035	184,140
5 April	5	..	..	..	..	..	..	135	..	..	..	..	55	4 April	81,140	188,950
1919—																
6 Nov.	6	..	..	..	..	..	..	..	..	23	..	..	51½	5 Nov.	114,798	426,430
1920—																
15 April	7	..	..	..	..	..	..	..	..	..	..	54	45⅞	14 April	140,485	439,547
1921—																
28 April	6½	..	..	..	..	..	..	..	..	..	8	..	48	27 April	155,036	444,949
23 June	6	..	..	..	..	..	..	..	..	4	..	..	45¾	22 June	155,048	430,938
21 July	5½	..	..	..	..	..	..	..	15	..	..	..	48	20 July	155,057	430,176
3 Nov.	5	..	..	..	..	..	..	15	..	..	..	..	48¾	2 Nov.	155,102	417,516
1922—																
16 Feb.	4½	..	..	..	..	..	8	..	..	..	..	..	53¼	15 Feb.	155,429	403,017
13 April	4	..	..	..	..	9	..	..	..	..	..	..	58¾	12 April	155,563	407,916
15 June	3½	..	..	..	4	..	..	..	..	..	..	..	54⅛	14 June	155,563	400,119
13 July	3	..	..	51	..	..	..	..	..	..	..	..	58	12 July	153,570	400,642
1923—																
5 July	4	..	..	..	..	87	..	..	..	..	..	..	58	4 July	152,797	392,296
1925—																
5 March	5	..	..	..	..	..	..	22	..	..	..	..	57	4 March	153,780	380,548
6 Aug.	4½	..	..	..	..	..	8	..	..	..	..	..	56¼	5 Aug.	162,655	394,223
1 Oct.	4	..	..	..	..	9	..	..	..	..	..	..	55½	30 Sept.	158,641	380,203
3 Dec.	5	..	..	..	..	..	..	72	..	..	..	..	55⅝	2 Dec.	143,868	375,133
1927—																
21 April	4½	..	..	..	..	..	94	..	..	..	..	..	54⅝	20 April	152,244	378,188
1929—																
7 Feb.	5½	..	..	..	..	..	..	..	33	..	..	..	56⅝	6 Feb.	149,626	357,519
26 Sept.	6½	..	..	..	..	..	..	..	..	..	5	..	53	25 Sept.	131,938	361,071
31 Oct.	6	..	..	..	..	..	..	..	..	3	..	..	54⅛	30 Oct.	131,017	358,820
21 Nov.	5½	..	..	..	..	..	..	..	3	..	..	..	53¼	20 Nov.	132,103	355,087
12 Dec.	5	..	..	..	..	..	..	8	..	..	..	..	52⅝	11 Dec.	137,007	365,158
1930—																
6 Feb.	4½	..	..	..	..	..	4	..	..	..	..	..	54	5 Feb.	150,784	348,690
6 March	4	..	..	..	..	2	..	..	..	..	..	..	53⅜	5 March	151,602	347,296
20 March	3½	..	..	..	6	..	..	..	..	..	..	..	56¼	19 March	153,458	348,890
1 May	3	..	..	54	..	..	..	..	..	..	..	..	54½	30 April	163,342	358,822
1931—																
14 May	2½	..	10	..	..	..	..	..	..	..	..	..	58 11/16	13 May	148,977	353,127
														8 July	164,619	359,258
23 July	3½	..	..	..	1	..	..	..	..	..	..	..	59½	22 July	148,774	356,098
30 July	4½	..	..	..	..	..	7 2/7	..	..	..	..	..	57¼	29 July	132,035	359,362
21 Sept.	6	..	..	..	..	..	..	..	..	21 3/7	..	..	·56¼	16 Sept.	135,574	351,618
														23 Sept.	133,628	352,676
1932—																
18 Feb.	5	..	..	..	..	..	..	3	..	..	..	..	55¼	17 Feb.	120,766	344,883
10 March	4	..	..	..	..	1	..	..	..	..	..	..	60	9 March	120,802	354,475
17 March	3½	..	..	..	5	..	..	..	..	..	..	..	59⅜	16 March	120,805	353,714
21 April	3	..	..	3	..	..	..	..	..	..	..	..	60⅝	20 April	120-815	354,271
12 May	2½	..	7	..	..	..	..	..	..	..	..	..	64⅛	11 May	120,816	358,313
30 June	2	..	..	..	..	..	..	..	..	..	..	..	67⅛	29 June	136,143	363,083

* Active circulation of Bank of England notes and Currency Notes.

APPENDIX II

Quarter Beginning		Reserve	Increase in Reserve	Net Imports of Gold	Interior Demand	Average Bank Rate	Twelve Months' Interior Demand
		£'000	£'000	£'000	£'000		£'000
2 Dec.	1857	2729	9320	8050	—3270‖	6·04	729
3 March	1858	12049	501	1470	969	3·00	4745
2 June		12550	—581	704	1285	3·00	6361
1 Sept.		11969	973	2718	1745	3·00	8145
1 Dec.		12942	808	1556	748	2·54	7724
2 March	1859	13750	—2603	—20	2583	3·19	7158
1 June		11147	—1353	1716	3069	2·75	5804
7 Sept		9794	467	1791	1324	2·50	3521
7 Dec.		10261	—1235	—1053	182	3·18	1967
7 March	1860	9026	144	1373	1229	4·46	— 652
6 June		9170	45	831	786	4·00	—2213
5 Sept.		9215	—1281	—2022	—230†	4·43	—3978
5 Dec.		7934	—692	—3466	—2437†	6·60	—3907
6 March	1861	7242	—692	—588	—332†	6·08	—708
5 June		6550	919	177	—979†*	5·46	1251
4 Sept.		7469	2310	2151	—159	3·42	2402
4 Dec.		9779	14	776	762	2·69	3596
5 March	1862	9793	—507	1120	1627	2·58	3756
4 June		9286	1680	1852	172	2·46	3851
3 Sept.		10966	—1060	—25	1035	2·88	5454
3 Dec.		9906	—442	480	922	3·78	6716
4 March	1863	9464	—857	865	1722	3·76	4690
3 June		8607	347	2122	1775	4·00	4704
2 Sept.		8954	—2278	19	2297	4·66	4782
2 Dec.		6676	1765	661	—1104	7·40	2106
2 March	1864	8441	—625	1111	1736	6·93	3395
1 June		7816	—1005	848	1853	6·96	3910
7 Sept.		6811	2037	1658	—379	8·54	5398
7 Dec.		8848	670	855	185	5·58	7131
1 March	1865	9518	—171	2080	2251	4·21	6967
7 June		9347	—2076	1265	3341	3·46	13158
6 Sept.		7271	1093	2447	1354	5·96	9800
6 Dec.		8364	—48	—377	21‡	7·31	7500
7 March	1866	8316	—5490	2952	8442	7·87	7296
6 June		2826	4148	4131	—17	9·15	—251
5 Sept.		6074	3550	2604	—946	4·46	1641
5 Dec.		10524	1353	1170	—183	3·42	5843
6 March	1867	11877	898	1793	895	2·95	7235
5 June		12775	2234	4109	1875	2·27	9109
4 Sept.		15009	—2134	1122	3256	2·00	9735
4 Dec.		12875	—332	877	1209	2·00	8406
4 March	1868	12543	200	2969	2769	2·00	7212
3 June		12743	—1204	1297	2501	2·00	5166
2 Sept.		11539	—1962	—35	1927	2·08	3465
2 Dec.		9577	—123	—108	15	3·00	4069
3 March	1869	9454	—158	565	723	3·85	3124
2 June		9296	3082	3882	800	3·31	3206
1 Sept.		12378	—2038	493	2531	2·65	7607
1 Dec.		10340	2030	1100	—930	3·00	5417
2 March	1870	12370	111	916	805	3·00	7437
1 June		12481	49	5250	5201	3·81	7993
7 Sept.		12530	1822	2163	341	2·65	5577
7 Dec.		14352	—1042	48	1090	2·50	1029
1 March	1871	13310	2764	4125	1361	2·71	—2020

† Silver included in Reserve :
  5 Dec. 1860 £511,000.
  6 March 1861 £848,000
  5 June 1861 £412,000.
‡ Fiduciary Issue increased by £350,000, 21 Feb., 1866.
* Fiduciary Issue increased by £175,000, 10 July, 1861.
‖Fiduciary Issue temporarily increased by £2,000,000 on 2 Dec., 1857.

Quarter Beginning	Reserve		Increase in Reserve	Net Imports of Gold	Interior Demand	Average Bank Rate	Twelve Months' Interior Demand
	£'000		£'000	£'000	£'000		£'000
7 June	16074		—1347	1438	2785	2·12	—1549
6 Sept.	14727		274	—3933	—4207	4·02	—2354
6 Dec.	15001		—1297	—3256	—1959	3·04	498
6 March	13704	1872	—1728	104	1832	3·88	—714
5 June	11976		—268	1712	1980	3·38	1
4 Sept.	11708		709	—646	—1355	5·48	—1347
4 Dec.	12417		2376	—795	—3171	4·35	1043
5 March	14793	1873	—4979	—2432	2547	4·41	3636
4 June	9814		2946	3578	632	4·69	3772
3 Sept.	12760		—1311	—276	1035	5·91	5305
3 Dec.	11449		1228	650	—578	3·96	8039
4 March	12677	1874	—1328	1355	2683	3·65	10119
3 June	11349		—183	1982	2165	2·96	9301
2 Sept.	11166		—2526	1243	3769	3·76	8474
2 Dec.	8640		1139	2641	1502	4·54	7317
3 March	9779	1875	297	2162	1865	3·50	2635
2 June	10076		5663	7002	1338	2·88	2454
1 Sept.	15739		—5043	—2481	2612	2·92	1554
1 Dec.	10696		1045	—2135	—3180	3·92	736
1 March	11741	1876	3126	4810	1684	2·79	1417
7 June	14867		6120	6558	438	2·00	1287
6 Sept.	20987		—4200	—2406	1794	2·00	1217
6 Dec.	16787		—2701	—5200	—2499	2·00	—1472
7 March	14086	1877	—1896	—342	1554	2·39	—1855
6 June	12190		—467	—99	368	2·45	—792
5 Sept.	11723		—118	—1013	—895	4·23	—1069
5 Dec.	11605		872	—2010	—2882	3·00	3710
6 March	12477	1878	—1626	991	2617	2·73	4704
5 June	10851		—550	—459	91	3·69	2388
4 Sept.	10301		1658	5542	3884	5·42	1307
4 Dec.	11959		6322	4434	—1888	4·08	—4205
5 March	18281	1879	531	832	301	2·23	—6175
4 June	18812		1890	900	—990	2·00	—5063
3 Sept.	20702		—5558	—7186	—1628	2·31	—3945
3 Dec.	15144		1417	—2441	—3858	3·00	—1398
3 March	16561	1880	—913	500	1413	3·00	—1123
2 June	15648		387	515	128	2·58	—1573
1 Sept.	16035		—1312	—393	919	2·50	—960
1 Dec.	14723		2107	—1476	—3583	3·15	—3041
2 March	16830	1881	—1922	—1709	963*	2·81	—1559
1 June	14908		—2486	—1745	741	2·75	51
7 Sept.	12422		—1332	—2494	—1162	4·69	554
7 Dec.	11090		1425	—676	—2101	5·29	2687
1 March	12515	1882	387	2960	2573	3·54	2026
7 June	12902		—1895	—651	1244	3·23	1385
6 Sept.	11007		—44	927	971	4·92	—733
6 Dec.	10963		2853	91	—2762	4·39	—759
7 March	13816	1883	—2872	—940	1932	3·31	—1231
6 June	10944		2999	2125	—874	4·00	37
5 Sept.	13943		—1446	—501	945	3·15	811
5 Dec.	12497		1431	—1803	—3234	3·15	—222
5 March	13928	1884	656	3856	3200	2·69	—1714
4 June	14584		—1486	—1586	—100	2·08	—4251
3 Sept.	13098		—1904	—1992	—88	3·31	—1898
3 Dec.	11194		5295	569	—4726	4·62	200
4 March	16489	1885	1403	2066	663	3·27	3177
3 June	17892		—2783	—530	2253	2·00	5131
2 Sept.	15109		—2946	—936	2010	2·23	3000
2 Dec.	12163		2259	510	—1749	3·23	1442
3 March	14422	1886	—3806	—1189	2617	2·31	—1247
2 June	10616		1547	1669	122	2·62	—1839
1 Sept.	12163		—799	—347	452	3·73	—1268
1 Dec.	11364		3936	—502	—4438	4·54	—1899
2 March	15300	1887	—903	1122	2025	2·69	293
1 June	14397		—3019	—2326	693	2·43	1554
7 Sept.	11378		1398	769	—179†	4·00	1863

* Fiduciary Issue increased by £750,000, 27 April, 1881.
† Fiduciary Issue increased by £450,000, 5 October, 1887.

Quarter Beginning		Reserve	Increase in Reserve	Net Imports of Gold	Interior Demand	Average Bank Rate	Twelve Months' Interior Demand
		£'000	£'000	£'000	£'000		£'000
7 Dec.		12776	3262	1016	—2246	3·31	1809
7 March	1888	16038	—3391	—105	3286	2·35	1350
6 June		12647	—228	774	1002	2·65	2286
5 Sept.		12419	—1767	—2000	—233	4·62	3499
5 Dec.		10652	4165	1460	—2705	3·95	4396
6 March	1889	14817	—712	3510	4222	2·73	3918
5 June		14105	—2021	194	2215	2·73	4065
4 Sept.		12084	—202	462	664	4·77	3171
4 Dec.		11882	4485	1052	—3183*	5·57	3329
5 March	1890	16367	—3180	1189	4369	3·46	5243
4 June		13187	1032	2353	1321	4·00	4215
3 Sept.		14219	2454	3276	822	5·07	8671
3 Dec.		16673	—1302	—2571	—1269	3·96	7980
4 March	1891	15371	2290	5631	3341	3·65	6022
3 June		17661	—943	4834	5777	2·81	6435
2 Sept.		16718	—1925	—1794	131	3·27	2733
2 Dec.		14793	1623	—1604	—3227	3·31	5403
2 March	1892	16416	—290	3464	3754	2·50	5797
1 June		16126	1674	3749	2075	2·00	7340
7 Sept.		17800	—2148	653	2801	2·54	6909
7 Dec.		15652	2972	189	—2833	2·58	3958
1 March	1893	18624	—1225	4072	5297	2·93	3115
7 June		17399	—847	797	1644	3·19	318
6 Sept		16552	254	104	—150	3·81	2116
6 Dec.		16806	6087	2061	—3676†	2·73	4160
7 March	1894	22893	5996	8496	2500	2·00	6322
6 June		28889	2005	5447	3442	2·00	6437
5 Sept.		30894	—5155	—3261	1894	2·00	4086
5 Dec.		25739	3177	1663	—1514	2·00	2788
6 March	1895	28916	—1180	1435	2615	2·00	2395
5 June		27736	4120	5211	1091	2·00	3883
4 Sept.		31856	3468	4064	596	2·00	9452
4 Dec.		35324	5059	3152	—1907	2·00	5635
4 March	1896	40383	—2107	1996	4103	2·00	4792
3 June		38276	—4954	1706	6660	2·00	7351
2 Sept.		33322	—7097	—10318	—3221	3·31	1954
2 Dec.		26225	3530	780	—2750	3·62	4615
3 March	1897	29755	—4509	2153	6662	2·58	4930
2 June		25246	—677	586	1263	2·00	4215
1 Sept.		24569	—2735	—3295	—560	2·65	4846
1 Dec.		21834	1772	—663	—2435	3·00	8873
2 March	1898	23606	2440	8387	5947	3·58	7829
1 June		26046	—2255	—361	1894	2·64	8131
7 Sept.		23791	—2922	545	3467	3·54	9991
7 Dec.		20869	2893	—586	—3479	3·58	10361

Quarter Beginning		Reserve	Increase in Reserve	Net Imports of Gold	Gold Set Aside	Interior Demand	Average Bank Rate	Twelve Month's Interior Demand
								£'000
1 March	1899	23762	—4231	2018	—	6249	3·00	18171
7 June		19531	4816	8570	—	3754	3·31	12957
6 Sept.		24347	—5395	—808	750	3837	4·64	11852
6 Dec.		18952	4944	5025	750	—669	4·88	10072
7 March	1900	23896	—3486	1074	—500	6035‡	3·92	6996
6 June		20410	3351	4500	—1000	2149	3·58	5967
5 Sept.		23761	—4236	—1679	—	2557	4·00	4838
5 Dec.		19525	5902	2157	—	—3745	4·46	2975
6 March	1901	25427	—740	4266	—	5006	4·00	3879
5 June		24687	2146	3166	—	1020	3·04	3813
4 Sept.		26833	—3187	—2493	—	694	3·38	6400
4 Dec.		23646	2650	—191	—	—2841	3·62	7920
5 March	1902	26296	—1492	3448	—	4940	3·00	8691

* Fiduciary Issue increased by £250,000, 19 February, 1890.
† Fiduciary Issue increased by £350,000, 21 February, 1894.
‡ Fiduciary Issue increased by £975,000, 21 March, 1900.

Quarter Beginning		Reserve	Increase in Reserve	Net Imports of Gold	Gold set Aside	Interior Demand	Average Bank Rate	Twelve Months' Interior Demand
		£'000	£'000	£'000	£'000	£'000		£'000
4 June		24804	1009	4216	—	3607*	3·00	8535
3 Sept.		25813	—4431	—2217	—	2214	3·69	5676
3 Dec.		21382	3790	1720	—	—2070	4·00	2559
4 March	1903	25172	—948	3836	—	4784	3·92	—806
3 June		24224	218	691	—	748†	3·08	—1000
2 Sept.		24442	—3345	—4248	—	—903	4·00	—2649
2 Dec.		21097	4454	—981	—	—5435	4·00	—2126
2 March	1904	25551	—2961	1629	—	4590	3·50	298
1 June		22590	4918	4017	—	—901	3·00	1958
7 Sept.		27508	—5042	—5422	—	—380	3·00	5048
7 Dec.		22466	7386	4375	—	—3011	3·00	4332
1 March	1905	29852	—2525	3725	—	6250	2·54	4675
7 June		27327	—2632	957	1400	2189	2·50	2987
6 Sept.		24695	—1526	978	3600	—1096	3·77	4357
6 Dec.		23169	4653	4080	2045	—2668	4·00	3020
7 March	1906	27822	—4797	—1835	—1600	4562	3·85	2651
6 June		23025	4342	6706	—1195	3559	3·58	3462
5 Sept.		27367	—4425	—6858	—	—2438	5·10	920
5 Dec.		22942	3467	2205	1775	—3087	5·46	4518
6 March	1907	26409	—2228	4825	1680	5373	4·46	4505
5 June		24181	2968	2485	—1500	1017	4·12	5170
4 Sept.		27149	—5240	—5075	—1000	1165	5·36	2427
4 Dec.		21909	7609	3059	—1500	—3050	5·31	—29
4 March	1908	29518	—2032	3006	—1000	6038	3·04	—406
3 June		27486	—185	—2911	—1000	—1726	2·50	1219
2 Sept.		27301	—3215	—4711	—205	—1291	2·50	3531
2 Dec.		24086	3519	92	—	—3427	2·77	4239
3 March	1909	27605	—1441	6222	—	7663	2·65	6811
2 June		26164	2764	3350	—	586	2·50	1696
1 Sept.		28928	—3152	—3735	—	—583	3·81	3066
1 Dec.		25776	360	—495	—	—855	3·88	4317
2 March	1910	26136	4381	9594	2665	2548	3·85	2201
1 June		30517	—829	1207	80	1956	3·04	5962
7 Sept.		29688	—3803	—3135	—	668	4·27	7929
7 Dec.		25885	3196	1025	800	—2971	4·21	7256
1 March	1911	29081	—114	6195	—	6309	3·04	7009
7 June		28967	1184	5107	—	3923	3·00	4611
6 Sept.		30151	—3393	—3398	—	—5	3·85	3899
6 Dec.		26758	2517	—46	655	—3218	3·85	4514
6 March	1912	29275	776	4687	—	3911	3·85	5009
5 June		30051	1317	4528	—	3211	3·08	8660
4 Sept.		31368	—5106	—2646	1850	610	4·54	10061
4 Dec.		26262	1552	—1061	110	—2723	5·00	9246
5 March	1913	27814	—403	7329	170	7562	4·73	9548
4 June		27411	4826	9548	110	4612	4·50	8752
3 Sept.		32237	—5953	—5978	180	—205	4·85	40604
3 Dec.		26284	5454	5333	2300	—2421	4·08	
4 March	1914	31738	—6290	576	100	6766	3·00	
3 June		25448	5487	15075	—1720	36464‡	4·13	
2 Sept.		30985						

* Fiduciary Issue increased by £400,000, 20 August, 1902.
† Fiduciary Issue increased by £275,000, 26 August, 1903.
‡ Currency Notes to the value of £25,156,000 issued up to 2 September, 1914.

APPENDIX III

	Unemployed per cent. in Trade Unions	Wage Index	Interior Demand		Unemployed per cent. in Trade Unions	Wage Index	Interior Demand
			£'000				£'000
1858	11·9	110	729	1886	10·2	148	1442
1859	3·8	112	7724	1887	7·6	149	—1889
1860	1·9	114	1967	1888	4·9	151	1809
1861	5·2	114	—3907	1889	2·1	156	4396
1862	8·4	116	3596	1890	2·1	168	3329
1863	6·0	117	6716	1891	3·5	163	7980
1864	2·7	124	2106	1892	6·3	162	5403
1865	2·1	126	7131	1893	7·5	162	3958
1866	3·3	132	7500	1894	6·9	162	4160
1867	7·4	131	5843	1895	5·8	162	2788
1868	7·9	130	8406	1896	3·3	163	5635
1869	6·7	130	4069	1897	3·3	166	4615
1870	3·9	133	5417	1898	2·8	167	8873
1871	1·6	138	1029	1899	2·0	172	10361
1872	0·9	146	558	1900	2·5	179	10072
1873	1·2	155	1043	1901	3·3	179	2975
1874	1·7	156	8039	1902	4·0	176	7920
1875	2·4	154	7317	1903	4·7	176	2559
1876	3·7	152	736	1904	6·0	176	—2126
1877	4·7	151	—1472	1905	5·0	175	4332
1878	6·8	148	3710	1906	3·6	181	3020
1879	11·4	146	—4205	1907	3·7	190	4518
1880	5·5	147	—1398	1908	7·8	187	—29
1881	3·5	147	—3041	1909	7·7	184	4239
1882	2·3	147	2687	1910	4·7	187	4317
1883	2·6	149	— 759	1911	3·0	188	7256
1884	8·1	150	— 222	1912	3·2	194	4514
1885	9·3	149	200	1913	2·1	197	9246

APPENDIX IV

DISCOUNT RATE OF THE BANK OF FRANCE

Date	Year	Rate	Date	Year	Rate	Date	Year	Rate
1 Feb.	1820	4	26 May		6	22 Feb.	1883	3
15 Jan.	1847	5	9 Sept.		7	16 Feb.	1888	2½
17 Dec.		4	13 Oct.		8	13 Sept.		3½
3 March	1852	3	3 Nov.		7	4 Oct.		4½
Oct.	1853	4	24 Nov.		6	10 Jan.	1889	4
30 Jan.	1854	5	8 Dec.		5	24 Jan.		3½
11 May		4	22 Dec.		4½	7 Feb.		3
4 Oct.	1855	5	9 Feb.	1865	4	19 May	1892	2½
25 Sept.	1856	6	9 March		3½	14 March	1895	2
25 June	1857	5½	1 June		3	20 Oct.	1898	3
12 Oct.		6½	5 Oct.		4	7 Dec.	1899	3½
20 Oct.		7½	9 Oct.		5	21 Dec.		4½
10 Nov.		8	23 Nov.		4	11 Jan.	1900	4
26 Nov.		7	4 Jan.	1866	5	24 Jan.		3½
5 Dec.		6	15 Feb.		4½	25 May		3
29 Dec.		5	22 Feb.		4	21 March	1907	3½
8 Feb.	1858	4½	22 March		3½	7 Nov.		4
19 Feb.		4	11 May		4	9 Jan.	1908	3½
11 June		3½	26 July		3½	23 Jan.		3
14 Sept.		3	30 Aug.		3	21 Sept.	1911	3½
4 May	1859	4	31 May	1867	2½	17 May	1912	3
5 Aug.		3½	20 July	1870	3½	17 Oct.		3½
12 Nov.	1860	4½	22 July		4	31 Oct.		4
2 Jan.	1861	5½	1 Aug.		5	29 Jan.	1914	3½
8 Jan.		7	9 Aug.		6	30 July		4½
14 March		6	20 July	1871	5	1 Aug.		6
21 March		5	3 Nov.		6	20 Aug.		5
26 Sept.		5½	27 Feb.	1872	5	8 April	1920	6
1 Oct.		6	14 Oct.	1873	6	28 July,	1921	5½
22 Nov.		5	8 Nov.		7	11 March	1922	5
21 Jan.	1862	4½	20 Nov.		6	10 Jan.	1924	5½
6 Feb.		4	27 Nov.		5	17 Jan.	1924	6
27 March		3½	5 March	1874	4½	11 Dec.	1924	7
6 Nov.		4	4 June		4	9 July	1925	6
8 Jan.	1863	5	26 May	1876	3	31 July	1926	7½
13 March		4½	5 April	1877	2	16 Dec.		6½
27 March		4	16 Oct.	1878	3	3 Feb.	1927	5½
7 May		3½	23 May	1879	2	14 April		5
11 June		4	23 Oct.		3	29 Dec.		4
8 Oct.		5	1 April	1880	2½	19 Jan.	28	3½
7 Nov.		6	14 Oct.		3½	30 Jan.	1930	3
13 Nov.		7	25 Aug.	1881	4	1 May		2½
24 March	1864	6	20 Oct.		5	2 Jan.	1931	2
6 May		7	23 Feb.	1882	4½	9 Oct		2½
9 May		8	2 March		4			
20 May		7	23 March		3½			

APPENDIX V

PRINCIPAL PERIODS OF NET GOLD EXPORTS

Period	Reserve at Beginning	Change in Reserve (— for decrease)	Net Exports of Gold (—)	Interior Demand	Bank Rate	Paris Bank Rate
	£'000	£'000	£'000	£'000		
8 Nov. 1859–14 March 1860	9501	—232	—1614	—1382	2½–4	3½
19 Sept. 1860–17 July 1861	9997	—4217	—7482	—3265	4–6–5–8–5–6	3½–7–5
7 May 1862–18 June, 1862	10867	—1447	—2491	—1044	2½–3	3½
4 Nov. – 9 Dec. 1863	6408	1058	—1295	—2353	5–8	5–7
28 Oct. –18 Nov. 1868	10669	—801	—1293	—492	2–2½	2½
26 July 1871–15 May 1872	17410	—7447	—10106	—2659	2–5–3–5	5–6–5
17 July –30 Oct. 1872	11498	—2439	—2072	367	3–6	5
8 Jan. –21 May 1873	13038	—2957	—4124	—1167	5–3½–6	5
10 Sept. –29 Oct. 1873	13178	—4723	—2704	2019	3–7	5–6
29 Sept. 1875– 5 Jan. 1876	13588	—5456	—4900	556	2–5	4
4 Oct. 1876– 9 May 1877	20567	—9276	—10517	—1241	2–3	3–2
11 July –10 Oct. 1877	13911	—4480	—3217	1263	2–5	2
2 Jan. –10 April 1878	12053	—1822	—2894	—1072	3–2–3	2
12 June –31 July 1878	11246	—2343	—1954	389	2½–4	2
30 July 1879– 3 March 1880	21372	—4811	—10353	—5542	2–3	2–3
3 Nov. 1880–19 Jan. 1881	15109	—2195	—3950	—1755	2½–3½	3½
2 March –13 April 1881	16830	—2311	—2042	269	3	3½
3 Aug. 1881– 8 Feb. 1882	13329	—3393	—7432	—4039	2½–6	3½–5
3 Oct. 1883– 6 Feb. 1884	12895	—682	—3115	—2433	3–3½	3
28 May –26 Nov. 1884	15552	—4525	—3801	724	2½–5	3
22 July – 6 Jan. 1886	17517	—6734	—3494	3240	2½–5	3
31 March –26 May 1886	13748	—2760	—1707	1053	2–3	3
25 Aug. 1886–12 Jan. 1887	12222	—1339	—2169	—830	2½–5	3
15 June 1887–14 Sept. 1887	15445	—3802	—2420	1382	2–4	3
31 Oct. –19 Dec. 1888	11841	—621	—2255	—1634	5	4½
27 Nov. 1889– 1 Jan. 1890	12564	—3255	—1699	1556	5–6	3
3 Sept. – 8 Oct. 1890	14219	—3628	—2126	1502	4–5	3
12 Aug. – 4 Nov. 1891	17106	—4506	—3959	547	2½–4	3
16 Dec. 1891–24 Feb. 1892	15704	1016	—2311	—3327	3½–3	3
2–23 Aug. 1893	16813	—1797	—2512	—715	3–5	2½
25 Oct. –20 Dec. 1893	16969	—818	—1551	—733	3	2½
5 Sept. –19 Dec. 1894	30894	—6057	—3921	2136	2	2½
5 Aug. –30 Dec. 1896	36122	—11827	—11396	431	2–4	2
1 Sept. 1897–26 Jan. 1898	24569	—1816	—4988	—3172	2–3	2
29 June –28 Sept. 1898	27071	—4608	—2086	2522	3–2½–3	2
27 Sept. –13 Dec. 1899	23424	—5416	—2287	3129	3½–6	3–3½
19 Sept. 1900– 9 Jan. 1901	25053	—7169	—3281	3888	4–5	3
21 Aug. 1901– 1 Jan. 1902	27057	—6947	—3744	3203	3–4	3
3 Sept. –10 Dec. 1902	25813	—4806	—3058	1748	3–4	3
29 July –23 Dec. 1903	24407	—6737	—5599	1138	3–4	3
21 Sept. –21 Dec. 1904	29005	—9264	—6892	2372	3	3
2 Aug. –18 Oct. 1905	25261	—3588	—3021	567	2½–4	3
6 Dec. 1905–24 Jan. 1906	23169	—555	—2244	—1689	4	3
4 April –23 May 1906	26447	—3260	—2720	540	4–3½–4	3
12 Sept. –24 Oct. 1906	24762	—6574	—10835	—4261	3½–6	3
18 Sept. – 6 Nov. 1907	28757	—11062	—9049	2013	4½–7	3½–4
6 May 1908–27 Jan. 1909	27195	—3145	—9257	—6112	3–2½–3	3
1 Sept. –27 Oct. 1909	28928	—6954	—7871	—917	3½–5	3
2 Feb. –16 March 1910	26956	— 2013	—3714	—1701	3½–3–4	3
10 Aug. –26 Oct. 1910	29173	—7163	—9463	—2300	3–5	3
28 Dec. 1910–11 Jan. 1911	21195	2257	—2183	—4440	4½	3
20 Sept. –15 Nov. 1911	32573	—6538	—5796	742	3–4	3–3½
4 Sept. –23 Oct. 1912	31368	—3867	—5366	—1499	4–5	3–3½
4 Dec. 1912–22 Jan. 1913	26270	290	—2333	—2623	5	4
3 Sept. –15 Oct. 1913	32240	—6648	—7907	—1259	4½–5	4
4 Feb. –20 May, 1914	33366	—7645	—3110	4535	3	3½

APPENDIX VI

WEEKLY AND MONTHLY RETURNS OF GOLD IMPORTS AND EXPORTS

COMPARISONS OF CO-TERMINOUS PERIODS

			Weekly		*Monthly*	
			Imports	Exports	Imports	Exports
			£'000	£'000	£'000	£'000
1 April	−30 June	1858	4575	3807	4577	3863
1 July	1858–31 Aug.	1859	26125	19556	26158	19674
1 Sept.	−30 Nov.	1859	5705	3428	5701	3428
1 Dec.	1859–29 Feb.	1860	2314	3460	2314	3460
1 March	−31 Oct.	1860	9138	8106	9139	8107
1 Nov.	1860–31 July	1861	9258	14716	9258	14717
1 Aug.	1861–30 April	1862	10329	4453	10328	4454
1 May	−31 Dec.	1862	14165	13223	14455	13286
1 Jan.	−30 Sept.	1863	14709	10967	14475	10980
1 Oct.	1863–31 Aug.	1864	16079	13999	16079	13091
1 Sept.	−30 Nov.	1864	3984	1943	3984	1937
1 Dec.	1864–31 May	1865	6633	4192	6634	4191
1 June	1865–28 Feb.	1866	10689	7262	10683	7275
1 March	−31 Oct.	1866	19892	11049	19892	11049
1 Nov.	1866–31 July	1867	10957	4325	10957	4322
1 Aug.	1867–30 Sept.	1868	21742	13310	21732	13333
1 Oct.	1868–31 March	1869	4539	5433	4538	5443
1 April	−30 June	1869	3364	1828	3364	1816
1 July	1869–31 Aug.	1870	20502	10924	20540	10928
1 Sept.	−30 Nov.	1870	5694	3057	5705	3084
1 Dec.	1870–31 May	1871	9771	5367	9760	5350
1 June	1871–31 Jan.	1872	13980	17548	14057	17482
1 Feb.	−31 July	1872	9420	10101	9424	10101
1 Aug.	1872–30 April	1873	13814	15926	13816	15962
1 May	−31 Dec.	1873	14458	11213	14327	11213
1 Jan.	−30 Sept.	1874	12349	8318	12356	8328
1 Oct.	1874–31 March	1875	9373	6564	9438	7606
1 April	−30 June	1875	7869	2386	7905	2384
1 July, 1875	−31 May	1876	18438	14895	18368	14904
1 June	1876–31 Jan.	1877	15953	15862	15962	16054
1 Feb.	−31 Oct.	1877	12458	14674	12482	14717
1 Nov.	1877–31 July	1878	10742	13303	10750	13293
1 Aug.	1878–30 April	1879	19008	6509	19020	6509
1 May	−31 Dec.	1879	6733	14919	6789	14919
1 Jan.	−31 March	1880	1222	1884	1185	1884
1 April	−30 June,	1880	1792	1402	1792	1402
1 July	1880–31 Aug.	1881	13372	17508	13483	18204
1 Sept.	−30 Nov.	1881	2559	5869	2559	5152
1 Dec.	1881–31 May	1882	7812	5469	7812	5469
1 June	1882–28 Feb.	1883	7779	7705	7792	7705
1 March	−31 Oct.	1883	6160	5081	6135	5122
1 Nov.	1883–30 April	1884	6951	5139	6925	5139
1 May	−31 Dec.	1884	4573	8365	4567	8379
1 Jan.	−30 Sept.	1885	9304	7075	9303	7121
1 Oct.	1885–31 March	1886	8244	7514	8244	7515
1 April	−30 June	1886	3445	4251	3445	4251
1 July	1886–31 Aug.	1887	12071	13157	12155	13155
1 Sept.	−30 Nov.	1887	2791	1886	2791	1881
1 Dec.	1887–29 Feb.	1888	2401	1881	2401	1882
1 March	−31 Oct.	1888	11414	10869	11436	10879
1 Nov.	1888–31 July	1889	14382	10935	14372	10933
1 Aug.	1889–30 April	1890	11920	9466	11924	9466
1 May	−31 Dec.	1890	17679	12162	17679	12162
1 Jan.	−30 Sept.	1891	24697	17867	24697	17867
1 Oct.	1891–31 Aug.	1892	21026	16012	20956	16013
1 Sept.	−30 Nov.	1892	4550	4347	4551	4347
1 Dec.	1892–31 May	1893	9248	6299	9246	6299

				Weekly		Monthly	
				Imports	Exports	Imports	Exports
				£'000	£'000	£'000	£'000
1 June	1893–28 Feb.		1894	19624	15565	20219	15495
1 March		–31 Oct.	1894	20719	8285	20713	8286
1 Nov.	1894–31 July		1895	21255	17967	21266	18315
1 Aug.	1895–30 Sept.		1896	38485	29226	38459	29226
1 Oct.	1896–31 March		1897	10256	14104	10258	14105
1 April		–30 June	1897	10490	8960	10499	8960
1 July	1897–31 Aug.		1898	47180	42181	47168	42183
1 Sept.		–30 Nov.	1898	8875	7368	8876	7368
1 Dec.	1898–31 May		1899	14176	14205	14179	14204
1 June	1899–31 Jan.		1900	25872	13176	25872	13177
Feb.	1900			1748	956	1748	956
1 March		–31 Oct.	1900	15486	11203	15482	11213
1 Nov.	1900–31 July		1901	17347	10019	17328	10011
1 Aug.	1901–30 April		1902	13292	12673	13309	12673
1 May		–31 Dec.	1902	15414	11532	15405	11533
1 Jan.		–30 Sept.	1903	20648	16739	20648	16780
1 Oct.	1903–31 Aug.		1904	29115*	27613	29119	27613
1 Sept.		–30 Nov.	1904	8744*	13332	8744	13332
1 Dec.	1904–31 May		1905	20107*	13096	20107	13031
1 June	1905–28 Feb.		1906	30261*	25839	30261	25779
1 March		–31 Oct.	1906	28373*	32205	28373	32331
1 Nov.	1906–31 July		1907	36851*	25367	36851	25167
1 Aug.	1907–30 Sept.		1908	65556*	65920	65568	65920
1 Oct.	1908–31 March		1909	26658	25840	26638	25840
1 April		–30 June	1909	12944	9388	12944	9388
1 July	1909–31 Aug.		1910	65978	57857	65978	57858
1 Sept.		–30 Nov.	1910	13546	17091	13546	17091
1 Dec.	1910–31 May		1911	23730	16945	23730	16945
1 June	1911–31 Jan.		1912	33382	31877	33382	31876
1 Feb.		–31 July	1912	24707	16337	24707	16329
1 Aug.	1912–30 April		1913	40244	37756	40244	37764
1 May		–31 Dec.	1913	42266	33438	42266	33438

* In this period the so called monthly returns of imports really related to periods of four and five weeks. When a weekly period ended on the last day of the month it was included in the total attributed to the *following* month. For comparison I have treated the weekly returns in the same way in this table. This applies only to imports, not to exports.

INDEX

For Product Safety Concerns and Information please contact our EU
representative GPSR@taylorandfrancis.com Taylor & Francis Verlag GmbH,
Kaufingerstraße 24, 80331 München, Germany

Printed and bound by CPI Group (UK) Ltd, Croydon, CR0 4YY

15/05/2025

01872757-0001